Proceedings of the Ninth Annual Conference of the British Association for Biological Anthropology and Osteoarchaeology

Department of Archaeology
University of Reading 2007

Edited by

Mary E. Lewis
Margaret Clegg

BAR International Series 1918
2009

Published in 2016 by
BAR Publishing, Oxford

BAR International Series 1918

Proceedings of the Ninth Annual Conference of the British Association for Biological Anthropology and Osteoarchaeology

ISBN 978 1 4073 0401 4

BAR Publishing is the trading name of British Archaeological Reports (Oxford) Ltd.
British Archaeological Reports was first incorporated in 1974 to publish the BAR
Series, International and British. In 1992 Hadrian Books Ltd became part of the BAR
group. This volume was originally published by Archaeopress in conjunction with
British Archaeological Reports (Oxford) Ltd / Hadrian Books Ltd, the Series principal
publisher, in 2009. This present volume is published by BAR Publishing, 2016.

Printed in England

BAR
PUBLISHING

BAR titles are available from:

BAR Publishing
122 Banbury Rd, Oxford, OX2 7BP, UK
EMAIL info@barpublishing.com
PHONE +44 (0)1865 310431
FAX +44 (0)1865 316916
www.barpublishing.com

Contents

Foreword   iii

Non-Adult Anthropology
A life course perspective of growing up in medieval London: evidence of sub-adult health
from St Mary Spital (London).   1
Rebecca Redfern and Don Walker

Preservation of non-adult long bones from an almshouse cemetery in the United States
dating to the late nineteenth to the early twentieth centuries.   13
Colleen Milligan, Jessica Zotcavage and Norman Sullivan

Childhood oral health: dental palaeopathology of Kellis 2, Dakhleh, Egypt.
A preliminary investigation.   19
Stephanie Shukrum and JE Molto

Skeletal manifestation of non-adult scurvy from early medieval Northumbria: the Black Gate cemetery,
Newcastle-upon-Tyne.   31
Diana Mahoney-Swales and Pia Nystrom

Infantile cortical hyperostosis: cases, causes and contradictions.   43
Mary Lewis and Rebecca Gowland

Biological Anthropology
Tuberculosis of the hip in the Victorian Britain.   53
Benjamin Clarke and Piers Mitchell

The re-analysis of Iron Age human skeletal material from Winnall Down.   61
Justine Tracey

Can we estimate post-mortem interval from an individual body part? A field study using
sus scrofa.   71
Branka Franicevec and Robert Pastor

The expression of asymmetry in hand bones from the medieval cemetery at Écija, Spain.   79
Lisa Cashmore and Sonia Zakrezewski

Ethics and Repatriation
Returning remains: a curator's view   93
Quinton Carroll

Authority and decision making over British human remains: issues and challenges   99
Piotr Bienkowski and Malcolm Chapman

Ethical dimensions of reburial, retention and repatriation of archaeological human
remains: a British perspective.   107
Simon Mays and Martin Smith

The problem of provenace: inaccuracies, changes and misconceptions.   119
Margaret Clegg

Native American human remains in UK collections: implications of NAGPRA to
consultation, repatriation, and policy development.   123
Myra J Giesen

Repatriation – a view from the receiving end: New Zealand.   131
Nancy Tayles

Foreword

The contributions in this volume represent a selection of papers and posters presented at the 9th Annual Meeting of the British Association of Biological Anthropology and Osteoarchaeology, in the Department of Archaeology, University of Reading, from the 14-16th September 2007. This publication joins a series of conference proceedings from the meetings of this Association.

The conference was attended by 128 delegates from the UK and all over the world, including New Zealand, Germany, Italy, USA, Canada, The Netherlands and Ireland. Themed sessions included papers on the bioarchaeology of children (their life course, health, dental development, trauma and preservation), and the recent issues of ethics and reburial of non-indigenous and indigenous skeletal remains in the UK. The ethics session presented papers from a variety of view points from within the UK, as well as the experiences of institutions from the US, New Zealand and Canada that showed the different approaches taken in these countries. The ever popular 'Open Session' included papers spanning archaeology, forensic anthropology, isotopic analysis, human evolution and palaeopathology. This publication therefore presents a representative sample of the diversity of research presented within the general themes of the conference. For ease of navigation, the papers have been divided into three sections: Non-adult Anthropology, Biological Anthropology (including papers on palaeopathology and forensic anthropology) and Ethics and Repatriation.

Mary Lewis, University of Reading
Margaret Clegg, Natural History Museum London

A life course perspective of growing up in medieval London: evidence of sub-adult health from St Mary Spital (London)

Rebecca Redfern and Don Walker

Museum of London Archaeology Service, Mortimer Wheeler House, 46 Eagle Wharf Road, London, N1 7ED
rredfern@museumoflondon.org.uk

Abstract

Our knowledge of the lives of medieval children is derived from medical, religious, legal and social texts, but these documents were written by adults and probably differed from the child's experience and world-view. Importantly, because medieval society acknowledged that childhood was a separate stage of life, with its own qualities and characteristics, we are able to employ a life course approach to the analysis of childhood in medieval London. This approach recognises that an individual's health, gender, status and location influence how they 'grow up'.

London was unique within medieval England in terms of population movement and social complexity, and primary texts have demonstrated that these factors influenced children's life-ways. The relationship between growing up in the city and sub-adult health has been explored by the bioarchaeological analysis of 1022 aged sub-adults from St Mary Spital; a hospital whose charter specified that it should care for children under the age of seven years old, and pregnant women. The results of this analysis revealed age-related increases in trauma and specific metabolic disease, while variations in mortality risk could be correlated to key stages in the life course, such as weaning in infancy, and employment during childhood and adolescence.

Keywords: medieval, sub-adult, health, life course

Introduction

Our approaches to understanding the life-ways of past children have been dominated by the Western perspective of childhood, which emphasizes dependency and social marginalization. Such a perspective has been challenged within recent archaeological research, which has integrated anthropological data on the pluralities of ageing. Baxter (2005:115) observes that 'archaeologists have always been excavating the remains of children. What is changing is our competence to interrogate the archaeological record'. This statement is supported by Lucy (2005), who notes that before their agency is accepted, evidence must be provided. Anthropological research has shown that a universal concept of childhood does not exist, and that an individual's biological age gives, as James (1998: 62) suggests, 'but a few guidelines from which to explore what children actually do'.

In order to investigate the life-ways of past children, a life course approach is used to study the relationship between chronological (i.e. calendar age), physiological (a medical construct, referring to the ageing process) and social age (gender ideology and socially prescribed behaviour) (Sofaer Derevenski 1997: 486). The approach examines how "chronological age, relationships, common life transitions, and social change shape people's lives from birth to death" (Hutchinson 2008: 9). Childhood is a cultural construct, which does not necessarily follow biological or mental development. Instead, it summarizes the temporal dimension of life, marked by rites of passage (Harlow and Laurence 2002: 3). Life courses are present in all societies; they are culturally specific and subject to change over time, often in response to wider economic and political events (Hareven 2001). Our knowledge of medieval childhood is mainly derived from religious literature, particularly hagiography, and emphasises spiritual development and moral behaviour. Sources from private letters, wills and childcare manuals, show that temporal, spatial and status differences existed in how childhood was understood and how children were treated. Contrary to the views of Ariès (1965), research has shown that parents did grieve the loss of their children, who were not considered to be simply 'little adults', as parental responsibilities and protection for children under law demonstrate (Pollack 1983; Shahar 1990).

A homogeneous life-way would not have existed in medieval London, due to the many political, catastrophic, social and environmental events that took place during this period. Recent reviews of medieval childhood have shown that an individual's life course was dictated by their socio-economic status and parental behaviour. Boswell (1988: 402) observes that many children were abandoned due to poverty, donated to the church, or sold as labour. Overall, the sources show that during the medieval period, childhood was regarded as the lowest stage of life, but was also appreciated for its own qualities and characteristics (Shahar 1990). Religious and social writings show that childhood was divided into three seven-year phases. Although regional and temporal variations in criminal responsibilities and differences between socio-economic groups show that the attainment of maturity was not uniform. The first stage of the life course was *infantia* (0-7 years old), which contained subdivisions based upon dental eruption, weaning and the acquisition of speech. This was followed by *pueritia* (7-12 years old) when children were able to properly express themselves and decide upon their career. *Adolescentia* (12 to 25 years old) was the stage where they became more independent and took on greater responsibility. This

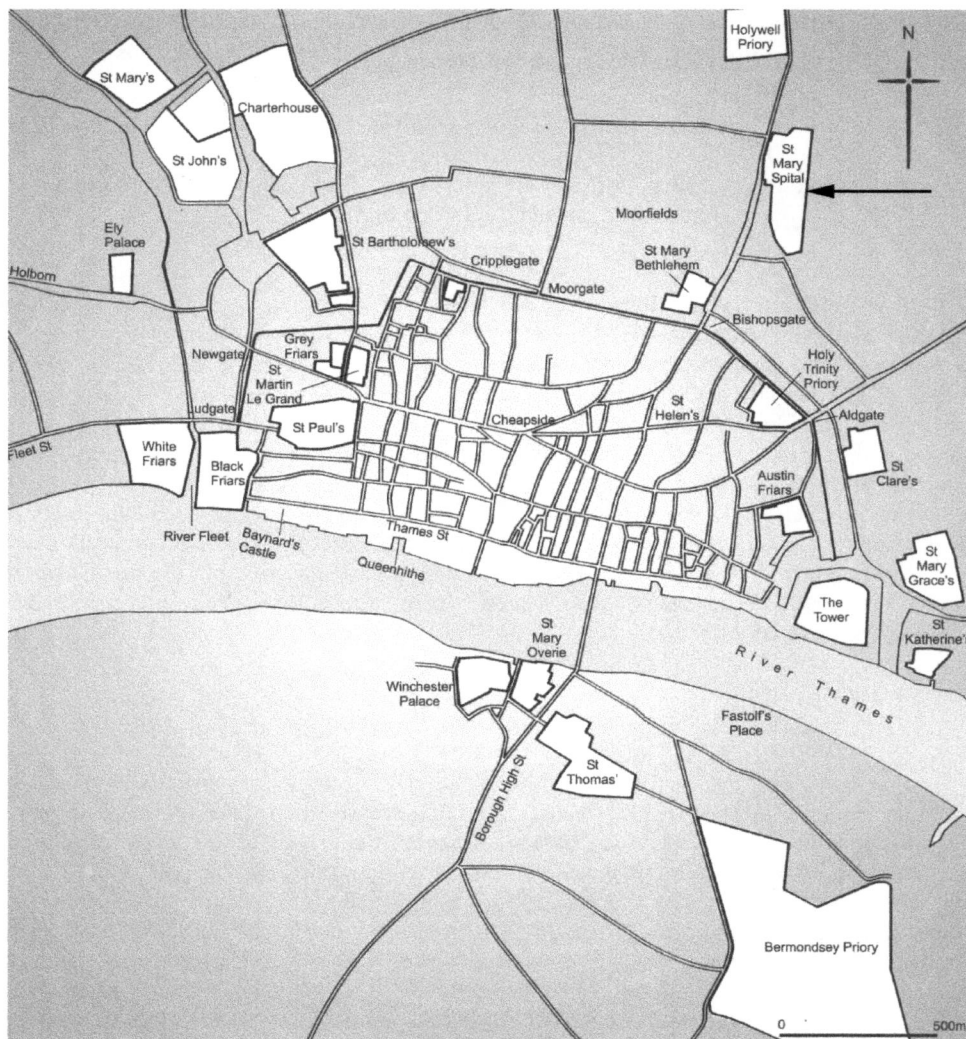

Figure 1. Map of the medieval city of London, showing the location of St Mary Spital (arrowed) in relation to other religious and government institutions (Thomas 1994: 64).

stage ended at approximately 25 years old in females and in males it could last until the age of 35 years (Shahar 1990). The osteological study of medieval sub-adults in Britain has been dominated by analyses of urban samples, particularly those from York, and the comprehensive work conducted by Mays (2007) on the rural sample from Wharram Percy. These have significantly improved our understanding of health during the medieval period. Detailed analyses of sub-adult health have been conducted on samples from Yorkshire and Northamptonshire (Lewis 2002). Other British palaeopathological studies of medieval sub-adults have focused on indicators of stress, specific infections, metabolic diseases, and growth and development (for example, McEwan et al. 2005). The present study provides an insight into the earliest life course stages of medieval Londoners, by focusing on the osteological study of St Mary Spital cemetery. In order to demonstrate how bioarchaeology can be used to explore the social life of archaeological populations, this study will focus upon infant demography, specific metabolic

diseases, trauma, and their relationship to phases of the medieval life course.

St Mary Spital

The priory and hospital of St Mary Spital was founded in the spirit of medieval charity in 1197 by Walter Brunus/Brown and his wife Roisia, together with several other benefactors who were wealthy London merchants. It was sited in east London outside the city walls and close to one of the main roads and gates (Bishopsgate) into the city (Figure. 1). Its location meant that it could be used by pilgrims and travellers, suburban/rural dwellers and those living in the city. In 1235, the priory was re-founded on a larger scale, with the construction of a new church and infirmary. The Browns invited Augustinian canons to operate the hospital and priory, together with lay brothers and sisters, and servants, all of whom inhabited and worked in the religious precinct. At the northern end of the site lay the cloister and canons' dormitory, and to the east a kitchen, the canons' infirmary and gardens, with the cemetery located to the south. This religious centre served the population of London and its suburbs until its dissolution in 1538. The hospital foundation charter stipulated that it must care for pregnant women and orphaned children until they were seven years old, making St Mary Spital unique within London (Thomas et al. 1997). This requirement may have been a response to the large servant population (particularly women) of London, prostitution and poverty, as well as its location outside the city walls. In other London hospitals, children were rarely cared for on a long-term basis, and primary sources note that poor pregnant women were left outside to die, as many of the institutions only accepted richer patients (Orme and Webster 1995).

Materials and Methods

As part of the regeneration of Spitalfields Market, the Museum of London Archaeology Service excavated the religious complex and cemetery, and recovered over ten and a half thousand burials, dating from approximately AD 1100 to 1539. The present study focuses upon individuals aged less than 18 years old (based upon dental and skeletal indicators) and whose skeleton was more than 35% complete (N=1022). Un-aged sub-adults were excluded from this study. These were recorded following the Museum of London methods and protocols described by Powers (2008).

For inter-uterine/neonate and early and later post-natal infants, age-at-death was determined using linear regression equations based upon long bone length (Scheuer and Black 2000). Individuals aged 1 year and over, age-at-death was determined using diaphyseal length and epiphyseal fusion based upon the data published by Scheuer and Black (2000). Dental eruption and formation were also recorded where observable using the methods of Gustafson and Koch (1974) and Moorrees et al. (1963ab). These methods were employed for teeth where the stage of crown or root completeness was visible, in loose teeth or those that could be removed from the socket for observation (Powers 2008, 13). When both dental and skeletal estimates were available, the dental age was chosen, as this has the most reliable correlation with chronological age (Lewis and Garn 1960). Sub-adult individuals were then divided into seven age categories described in Table 1.

Table 1. Summary of age categories at St Mary Spital (after Powers 2008: 14-15).

Terminology	Age category
Inter-uterine/neonate	< four weeks
Early post-natal infant	1-6 months
Later post-natal infant	7-11 months
Early childhood	1-5 years
Later childhood	6-11 years
Adolescent	12-17 years
Unaged sub-adult	<18 years

The diagnosis of specific metabolic diseases was based upon macroscopic bone changes and the distribution of these changes in the skeleton; care was taken to distinguish 'normal' vascularity and bone changes stimulated by growth from those caused by haemorrhage (Brickley and Ives 2006; Ditkowsky et al. 1970; Scheuer and Black 2000; Shopfner 1966). Wherever possible, attempts were made to recognize cases active at the time of death. These were identified when osseous remodelling was absent and active new bone formation was present (Ortner 2003), providing the changes corresponded to the diagnostic criteria.

Rickets is caused by a deficiency in vitamin D, predominantly caused by inadequate exposure of the skin to ultraviolet light. It can also be produced by dietary deficiency and failings in the digestion system and kidneys (Ortner 2003, 393). The disease was diagnosed as present if the osseous changes conformed to the criteria published by Ortner and Mays (1998) and Mays et al. (2006), which include porosity and deformation of skull bones, long bone and rib deformity, and porosity of bone underlying long bone growth plates. Scurvy is a vitamin C deficiency disease arising from a poor or compromised diet, with bone changes varying by age group. In sub-adults (usually between the ages of 2-24 months), the patterning of abnormal porosity in the skeleton is observed in the skull and scapulae (Brickley and Ives 2006; Mays et al. 2006; Ortner 2003, 394). The disease was diagnosed according to the criteria described by Brickley and Ives (2006), with abnormal cortical porosity in the cranium and periosteal new bone formation on the long bones, together with expansion of long bone metaphyses and costo-cartilage rib junctions.

Trauma is defined as "…an injury to living tissue that is caused by a force or mechanism extrinsic to the body" (Lovell 1997: 139), and was identified if a break in bone was observed (Resnick and Goergen 2002: 2636). Peri-mortem trauma was not identified in the sample and dental trauma is excluded from this study. Antemortem injuries were identified if a fracture callus (ranging from initial fracture bridging to callus remodelling) was present (Lovell 1997). Trauma was recorded following the protocol and guidance described by Roberts (2000), where the bone, segment, side affected and fracture type were recorded, as well as the presence of secondary changes (e.g. infection), deformity, degree of apposition and overall alignment.

Results

Demography

A total of 1022 sub-adults were recorded, with the majority of individuals (87.3%) aged 6 years or over. The smallest sample of individuals were those aged between 1 to 11 months (n=4; 0.4%), with over half of all the sub-adults aged between 12 to 17 years (53.2%). Seventy-two (7%) individuals were aged between inter-uterine/neonate and later post-natal infant. Table 2 shows that the sample size increases between these groups and those aged between one to eleven years old. The greater numbers of those between 6 and 17 years old (N= 892)

Table 2. Sub-adult demography by age category.

Body area	Age category (years)	N. affected	% age-group	% sample
Skull	6-11	2	0.6	0.2
	12-17	3	0.5	0.3
Ribs	6-11	1	0.3	0.1
	12-17	4	0.7	0.4
Spine	6-11	-	-	-
	12-17	5	1.2	0.5
Arm	6-11	1	0.3	0.1
	12-17	4	0.7	0.4
Hand	6-11	-	-	-
	12-17	1	0.2	0.1
Leg	6-11	2	0.6	0.2
	12-17	5	1.2	0.5
Foot	6-11	1	0.3	0.1
	12-17	4	0.7	0.4

Specific metabolic diseases
Scurvy was only evident in the four children (0.4%), all from the older age categories. Of the 348 children in the 6-11 year category, two (0.6%) had scurvy: one had cranial and post-cranial changes present, while the other only displayed skull changes. Both cases appear to have been active at the time of death, as the porotic margins were sharp (Ortner 2003). Two adolescents (0.4%) also demonstrated lesions indicative of scurvy and in both cases the skeletal lesions appear to have been healing at the time of death. These changes conform to the later stages of the disease when remodelling takes place, suggesting that the deficiency had been sustained for period of time before death – perhaps beginning during later childhood (Brickley and Ives 2006: 169-171; Ortner 2003: 386).

Five sub-adults (0.5%) had evidence of vitamin D deficiency, with 3 cases in the 1-5 year age category (5.2%). The first of these had cranial and post-cranial changes while the second and third had changes to the upper and lower limbs, but only in the third case was lesion remodelling present (Ortner 2003: 398). Two 6-11 year olds (0.6%) had rickets, and both individuals had anterior bowing to the distal humerii.

Trauma
Within the sample as a whole, a small number of sub-adults (33 or 3.2%) had antemortem bone fractures (39 fractures in all), which affected all body areas, with the spine, foot, ribs and arm most frequently involved (Table 3). No fractures were observed in individuals less than 6 years old. In the later childhood (6-11 year) age category, 2% (7) had trauma present, and the crude prevalence rate shows that this figure doubled in the adolescent age-group with 26 (4.8%) cases of trauma.

The distribution of trauma for those in later childhood (6-11 years) was focused upon the skull and leg (0.6% or 0.2%), and fractures were also observed to affect the ribs, arm and foot bones (0.3% or 0.1%). Adolescents also had these body areas affected by fractures but were the only sub-adult age-group to have spine and hand fractures. The majority of individuals had fractures to the spine and leg (1.2% or 0.5%), followed by the ribs, arm and foot (0.7% or 0.4%) and hand (0.2% or 0.1%).

Table 3. Crude prevalence rate of sub-adult trauma by age and body area (n= number of individuals with a fracture/s in that body area).

Age category	Number of individuals	% of total
< four weeks	68	6.6
1-6 months	2	0.2
7-11 months	2	0.2
1-5 years	58	5.7
6-11 years	348	34
12-17 years	544	53.2
Total	**1022**	**100**

Discussion

Surviving birth and weaning: the critical phase of infantia
The analysis of sub-adult age-at-death provides a unique insight into the well-being and general health of the population from which they were derived, because younger sub-adults are more dependent upon others for care and their morbidity risk is greater due to local environmental conditions (Bogin 1998; Goodman and Armelagos 1989; Saunders and Barrans 1999). The demographic profile of the St Mary Spital sub-adults shows that the mortality rate of perinates was higher than those who had reached one month of life. In order to investigate whether genetic, maternal and parturition factors, or external hazards were the cause of death in these age groups, it is common practice for the percentage of neonatal and post-neonatal deaths to be compared (Lewis 2007; Lewis and Gowland 2007; Konigsberg et al. 2008). Due to the ageing categories used in this study, it was only possible to compare the number of inter-uterine/neonates, and early and late post-natal infants, and it is acknowledged that the use of linear regression age-at-death estimation may produce a peak in mortality at 38 weeks (Lewis and Gowland 2007). It was found that 94% (63/67) reached < 4 weeks old and 3.1% (2/67) were aged 1-6 months. This result indicates that endogenous or genetic factors, such birth defects (Barnes 1994), maternal disease such as influenza (Holzel 1993), and traumatic parturition were more influential than the general living environment (exogenous factors).

The mortality rate of those less than a year old was lower (72/1022, 7%) than other urban centres in England (Lewis 2002: 40). For example, in the later medieval sample from St Helen-on-the-Walls in York, 22.5%

(45/200) of sub-adults were aged between 0.6-2.5 years old, and 5% (5/200) were aged between birth and 0.5 years old (Lewis 2002:40). It should be noted that only part of the York cemetery was excavated and, infanticide may have been practiced by the inhabitants of local area (Lewis and Gowland 2007, 120-121).

The extent to which meaningful comparisons may be made is problematic, as the St Mary Spital results may not reflect a real trend due to a number of factors specific to the site. The hospital had a mandate to care for confined mothers and orphans, which may have enabled a greater number of individuals to survive the risky post-partum stage, and the cemetery was also used for attritional and catastrophic burials in response to the many epidemic disease events that occurred in the medieval period (Connell et al. in review). Additionally, it should be noted that sample excluded individuals less than 35% complete and during recording, it was not possible to record the entire excavated sample (Connell et al. in review). Additionally, it should be considered that medieval sub-adult demography was influenced by social and funerary biases that affect all cemeteries of this period, such as the exclusion of un-baptised babies and the loss of their remains due to cemetery use and other taphonomic factors (Gilchrist and Sloane 2005: 72).

Rousham and Humphrey (2002) observed that the physical vulnerability of those less than a year old increases their susceptibility to disease, because they have an immature immune system, and a high energy and nutrient requirement relative to body weight. The majority of deaths result from exogenous factors, such as the synergism between infectious disease and nutrition. The demographic profile from St Mary Spital demonstrates that the number of sub-adults who died between 7-11 months (0.2%) equalled those who had only lived for 6 months (0.2%). However, their numbers are unusually low when compared to other palaeodemographic studies that compare the proportion of deaths by age. For example, using computer modelling and Leslie matrices, Paine and Boldsen (2002) showed that 0.4% of infants are expected to die in a stable year and 0.08% in a plague year compared equally amounts (0.1%) of 1-5 year olds in stable and plague years respectively.

Breastfeeding is an important aspect of biological development; it influences long-term health and confers immunity from disease (particularly through the colostrum) (Stuart-Macadam 1995a). Medieval breastfeeding practices were influenced by Classical medical and philosophical texts, and medical treatise recommended that wet-nurses were used, although women's diaries show that they usually fed their babies for a few weeks before employing wet-nurses. Babies of wealthy parents were often fed by numerous wet-nurses, usually upon request (Fildes 1986). This practice would have increased their risk of morbidity as the nurse could have passed on rubella or pneumonitis (Hall and Peckham 1997:19). Newborns whose mothers could not breastfeed, or had died during parturition, would have

had a higher morbidity risk from wet-nursing or being fed animal milk from a vessel (Fildes 1986). The risk of disease and sickness was increased by the use of feeding vessels that were not sterilised between feeds, and were made from a variety of materials including pottery, wood and horn (Fildes 1986). Medieval hospital records from Europe show that the use of wet-nurses and feeding vessels resulted in a high death rate amongst infants. In Florence (Italy) between the years of 1300-1530, 17% of wet-nursed infants died (Boswell 1988: 421).

European and British medieval medical sources advised that boys should be weaned 6-12 months later than girls, with weaning typically taking place at 1 to 2 years (Fildes 1986). The demographic data from St Mary Spital shows a sharp increase in the burial of sub-adults mortality between 1-5 years, which conforms to the expected increased morbidity risks associated with weaning and childhood diseases (Lewis 2007: 86). The cessation of breastfeeding, and therefore protection from poor environmental conditions (Stuart-Macadam 1995b), would have forced nurslings into the 'weanling's dilemma'. Defined as, "the health toss-up faced by an infant confronted with complementary foods contaminated with diarrheal pathogens when hygiene is poor against the probability that growth faltering will result when exclusive breast-feeding continues for too long" (Katzenberg et al. 1996: 180). Medieval medical and instructional texts recommended a rapid weaning, feeding infants pap (flour or breadcrumbs cooked in water or milk) or panda (bread, broth, milk and/or eggs) (Fildes 1986). This type of food is necessary because of children's small gastrointestinal tracts, and requires considerable time investment in preparation (Bogin 1998:34).

Weaning in poor environmental conditions increases the risk of death; at St Mary Spital there is an increase in mortality rate at the age of 1-5 years (Table 2). This mortality profile may also reflect the widespread practice of breast-feeding that reduces mortality risk until weaning (Knodel and Kinter 1977). The proposed rapid weaning during the British medieval period (Richards et al. 2002) would have intensified morbidity risk, particularly from infectious diseases (Rousham and Humphrey 2002: 124). The associations between diarrhoea, weaning and mortality risk were recognised in the medieval period, as medical and social texts advised that weaning begin in the spring or autumn to avoid the gastrointestinal diseases that commonly occurred in the summer (Fildes 1986: 366). The critical period of weaning and associated risk of morbidity were recognised as an important aspect of the medieval life course, and surviving the weaning period marked the ending of one subdivision of infantia (Orme 2001; Shahar 1990).

The use of documentary evidence allows us to understand the wider social contexts that influenced the survival of those in the first stage of the life course. In the medieval period, newborns were often abandoned (particularly in times of famine) at religious institutions and hospitals (e.g. St Mary Spital) in the hope that they would have a better chance of survival (Boswell 1988, 402). However, this increased their mortality risk, 14th century documentary sources from the San Gallo hospital (Florence, Italy) show that 20% of infants died within one month of arrival (Boswell 1988: 421). Documentary sources, particularly those from coroners, provide a unique insight into additional socio-cultural causes of morbidity and mortality that include misadventure, neglect or animal attack; for example a one year old boy managed to wound himself in the throat with a pair of shears and died later from his injuries (Butler 2006, 263).

Can the presence of specific metabolic diseases be explained by the life course?
Specific metabolic diseases present in the sub-adult sample demonstrate that for a small minority (0.9%), their diet was insufficient in vitamins C or D. Sub-adults are particularly vulnerable to developing a metabolic disease within a relatively short space of time, as they have rapid bone remodelling (Brickley and Ives 2006). However, the role of the osteological paradox should be taken into consideration, in that diseases may only identified in those who were capable of surviving with deficiencies long enough to stimulate a diagnostic osseous response (Brickley 2000; Wood et al. 1992).

Five individuals had evidence of rickets, caused by insufficient exposure to daylight and less typically, disorders of the gut, liver disease, or kidneys (Mays et al. 2006). Mays et al. (2006) emphasise the co-existence of diseases in the development of rickets, and suggest that in the medieval period, sickly infants could have been kept indoors for long periods, thereby restricting the amount of sunlight they could effectively metabolize. Although, the majority of vitamin D is produced by sunlight, the 'weanling's dilemma' may have compromised the amount of vitamin D absorbed through the diet, as weaning food (as described in the primary sources) did not include oily fish (Oxford Medical Dictionary 2000: 703). Their risk during weaning may have been heightened if they had previously consumed breast-milk low in vitamin D (Lewis 2007:120). Socio-economic factors are important cultural buffers against disease and as in later historical periods, high status children may have had higher rates of metabolic diseases because they spent more time indoors (Molleson and Cox 1993). As the disease was present in rural and urban communities in medieval England (Roberts and Cox 2003), it suggests that risk factors (not excluding wealth) present in both environments led to the development of rickets in this period.

Key changes in the life course may have increased the risk of developing metabolic diseases, particularly those in adolescence and later childhood. However, it should be noted that our ability to recognise rickets in these individuals is influenced by their activity levels, as those who keep mobile often display the most severe deformities (Lewis 2007:122). These older individuals would have been regarded as reaching pueritia or adolescentia, and many could have changed households

or migrated to London as apprentices (Hanawalt 1993), as their greater numbers suggest (Table 2). We should also consider that many could have been entirely self-reliant and/or independent of their families (see Panter-Brick 2000). This life-way change may have resulted in many having a nutritionally compromised diet or a downturn in their economic circumstances which prevented them from purchasing adequate food; as they would have had to be nutritionally compromised for a long period of time before an osseous response was initiated (Brickley and Ives 2006). Ortner (2003: 384) notes that populations who predominantly consume cooked food are at greater risk of developing scurvy; and unlike their rural counter-parts, urban dwellers had a greater opportunity to purchase cooked food from cookshops, piebakers and taverns (Hammond 1998:50).

'Sticks and stones': sub-adult trauma
The analysis of trauma sustained during childhood provides an insight into the risks encountered in the living environment. Sub-adult fracture risk and patterning has been demonstrated to correlate with increasing development and their level of dependence (Agran et al. 2001; 2003). For example, pre-mobile infants are more likely to fall from furniture and sustain head injuries (Warrington and Wright 2001).

The sub-adult fracture prevalence was very low, at 0.05% of all observed sub-adult bones. This result is typical of archaeological populations, as sub-adult bones are less likely to fracture because their bones are more elastic and able to absorb more energy before fracturing. The fracture mechanism causes plastic deformation of the bone or a greenstick fracture, which can be rapidly remodelled and obliterated during growth (Currey and Butler 1975; Lovell 1997; Roberts and Manchester 2005). Sub-adults are also more likely to sustain lacerations or abrasions, which are unobservable in skeletonized material (Gratz 1979). As in adults, sex differences in trauma rates exist in sub-adults, with males more likely to sustain an injury (Klauber et al. 1986).

No infants or individuals in early childhood had evidence for fractures, which may be due to the rapid skeletal remodelling in these age groups, but also suggests that trauma associated with birth and from abuse was very low. Clinical data has also shown that accidental trauma has a low risk of death in these age groups (Lewis 2007; Rivara 1982). Falls in pre-mobile infants are unlikely to result in fracture or result in an osseous change, and any injuries they do sustain are less severe as the fall drop is usually less than 10 feet (Warrington and Wright 2001). In later childhood, the majority of fractures were sustained to the skull by a blunt force mechanism, which is a common clinical finding. Sub-adults often have a higher skull fracture rate compared to adults, because the neck muscles are weaker and the head is relatively large compared to the remainder of the body (Gratz 1979: 551). Limb bone fractures are commonly associated with increasing mobility (Agran et al. 2001; 2003). The higher rate of arm fractures conforms to clinical data, which found that the upper limb is more frequently involved in severe injuries (Gratz 1979: 551). Where upper limb fracture mechanisms could be identified, they show that injuries were produced by a fall onto a flexed elbow causing the humerus to fracture, usually during falls from a height or during play (Apley and Solomon 2000: 275; Galloway 1999: 120). Although falls are usually considered accidental, the context of this injury may also include inter-personal violence (Judd 2004: 47). One individual had a healed fracture to the second left rib and Barness et al. (2003) suggest that a rib fracture is a positive predictor of non-accidental trauma. For a sub-adult to sustain a fracture to the ribs, considerable compression or crushing must have taken place (Galloway 1999: 107).

The lower limb fractures were observed in two tibiae, and were produced by torsion and fatigue mechanisms. Tibial fractures are very common in children and are most frequently sustained during sports activities (Galloway 1999: 193). Torsion fractures of the tibia are usually caused by a fall when the individual is a toddler (Resnick and Goergen 2002). Fatigue fractures are produced by repetitive stress (Apley and Solomon 2000: 334), and recent clinical literature suggests that this fracture type is within the trauma spectrum sustained by toddlers (Moorthy and Swischuk 1997; Niemeyer et al. 2006) and was probably sustained when this individual was learning to walk. One individual had a healed fracture to the fourth left metatarsal produced by direct force; this foot bone is less frequently fractured in sub-adults compared to the first and fifth metatarsals (Owen et al. 1995). As the fracture type is not fatigue, it was most likely caused by a heavy object falling onto their foot (Apley and Solomon 2000: 343).

Adolescent individuals generally had fractures to the same body areas as those in later childhood. Many were most probably sustained between the ages of 6 to 11 years; however, only adolescents have spinal fractures to the thoracic and lumbar vertebrae. These fractures were caused by compression or avulsion forces, either by extreme movement of the body or blows to other areas of the body, the force of which was transmitted through the spine. In a clinical setting, such fractures are often associated with child abuse (Galloway 1999); however, other clinical data demonstrates that they are most frequently caused by falls, sports or play, particularly in those aged between 10-14 years (Stulik et al. 2006).

The sample from St Mary Spital had the only reported sub-adult hand fracture in Britain (Table 3), a result possibly biased by differences in recovery practices and developments in the study of sub-adult trauma over time (Lewis 2007). These fractures reflect their employment including manual tasks, making the hands vulnerable to trauma (Galloway 1999: 152). Clinical studies have shown that trauma to the hand phalanges are the second most frequently occurring fracture in children (Landin 1983). Like their peers who had died during later childhood, those surviving to adolescence had sustained fractures to pedal bones, particularly to the first pedal phalange, which was most likely sustained before the age

of 5 years (Owen et al. 1995). The majority of hand and foot fractures did not heal satisfactorily; this may be because such fractures are hard to set, or that the adolescents did not consider that they warranted treatment (Grauer and Roberts 1996). The majority of the remaining fractures observed in adolescents were produced by mechanisms encountered in later childhood. There is also the only example of a healed fracture with osteomyelitis (to a humerus) within the sub-adult sample: the long-term survival of infected fractures by sub-adults is attested in miracle narratives (Gordon 1991).

Gordon's (1991) analysis of accidental trauma using six miracle narratives has shown that the most frequently affected individuals were males under 13 years old; the minority of accidents resulted in fractures, sprains or dislocations; and the majority of accidents were sustained at home or nearby. It is very interesting to note that these findings correlate to those reported in clinical data (e.g. Gratz 1979; Rivara 1982), allowing us to postulate that the majority of fractures observed in the St Mary Spital sample were sustained around the home and local environs, particularly for those classed as *infantia* (0-2 years). The majority of individuals included in the miracle narratives had been involved in an accident before the age of four, usually because of poor care by their parents or siblings (Gordon 1991). The number of healed 'toddler's' fractures to the head, arms and legs observed in the older children in the sample possibly reflects the risk from falls before the age of four. It is significant that in the miracle narratives, adolescents (Gordon's criteria, > 13 years old) have the lowest risk of accident; this may be because they were no longer at home, or were deemed old enough to take care of themselves. In contrast, the osteological data suggests that they had a high risk of trauma.

The analysis of fracture location and mechanism in sub-adults from St Mary Spital has demonstrated that the majority of fractures were those commonly sustained during *infantia* and associated with growth, greater mobility and play. The evidence from the miracle narratives and clinical data suggests that the majority of trauma was sustained in the local environment that contained many hazards, from open hearths to animals (Gordon 1991). The changing pattern of trauma with age reflects the medieval life course. *Adolescentia* would have resulted in many sub-adults beginning employment in occupations that relied upon manual labour (particularly males, as attested in the clinical literature), and many fractures could have been sustained before undertaking rural-to-urban migration. By taking a life course approach to the trauma data, it has been shown that adolescents were engaging in repetitive and strenuous activity that often resulted in stress fractures.

Conclusions

The results from St Mary Spital indicate that the urban environment presented a risk to all age groups, but particularly in *adolescentia* and to those being weaned. The data show that for many, the dependent period of their life course was hazardous, resulting in compromised nutrition (causing rickets and scurvy) and risk of injury. The demographic results, although influenced by medieval funerary practices and catastrophic events, is suggested to indicate a number of factors; endogenous risks early in life, and the increased numbers of those in later childhood and adolescence may reflect their migration to the city as workers (Hanawalt 1993). The trauma data indicate that *adolescentia* was a key period in the life course, with health directly influenced by cultural change.

These results show that the stressors of medieval London, particularly during episodes of social and environmental catastrophe, were such that the frailer members of the community could not adapt (Wood et al. 1992). The most important findings were the relationship between the medieval life course and changing patterns of health with age, supporting the documented migration of young workers to the city and the often-hazardous nature of city life, showing that 'growing up' in London was a unique experience.

Acknowledgements

Express thanks are given to the other members of the Spitalfields osteology team (Brian Connell and Amy Gray Jones), Natasha Powers and Chris Thomas. We are also grateful to the Spitalfields Development Group, the Corporation of London and Hammerson for their support.

Literature cited

Ariès, P. 1965. *Centuries of Childhood*. London: Vintage.

Agran, PF, Winn, D, Anderson, C, Trent, R and Walton-Haynes, L. 2001. Rates of pediatric and adolescent injuries by year of age. *Pediatrics* 108 (3) 1-11.

Agran, PF, Winn, D, Anderson, C, Trent, R, Walton-Haynes, L and Thayer, S. 2003. Rates of pediatric injuries by 3-month intervals for children 0 to 3 years of age. *Pediatrics* 111 (6):683-692.

Apley, AG and Solomon, L. 2000. *Concise System of Orthopaedics and Fractures*. London: Arnold.

Barnes, E. 1994. *Developmental Defects of the Axial Skeleton in Paleopathology*. Boulder: Colorado University Press.

Barness, KA, Cha, ES, Bensard, DD, Calkins, CM, Partrick, DA, Karrer, FM and Strain, JD. 2003. The positive predictive value of rib fractures as an indicator of nonaccidental trauma in children. *Journal of Trauma* 54 (6): 1107-1110.

Baxter, JA. 2005. *The Archaeology of Childhood. Children, Gender, and Material Culture*. Oxford: Altamira Press.

Bogin, B. 1998. Evolutionary and biological aspects of childhood. In: Panter-Brick C. (ed.) *Biosocial Perspectives on Children*. Cambridge: Cambridge University Press, 10-43.

Boswell, J. 1988. *The Kindness of Strangers: The Abandonment of Children in Western Europe from Late Antiquity to the Renaissance*. Chicago: The University of Chicago Press.

Brickley, M. 2000. The diagnosis of metabolic disease in archaeological bone. In Cox, M and Mays, S (eds.) *Human Osteology in Archaeology and Forensic Science*. Cambridge: Cambridge University Press, 183-198.

Brickley, M and Ives, R. 2006. Skeletal manifestations of infantile scurvy. *American Journal of Physical Anthropology* 129 (2): 163-172.

Butler, S.M. 2006. Degrees of culpability: suicide verdicts, mercy, and the jury in medieval England. *Journal of Medieval and Early Modern Studies* 36.2, 263-290.

Connell, B, Gray Jones, A, Redfern, RC and Walker D. in review. *Spitalfields: A Bioarchaeological Study of Health and Disease from a Medieval London Cemetery*. Archaeological excavations at Spitalfields Market 1991–2007, Volume 3. London: MoLAS Monograph.

Currey, JD and Butler, G. 1975. The mechanical properties of bone tissue in children. *The Journal of Bone and Joint Disease* 57 (6): 810-184.

Ditkowsky, SP, Goldman, A, Barnett, H, Baker, M, and Sammett, J. 1970. Normal periosteal reactions and associated soft-tissue findings. *Clinical Pediatrics* 9 (9): 515-524.

Fildes, VA. 1986. *Breasts, Bottles and Babies: A History of Infant Feeding*. Edinburgh: Edinburgh University Press.

Galloway, A. (ed.) 1999. *Broken Bones. Anthropological Analysis of Blunt Force Trauma*. Illnois: Charles C Thomas.

Gilchrist, R. and Sloane, B. 2005. *Requiem: The Medieval Monastic Cemetery in Britain*. London: Museum of London Archaeology Service.

Goodman, AH and Armelagos, GJ 1989. Infant and childhood morbidity and mortality risks in archaeological populations. *World Archaeology* 21 (2): 225-243.

Gordon, EC. 1991. Accidents among medieval children as seen from the miracles of six English Saints and Martyrs. *Medical History* 35 (2): 145-163.

Gratz, RR. 1979. Accidental injury in childhood: a literature review on pediatric trauma. *The Journal of Trauma* 19(8): 551-555.

Grauer, AL and Roberts, CA. 1996. Paleoepidemiology, healing, and possible treatment of trauma in the medieval cemetery population of St. Helen-on-the-Walls, York, England. *American Journal of Physical Anthropology* 100 (4): 531-544

Gustafson, BE and Koch, G. 1974. Age estimation up to 16 years of age based on dental development. *Odontologisk Revy* 25: 297-306.

Hall, AJ and Peckham, CS. 1997. Infections in childhood and pregnancy as a cause of adult disease - methods and examples. *British Medical Bulletin* 53 (1): 10-23.

Hammond, PW. 1998. *Food and Feast in Medieval England.* Stroud: Sutton Publishing Ltd.

Hanawalt, BA. 1993. *Growing Up in Medieval London.* Oxford: Oxford University Press.

Hareven, TK. 2001. Historical perspectives on aging and family relations. In: Binstock, RH and George, LK (eds.) *Handbook of Aging and the Social Sciences.* New York: Academic Press, 141-159.

Harlow, M and Laurence, R. 2002. *Growing Up and Growing Old in Ancient Rome, A Life Course Approach.* London: Routledge.

Holzel, H. 1993. Infection in pregnancy and the neonatal period. In: Keeling, JW. (ed.) *Fetal and Neonatal Pathology.* London: Springer-Verlag, 295-321.

Hutchinson, ED. 2008. A life course perspective. In: Hutchinson, E.D. (ed.) *Dimensions of Human Behaviour: The Changing Life Course, Third Edition.* London: Sage Publications Ltd., 1-38.

James, A. 1998. From the child's point of view: issues in the social construction of childhood. In: Panter-Brick C. (ed.) *Biosocial Perspectives on Children.* Cambridge: Cambridge University Press. 45-65.

Judd, M. 2004. Trauma in the City of Kerma: ancient versus modern injury patterns. *International Journal of Osteoarchaeology* 14 (1): 34-51.

Katzenberg, MA, Herring, DA and Saunders, SR. 1996. Weaning and infant mortality: evaluating the skeletal evidence. *Yearbook of Physical Anthropology* 39 (S23): 177-199.

Klauber, MR, Barrett-Connor, E, Hofsetter, CR and Micik, SH. 1986. A population-based study of nonfatal childhood injuries. *Preventative Medicine* 15: 139-149.

Knodel, J. and Kinter, H. 1977. The impact of breast feeding patterns on the biometric analysis of infant mortality. *Demography* 14 (4): 391-409.

Konigsberg, LW, Owsley, DW and Jantz, R.L. 2008. Maximum likelihood estimation of perinatal mortality in paleodemography. *American Journal of Physical Anthropology* 46, 133.

Landin, LA. 1983. Fracture patterns in children. Analysis of 8,682 fractures with special reference to incidence, etiology and secular changes in a Swedish urban population 1950-1979. *Acta orthopaedica Scandinavica, Supplementum* 202: 1-109.

Lewis, AB and Garn, SM. 1970. The relationship between tooth formation and other maturational factors. *Angle Orthodontist* 30: 70-77.

Lewis, ME. 2002. *Urbanisation and Child Health In Medieval and Post-Medieval England. An Assessment of the Morbidity and Mortality of Non-Adult Skeletons from the Cemeteries of Two Urban and Two Rural Sites in England (AD 850-1859).* Oxford: British Archaeological Reports 339.

Lewis, ME. 2007. *The Bioarchaeology of Children, Perspectives from Biological and Forensic Anthropology.* Cambridge: Cambridge University Press.

Lewis, ME and Gowland, R. 2007. Brief and precarious lives: infant mortality in contrasting sites from medieval and post-medieval England (AD 850-1859). *American Journal of Physical Anthropology* 134, 117-129.

Lovell, NC. 1997. Trauma analysis in palaeopathology. *Yearbook of Physical Anthropology* 40 (S25), 139-170.

Lucy, S. 2005. The archaeology of age. In: Diaz-Andreu M, Lucy S, Babic, S and Edwards, DN (eds.). *The Archaeology of Identity, Approaches to Gender, Age, Status, Ethnicity and Religion.* London: Routledge. 43-66.

McEwan, JM, Mays, S and Blake, GM. 2005. The relationship of bone mineral density and other growth parameters to stress indicators in a medieval juvenile population. *International Journal of Osteoarchaeology* 15 (3): 155-163.

Mays, S. 2007. The human remains. In: Mays, S, Harding, C and Heighway, C. (eds.) *Wharram XI: The Churchyard. A Study of Settlement on the Yorkshire Wolds XI.* York: York University, Department of Archaeology, 77-192.

Mays, S, Brickley, M and Ives, R. 2006. Skeletal manifestations of rickets in infants and young children in a historic population from England. *American Journal of Physical Anthropology* 129 (3): 362-374.

Molleson, T and Cox, M. 1993. *The Spitalfields Project, Volume 2: The Anthropology: The Middling Sort.* York: Council for British Archaeology Research Report 86.

Moorrees, CFA, Fanning, EA and Hunt, EF. 1963a. Age variation of formation stages for ten permanent teeth. *Journal of Dental Research* 42 (6): 1490-1502.

Moorrees, CFA, Fanning, EA and Hunt, EF. 1963b. Formation and resorption of three deciduous teeth in children. *American Journal of Physical Anthropology* 21 (2): 205-213.

Moorthy, JSD and Swischuk, LE. 1997. Expanding the concept of the toddler's fracture. *Radiographics* 17 (2): 367-376.

Niemeyer, P, Weinberg, A, Schmitt, H, Kreuz, PC, Ewerbeck, V and Kasten, P. 2006. Stress fractures in the juvenile skeletal system. *International Journal of Sports Medicine* 27 (3): 242-249.

Orme, N. 2001. *Medieval Children*. Yale: Yale University Press.

Ortner, DJ. 2003. *Identification of Pathological Conditions in Human Skeletal Remains. 2nd Ed.* London: Academic Press.

Ortner, DJ and Mays, S. 1998. Dry-bone manifestations of rickets in infancy and early childhood. *International Journal of Osteoarchaeology* 8 (1): 45-55.

Owen, RJ, Hickey, FG and Finlay, DB. 1995. A study of metatarsal fractures in children. *Injury* 26 (8): 537-538.

Oxford Medical Dictionary. 2000. Oxford: Oxford University Press.

Paine, RR and Boldsen, JL. 2002. Linking age-at-death distributions and ancient population dynamics: a case-study. In: Hoppa, RD and Vaupel, JW. (eds.) *Paleodemography. Age Distributions from Skeletal Samples.* Cambridge: Cambridge University Press, 169-180.

Panter-Brick, C. 2000. 'Nobody's children? A reconsideration of child abandonment. In: Panter-Brick, C and Smith, MT. (eds.) *Abandoned Children.* Cambridge: Cambridge University Press, 1-26.

Pollack, L.A. 1983. *The Forgotten Children.* Cambridge: Cambridge University Press.

Powers, N. (ed.) 2008. *Human Osteology Method Statement.* Museum of London.

Resnick, D and Goergen, TG. 2002. Traumatic diseases. In: Resnick, D. (ed.) *Diagnosis of Bone and Joint Disorders. 4th Ed.* Philadelphia: WB Saunders, 2627-3015.

Richards, MP, Mays, S and Fuller, BT. 2002. Stable carbon and nitrogen isotope values of bone and teeth reflect weaning age at the medieval Wharram Percy site, Yorkshire, UK. *American Journal of Physical Anthropology* 119 (3): 205-210.

Rivara, FP. 1982. Epidemiology of childhood injuries. *American Journal of Diseases of Children* 136 (5): 399-405.

Roberts, C. 2000. Trauma in biocultural perspective: past, present and future work in Britain. In: Cox, M and Mays, S. (eds.) *Human Osteology in Archaeology and Forensic Science.* Cambridge: Cambridge University Press, 337-356.

Roberts, C and Cox, M. 2003. *Health and Disease in Britain. From Prehistory to the Present Day.* Stroud: Sutton Publishing.

Roberts, C and Manchester, K. 2005. *The Archaeology of Disease.* Stroud: Sutton Publishing.

Rousham, EK and Humphrey, LT. 2002. The dynamics of child survival. In: Macbeth, H and Collison, P. (eds.) *Human Population Dynamics. Cross-Disciplinary Perspectives.* Cambridge: Cambridge University Press, 124-140.

Saunders, SR and Barrans, L. 1999. What can be done about the infant category in skeletal samples? In: Hoppa, RD and Fitzgerald, CM. (eds.) *Human Growth in the Past. Studies from Bones and Teeth.* Cambridge: Cambridge University Press, 183-209.

Scheuer, L and Black, S. 2000. *Developmental Juvenile Osteology.* London: Academic Press.

Shahar, S. 1990. *Childhood in the Middle Ages.* London: Routledge.

Shopfner, CE. 1966. Periosteal bone growth in normal infants. A preliminary report. *American Journal of Roentgenology, Radium Therapy and Nuclear Medicine* 97 (1): 154-163.

Sofaer Derevenski, J. 1997. Linking age and gender as social variables. *Ethnographisch Archäologischen Zeitschrift* 38 (3&4): 485-493.

Stuart-Macadam, P. 1995a. Biocultural perspectives on breastfeeding. In: Stuart-Macadam, P and Dettwyler, KA. (eds.) *Breastfeeding. Biocultural Perspectives.* New York: Transaction Publishers, 1-37.

Stuart-Macadam, P. 1995b Breastfeeding in Prehistory. In: Stuart-Macadam, P and Dettwyler, KA. (eds.) *Breastfeeding. Biocultural Perspectives.* New York: Transaction Publishers, 75-99.

Stulik, J, Pesl, T, Kryl, J, Vyskocil, T, Sebesta, P and Havranek, P. 2006. Spinal injuries in children and adolescents. *Acta Chirurgiae Orthopaedicae et Traumatologiae Cechoslovaca* 73 (5): 313-320.

Thomas, C, Sloane, B and Phillpotts, C, (eds.). 1997. *Excavations at the Priory and Hospital of St Mary Spital, London*: MoLAS Monograph.

Thomas, C. 2004. *Life and Death in London's East End.* Museum of London.

Warrington, SA and Wright, CM. 2001 Accidents and resulting injuries in premobile infants: data from the ALSPAC study. *Archives of Diseases in Childhood* 85: 104-107.

Wood, J W, Milner G R, Harpending, H C and Weiss, K M. 1992. The Osteological Paradox. Problems of Inferring Prehistoric Health from Skeletal Samples, *Current Anthropology* 33 (4): 343-370.

Preservation of Non-adult Long Bones from an Almshouse Cemetery in the United States dating to the Late Nineteenth and Early Twentieth Centuries

Colleen Milligan,[1] Jessica Zotcavage[2] and Norman Sullivan[3]

[1]Department of Anthropology, Michigan State University, 354 Baker Hall, East Lansing, MI, USA 48824

[2]Department of Anthropology, University of Colorado at Denver, Campus Box 103, P.O. Box 173364
Denver, CO, USA 80217-3364

[3]Department of Social and Cultural Sciences, Marquette University, Lalumiere Language Hall, Room 340
P.O. Box 1881, Milwaukee, WI, USA 53201-1881

norman.c.sullivan@mu.edu
millig25@msu.edu

Abstract

An analysis was conducted on 588 non-adult skeletal remains from an almshouse cemetery, in use between AD1884 and 1924. A sample of 152 non-adults was further studied with the intent of determining the contribution of various factors in the preservation of the skeletal remains. A preservation coding system was developed for this analysis, with a total preservation score was determined for each individual. The degree of preservation was tested against age of the individual, soil pH, and locus of the burial relative to an area of standing water adjacent to the cemetery. Each of these factors had an effect on preservation. However, only 32.3% of the variance in preservation is explained by the interaction of these factors, and further work will be required to identify additional causes of variation in preservation.

Keywords: Skeletal preservation, infant taphonomy, almshouse cemetery

Introduction

The state of preservation of human skeletal remains is a critical factor in determining the degree to which bioarchaeologists can offer complete and reliable reconstructions of past populations (Boddington et al. 1987). Differential preservation of skeletal elements has important implications in the reconstruction of demographic features (Garland 1989; Walker et al. 1988), and palaeopathological diagnoses (Waldron 1987). Beyond this, preservation plays a determinate role in forensic identification and the circumstances of death (Correia and Beattie 2002; Darwent and Lyman 2002; Saul and Saul 2002).

The taphonomic factors affecting preservation of skeletal remains have been well studied (a thorough discussion is provided by Henderson 1987). The durability of specific anatomical elements has been documented from differing burial contexts (Ubelaker 1974; Waldron 1987; Mays 1991; Larsen 2002). Factors such as the chronological age of the individual are strongly linked with preservation as a result of the amount and density of mineralized tissue (Walker et al. 1988; Guy et al. 1997; Galloway et al. 2002). Furthermore, soil pH has long been known to significantly affect bone preservation, and the degree of its effects has been studied previously (Gordon and Buikstra 1981). Additional factors playing a role in skeletal preservation include; exposure to water in the burial environment (Goffer 1980), temperature (Von Endt and Ortner 1984), depth of the burial (Stewart 1979), and burial with or without a coffin (Evans 1963). However, the degree to which these factors interact and collectively affect the preservation of skeletal remains is more difficult to discern and forms the basis of this study.

Earlier works on skeletal preservation in the United States (Walker et al. 1988; Saunders et al. 1995) have tended to focus on adults, particularly with regard to both age and sex dimensions. When non-adults are analyzed, factors such as soil pH, bone mineral content, age at death, and location of burial are often cited factors in preservation (Gordon and Buikstra 1981; Larsen 2002; Stojanowski et al. 2002). The available sample size of these studies tends to be relatively small, with ages ranging from birth to adolescence. A notable exception has been the more recent work on the non-adults from the Spitalfields collection and the comparison of other historical samples (Bello et al. 2006; Lewis and Gowland 2007). The current work expands the data on preservation in non-adults. The variables included in this study were selected because of their use in other similar studies, and also because of the availability of such data from the original archaeological excavations.

Materials and Methods

Skeletal preservation is documented in this study by analysis of the long bones in a sample of non-adults from the Milwaukee County Institutional Grounds Cemetery, located in Wauwatosa, Wisconsin, US. The overall skeletal collection is comprised of 1649 individuals.

These represent the interments in the cemetery made between AD1884 and 1924, and include the remains of residents of an orphanage, tuberculosis sanatorium, insane asylum and the county almshouse, as well as unclaimed bodies from the city of Milwaukee (Richards and Kastell 1993). The collection includes the skeletal remains of 588 non-adults. It was possible to provide dental ages for 173 of the non-adults, and of these 76% were younger than six months of age at their time of death (Sullivan et al. 2007).

The non-adults were interred in coffins, typically made from pine or poplar, which were placed in the ground without the construction of crypts (Richards and Kastell 1993). The depth of the burials cannot be determined since the landscape of the cemetery area was modified on a number of occasions subsequent to the interments. Excavations of the non-adults demonstrated that the coffins had, in most instances, deteriorated to the point where their presence was marked only by soil colour differences. However, in a few burials, small fragments of badly decayed wood remained. The remains of all the interments were completely reduced to skeletons. During excavation, the non-adult burials were fully exposed *in situ*, photographed, and then removed in a block. The block was water screened on a 1/8 inch mesh.

Only 152 individuals, from the total collection of non-adults, were included in this study. The selection of non-adult burials included those for which the following variables were present: estimated age at death; preservation score for both the articular portion and shaft of long bones; measure of soil pH; and measure of feet above mean sea level for the burial itself. The age of the non-adults was determined from observations of the mineralization of both the crown and root of teeth (Moorrees et al. 1963ab). These observations were obtained from radiographs of both available single-rooted and multiple-rooted teeth (Sullivan et al. 2007). In addition, teeth that were no longer secured in the sockets were measured for dental crown dimensions (Liversidge et al. 1993). Observations of the appearance and fusion of epiphyses (Scheuer and Black 2000) and measurements of various cranial and postcranial bones (Fazekas and Koza 1978) were included in the overall age assessments used in this study. Observations of dental pathologies, such as linear enamel hypopolasias and neonatal lines, were also considered when possible (Prindiville 1993). Estimations of fetal age were divided into 12 week intervals, starting with 0-12 gestational weeks and ending with 36-44 gestational weeks. Of these, 73 burials were estimated to have died at or around birth, between 36-44 gestational weeks, or 9 months fetal and 1 month post-partum. Given the high number of non-adults with an age-at-death of less than 1 year, estimations of age were divided into 3 month intervals, starting with 1-3 months for the first 2 years of life. Classifications based on two-year intervals were used for age estimations past 24 months (Ubelaker 1989). The age classifications were established to address issues related to preservation at the prenatal, neonatal, and post-neonatal stages.

For statistical purposes, each age category was then given a 'score' between 1-15. When an age estimation for an individual burial encompassed two categories, a score that averaged those categories was used instead. For example, an age estimation of 3-9 months post-partum which would include both the 3-6 month age category (score 6) and 6-9 month age category (score 7), was averaged to score 6.5. Table 1 outlines the age categories used, the number of individuals included in each, and the scores given to the age categories. Score averages, such as '6.5', are shown as grouped with the lowest age category included in the average, which in the example mentioned previously would be 3-6 months post-partum.

Table 1: Non-adult age categories

Age Categories	N.Individuals (n=152)	Categorical Score for Age
0-12 weeks	0	1
12-24 weeks	3	2
24-36 weeks	19	3
36-40 weeks	73	4
1-3 months	21	5
3-6 months	10	6
6-9 months	15	7
9-12 months	2	8
12-15 months	3	9
15-18 months	1	10
18-21 months	3	11
21-24 months	0	12
2-4 years	1	13
4-6 years	1	14
6-8 years	0	15
Total	152	

Soil samples, taken during excavation of each burial, were recorded for pH using the Oakton pH tester. Table 2 shows the range of pH scores and the number of individual burials included in each.

Table 2: Soil pH categories

Soil pH	Number of burials
6.5	7
6.6	17
6.7	30
6.8	40
6.9	24
7	13
7.1	19
7.2	2

During excavation, the depth of each burial was recorded as Feet Above Mean Sea Level (FAMSL), with a minimum measure of 722.073 feet and a maximum measure of 749.490 feet. These data were categorized in 0.999-foot increments (Table 3).

Table 3: Feet above mean sea level

FAMSL	Categorical Score for FAMSL	Number of Burials
722-722.999	22	1
723-723.999	23	0
724-724.999	24	17
725-725.999	25	11
726-726.999	26	24
727-727.999	27	16
728-728.999	28	6
729-729.999	29	8
730-730.999	30	1
731-731.999	31	2
732-732.999	32	6
733-733.999	33	7
734-734.999	34	0
735-735.999	35	0
736-736.999	36	0
737-737.999	37	1
738-738.999	38	1
739-739.999	39	6
740-740.999	40	10
741-741.999	41	15
742-742.999	42	10
743-743.999	43	9
744-744.999	44	0
745-745.999	45	0
746-746.999	46	0
747-747.999	47	0
748-748.999	48	0
749-749.999	49	1

Burials near the minima were located in proximity to permanent standing water, and as a burial locus was further upslope and more distant from standing water, a higher number was recorded for FAMSL.

The preservation scoring system was developed specifically for this study. This particular system, unlike other commonly used approaches to preservation coding, generates a number which reflects not only the degree to which the skeletal element is present, but also is indicative of the degree to which the element is intact and useful for additional analyses.

Preservation scores were calculated for both the articular surfaces and the shaft of each long bone. For each major long bone in each burial, a preservation score was calculated based on a percentage scale:

Articular Surfaces:
- Score of 1.0 (100%) – no damage to the cortical bone and no cancellous bone visible
- Score of 0.75 (75%) – at least 75% of cortical bone present
- Score of 0.50 (50%) – at least 50% but less than 75% of cortical bone present
- Score of 0.25 (25%) – at least 25% but less than 50% of cortical bone present
- Score of 0.10 (10%) – trace amounts of cortical bone present
- Score of 0.0 (0%) – no cortical bone present

Shaft:
- Score of 1.0 (100%) – shaft complete with minimal weathering on surface
- Score of 0.75 (75%) – at least 75% of shaft present
- Score of 0.50 (50%) – at least 50% but less than 75% of shaft present
- Score of 0.25 (25%) – at least 25% but less than 75% of shaft present
- Score of 0.10 (10%) – shaft identifiable but less than 25% present
- Score of 0.0 (0%) – shaft absent

Individual preservation scores were recorded for all articular surfaces and the proximal third, middle third, and distal third of each shaft present. For each burial, these scores were added together for an overall preservation score (PreservS). The maximum possible score is 36, where all twelve major long bones are intact and have suffered no cortical bone loss.

Statistical analysis of the variables looked at the associations between variables and the amount of variance, in regards to preservation of non-adult long bones that can be explained by soil pH, feet above mean sea level, and estimated age. The strength of the relationship between all variables was tested with Pearson product-moment correlation coefficients (r_p) (Hinton et al. 2004). All tests were conducted using the SPSS statistical program.

Results

Based on previous studies related to the preservation of immature remains, the strength of the relationships between variables was tested. Using Pearson's product-moment correlation coefficients (r_p), the correlation between preservation of long bones and age was tested. The result was significant at an alpha level of 0.05 (r_p=-0.164; p=0.044; n=152). The calculation of r^2 shows that only 2.7% of the variation in long bone preservation is explained by the relationship between age and preservation (Garson n.d.). The preservation of long bones was found to have a negative correlation with age. As the estimated age increased, the level of preservation decreased. This relationship could be a product of the large number of non-adults aged at less than 1 year. Previous studies (Guy et al. 1997) have suggested that the mineral content of non-adult bones is higher during fetal development than during the first two years of life.

The correlation between preservation of the long bones and feet above mean sea level (FAMSL) was also found to be significant. However, the strength of the association with FAMSL was stronger than that found with age at death. The results were significant at an alpha level of 0.01 (r_p=0.534, p=0.000; n=152). The calculation of r^2 shows that 28.5% of the variation in long bone preservation is explained by the relationship between FAMSL and preservation. The resulting observations show that as FAMSL increases so does the preservation of long bones in non-adult burials.

Of the three independent variables tested, the correlation between soil pH and long bone preservation was the only one not found to be significant. The results showed an r_p value of -0.157 with p=0.054 and n=152. However, the calculation of r^2 shows that 2.5% of the variation in long bone preservation is explained by this relationship. While the relationship between soil pH and long bone preservation was not found to be significant, the impact of this variable on preservation was found to be similar to the impact of age. Both variables represented less than 3% of the variation seen in the preservation of long bones.

Each of the correlations conducted showed at least a minimal amount of influence over the preservation of non-adult long bones. To further examine the relationship between the variables and preservation, a SPSS linear regression analysis was used. Specifically, the additional analysis was used to address the ability of the combined independent variables to predict the dependent variable of preservation (Garson n.d.). FAMSL, estimated age, and pH were found to have an r^2 value of 0.323. In addition, an F value of 23.500 with p = 0.000 was calculated using the regression model. When considered together, 32.3% of the variance in preservation can be reliably predicted from the independent variables. When considered separately, soil pH and FAMSL were found to be significant in their ability to predict preservation. Table 4 lists the coefficients and significance levels for FAMSL, soil pH, and age from the linear regression analysis.

Conclusions

Most of the variation observed in the preservation of this sample is unexplained by factors that have, in other studies, been shown to have a determinative effect. As shown by Gordon and Buikstra (1981), the affect of one variable, such as soil pH, on the preservation of non-adults is minimal. However, the use of several variables has a much higher predictive value in regards to states of preservation. The current study found that the combination of soil pH, age, and location of the non-adult burials represented only about a third of the variation seen. This is in part due to the age structure of the sample, with the majority of the non-adults under 1 year of age providing only limited data. Guy et al. (1997) point to the fact that in archaeological contexts, the lack of preservation often observed for non-adult remains may be a factor of both biological constraints (age-related mineral content of bones), and cultural practices regarding the burials themselves. The results of the current study would benefit from a more complex analysis of the burial practices of the Milwaukee County Institutional Grounds, specifically in regards to the burial of the very young. As more of the archival research is completed, it is expected that data will become available on the specific month and year of interment for each of the burials, and possibly the type of wood used in the manufacture of coffins for individual burials as well. Beyond this, GIS work is underway that will allow us to better understand at least some aspects of the landscape modifications in the cemetery area, and to overlay access drives and cart paths over the internment areas to determine any possible contribution from soil compaction in affecting preservation.

Acknowledgements

This analysis was made possible with a grant from the Hewlett Foundation and the considerable assistant given by Rev. SJ Thaddeus Burch, Dean of the Graduate School (retired), Marquette University and Dr Erik Thelen, Director, Office of Research Support and Sponsored Programs, Marquette University. The authors also very much appreciate the helpful comments on the manuscript given by Professor William Lovis, Michigan State University.

Table 4: Results from the linear regression analysis

	unstandardized coefficients		standardized coefficients		Sig. (alpha level = .05)
	B	SE	Beta	t	
Constant	-8.216	3.284		-2.502	0.013
Age	-0.561	0.291	-0.131	-1.927	0.056
pH	8.893	4.127	0.171	2.155	0.033
FAMSL	0.756	0.098	0.614	7.743	0.000

Literature Cited

Bello SM, Thomann A, Signoli M, Dutour O, and Andrews P. 2006. Age and sex bias in the reconstruction of past population structures. *American Journal of Physical Anthropology* 129: 24-38.

Boddington, A, Garland, AN and Janaway, RC. 1987. Flesh, bones dust and society, in A Boddington, AN Garland and RC Janaway (eds.): *Death, Decay and Reconstruction. Approaches to Archaeology and Forensic Science.* Manchester: Manchester University Press, 3-9.

Correia, PM and Beattie O. 2002. A critical look at methods for recovering, evaluating, and interpreting cremated human remains, in WD Haglund and MH Sorg (eds.): *Advances in Forensic Taphonomy: Method, Theory, and Archaeological Perspectives.* Boca Raton: CRC Press, 435-450.

Darwent, CM and RL Lyman. 2002. Detecting the postburial fragmentation of carpals, tarsals, and phalanges, in WD Haglund and MH Sorg (eds.): *Advances in Forensic Taphonomy: Method, Theory, and Archaeological Perspectives.* Boca Raton: CRC Press, 355-389.

Evans, WED. 1963. *The Chemistry of Death.* Springfield: Charles C Thomas.

Fazekas IG, and Kósa F. 1978. *Forensic Fetal Osteology.* Budapest: Academic Press.
Galloway A, Willey P, and Snyder L. 2002. Human bone mineral densities and survival of bone elements: a contemporary sample, in WD Haglund and MH Sorg (eds.): *Advances in Forensic Taphonomy: Method, Theory, and Archaeological Perspectives.* Boca Raton: CRC Press, 295-317.

Garland, AN. 1989. The taphonomy of inhumation burials, in CA Roberts, F Lee and J Bintliff (eds.): *Burial Archaeology: Current Research, Methods and Developments.* Oxford: BAR British Series 211, 15-37.

Garson GD n.d. *Statnotes: Topics in Multivariate Analysis.* Retrieved 11/10/2007 from http://www2.chass.ncsu.edu/garson/pa765/statnote.htm

Goffer, Z. 1980. *Archaeological Chemistry.* New York: John Wiley and Sons.

Gordon, CC and Buikstra JE. 1981. Soil pH, bone preservation and sampling bias at mortuary sites. *American Antiquity* 46: 566-571.

Guy H, Masset C, and Baud CA. 1997. Infant taphonomy. *International Journal of Osteoarchaeology* 7:221-229.

Henderson, J. 1987. Factors determining the state of preservation of human remains, in A Boddington, AN

Garland and RC Janaway (eds.): *Death, Decay and Reconstruction. Approaches to Archaeology and Forensic Science.* Manchester: Manchester University Press, 43-54.

Hinton PR, C Brownlow, I McMurray, and B Cozens. 2004. *SPSS Explained.* New York: Routledge.

Larsen, CS. 2002. *Bioarchaeology of the Late Prehistoric Guale: South End Mound I, St. Catherine's Island, Georgia.* New York: American Museum of Natural History, Anthropological Papers, Number 84.

Lewis ME and R Gowland. 2007. Brief and precarious lives: infant mortality in contrasting sites from medieval and post-medieval England (AD 850-1859). *American Journal of Physical Anthropology* 134: 117-129.

Liversidge, HM, Dean MC and Molleson. TI. 1993. Increasing human tooth length between birth and 5.4 years. *American Journal of Physical Anthropology* 90: 307-313.

Mays, S. 1991. Taphonomic factors in a human skeletal assemblage. *Circea* 9: 54-58.

Moorrees CFA, Fanning E, and Hunt EE. 1963a. Age variation of formation stages for ten permanent teeth. *Journal of Dental Research* 42: 1490-1502.

Moorrees CFA, Fanning E, and Hunt EE. 1963b. Formation and resorption of three deciduous teeth in children. *American Journal of Physical Anthropology.* 21: 205-213.

Prindiville T 1993. *Enamel Hypoplasia in the Remains of Non-adults in the Milwaukee County Institutional Grounds' Pauper Cemetery.* Anthropology Senior Thesis, Marquette University. Milwaukee, Wisconson.

Richards, PB and Kastell MW. 1993. *Archaeological Excavations at the Almshouse Burial Ground, Milwaukee County Poorhouse, Wauwatosa, Wisconsin.* Reports of Investigation No. 333, Great Lakes Archaeological Research Center, Inc.

Saul, JM and Saul FP. 2002. Forensics, archaeology, and taphonomy: The symbiotic relationship, in WD Haglund and MH Sorg (eds.): *Advances in Forensic Taphonomy: Method, Theory, and Archaeological Perspectives.* Boca Raton: CRC Press, 71-98.

Saunders SR, Herring DA, and Boyce G. 1995. Can skeletal samples accurately represent the living population they come from? The St. Thomas' cemetery site, Belleville, Ontario, in AL Grauer (ed): *Bodies of Evidence: Reconstructing History Through Skeletal Analysis.* New York: Wiley-Liss, 69-89.

Scheuer L, and Black S. 2000. *Developmental Juvenile Osteology.* London: Elsevier Academic Press.

Stewart TD. 1979. *Essentials of Forensic Anthropology*. Springfield: Charles C Thomas.

Stojanowski CM, Seidemann RM, and Doran GM. 2002. Differential skeletal preservation at Windover Pond: causes and consequences. *American Journal of Physical Anthropology* 119: 15-26.

Sullivan, NC, Milligan C and Dougherty S. 2007. *A Report on the Non-adult Burials from the Milwaukee County Institutional Grounds Cemetery*. Unpublished Report, on file with the State Historical Society of Wisconsin, Madison.

Ubelaker, DH. 1974. *Reconstruction of Demographic Profiles from Ossuary Skeletal Data*. Smithsonian Contributions to Anthropology, Number 18. Washington, DC: Smithsonian Institution Press.

Ubelaker DH. 1989. *Human Skeletal Remains*. Washington, DC: Taraxacum

Von Endt, DW and Ortner DJ. 1984. Experimental effects of bone size and temperature on bone diagenesis. *Journal of Archaeological Science* 11:247-253.

Waldron, T. 1987. The relative survival of the human skeleton: implications for palaeopathology, in A Boddington, AN Garland and RC Janaway (eds.): *Death, Decay and Reconstruction. Approaches to Archaeology and Forensic Science*. Manchester: Manchester University Press, 55-64.

Walker, PL, Johnson JR and Lambert PR. 1988. Age and sex biases in the preservation of human skeletal remains. *American Journal of Physical Anthropology* 76:183-88.

Child Oral Health: Dental Palaeopathology of Kellis 2, Dakhleh, Egypt
A Preliminary Investigation

Stephanie Shkrum and J.E. Molto

Department of Anthropology, University of Western Ontario, London, Ontario, N6A 5C2
sshkrum@uwo.ca

Abstract

Recently, bioarchaeological research has witnessed an emerging trend, namely reconstructing the role of infants and children in antiquity. A neglected aspect of this trend is the systematic study of dental disease in deciduous teeth relative to age. This is concomitant of the assumption that non-adult dentitions are invariably healthy and of little consequence to their adaptability, an assumption that is primarily based on the limited time for dietary agents to effect change in tooth structure. This paper tests this hypothesis by examining the oral health of infants and children in an agriculturally based population sample from the Kellis 2 cemetery in the Dakhleh Oasis, Egypt.

A sample of 843 deciduous teeth was analyzed using a cohort comparison. The results indicate that there is an association between the development of dental disease and age, as the prevalence of most dental pathology (i.e. caries, periapical abscessing, antemortem trauma and tooth loss) increases with each successive cohort. For example, the prevalence of carious teeth increased from 3.3% to 19.3% between the first (i.e. 1.0 to 3.5 years) and third cohorts (i.e. 6.6 to 9.5 years). Overall, non-adult health appears to be compromised in this sample due to the relatively high prevalence of dental disease, particularly in late childhood.

Keywords: dental disease; children; weaning diet; Roman Egypt

Introduction

The place and contribution of infants and children in society were long neglected topics in anthropology, although this relative lack of research has now fortunately been addressed (Gottlieb 2000). Bioarchaeological research has also witnessed an emerging trend, namely reconstructing the role of infants and children in antiquity. In terms of non-adult health, this emphasis has primarily focused on skeletal manifestations of disease (e.g. periosteal new bone reactions, porotic hyperostosis) with the 'Osteological Paradox' receiving considerable attention in terms of non-adult frailty (Wood et al. 1992). Enamel hypoplasias have often been used as markers of non-adult disease stress (Goodman et al. 1980). However, there are relatively few archaeological studies that focus on the oral health of children. Specifically, there is relatively little information regarding the dental health of the deciduous dentition (Oyamada et al. 2008). The majority of these studies focus on dental caries in medieval children (James and Miller 1970; Williams and Curzon 1985; Watt et al. 1997). Deciduous teeth have also been included in a number of studies regarding caries prevalence in prehistoric England (Moore and Corbett 1971, 1973, 1975; Corbett and Moore 1976; Varrela 1991; O'Sullivan et al. 1993). However, few examples of caries were reported in the deciduous teeth (Moore and Corbett 1971). A number of studies examine enamel defects of the deciduous dentition (e.g. Lunt 1972; Cook and Buikstra 1979; Blakey and Armelagos 1985; Duray 1990; Schulz 1992; Stodder 1997; Halcrow and Tayles 2008). In addition, the relationship between dental disease and general health is not often acknowledged (Schulz 1992; Papathanasiou 2005). The exclusion of deciduous dentitions from analysis appears to be consequence of poor preservation, as deciduous teeth are more fragile (Oyamada et al. 2008) and may be lost from the jaws more easily. Deciduous teeth are also sometimes excluded because these dentitions often lack age-accumulated indicators of diet and disease (Seidemann and McKillop 2007).

Here, a pilot study is conducted to evaluate the oral health of non-adults at Kellis. Specifically, the research will document and interpret dental pathology in a sample (i.e. 64 burials) of non-adults in a Roman period population from the Kellis 2 cemetery in the Dakhleh Oasis, Egypt. The present study uses an epidemiological design known as a 'cohort approach' to analyze dental pathology prevalence in children, including both permanent and deciduous teeth. Defined cohorts (age categories) assess dental disease and general health at different life stages; for non-adults these include early childhood, late childhood and adolescence (Boldsen 2007:62). The categories of dental pathological conditions used to assess oral health include caries, periapical abscessing, antemortem trauma, enamel hypoplasia, attrition and antemortem tooth loss. The analysis of a number of pathological dental conditions addresses questions regarding Kellis 2 non-adult oral health at different ages, factors that contribute to their development (e.g., host resistance, diet, weaning practices), and implications to overall non-adult health. Specific research objectives include: (1) determining the age distribution of dental pathology in non-adults (2) determining the affects of a changing diet throughout childhood to dental pathology prevalence at different ages; and, (3) emphasizing the influence of oral health on general health, especially during childhood. By considering the defined path of dental development in children, and the changing dietary regimens throughout childhood (i.e. breastfeeding, weaning, etc.), this preliminary investigation describes the age-related dental disease patterns observed in the primary dentition of the Dakhleh sample.

The site and burial sample

The Dakhleh Oasis is located in the Western Desert of Egypt, approximately 600 kilometres south-southwest of Cairo (Dupras et al. 2001). Since 1977, this site has been the focus of a multi-field research project, the Dakhleh Oasis Project (DOP). The bioarchaeological component of the DOP focuses on two cemeteries associated with the ancient town of Kellis: Kellis 1 and Kellis 2. The dental sample examined in this study is from Kellis 2, located immediately north of the town site and associated with the site's Roman period occupation (circa AD100 to AD400).

The Dakhleh Oasis is an ideal setting for this type of study, as the arid climate in combination with cultural factors (i.e. Christian burials and wrappings) has produced a large population sample of non-adult remains (Tocheri et al. 2005). The Kellis 2 cemetery offers a unique archaeological circumstance, the examination analysis of 64 well-preserved human non-adult dentitions (i.e. infants to age fifteen) and 806 deciduous teeth. Due to the excellent preservation at Kellis 2, it is possible to analyze both the teeth and the supporting alveolar bone. This is important in dental analyses because dental diseases are interrelated, and affect the entire dentition (Roberts and Manchester 2005). In addition, the individual burial pattern of Kellis 2 has resulted in the recovery of maxillae and mandibles in association with each other and per individual, with no commingling present.

Childhood diet at Kellis, Roman period

The primary function of the mouth is to process food (Lukacs 1989); therefore, it is important to identify available food items at Kellis that influence dietary choices. Dietary choice is important; since the types of food being consumed by children at a young age influences their health and survival. A number of sources exist that provide background dietary information for Kellis. These include a previous isotopic analysis of diet (Dupras 1999), an ancient documentary text recovered from the Kellis town site, and Roman period infant feeding practices. A brief outline of these is provided in order to interpret the dental pathology data. The significance of diet to non-adult oral health is detailed in the discussion.

It is possible that Roman ideologies concerning infant feeding and weaning influenced early childhood diet at Kellis. Infant feeding and weaning practices are specifically mentioned in two documentary sources dating from the Roman period: *Gynecology* (ca. AD98 to AD177) written by the Greek physician Soranus (Temkin 1956), and *De sanitate tuenda* (*"Hygiene"*) (ca. AD130 to AD200) by Galen, a Roman physician who wrote at

length about infant and child care (Green 1951). Soranus recommended infants be exclusively fed breastmilk during the first six months of life. Both Soranus and Galen suggested supplementary foods should be introduced at approximately 6 months, or with the eruption of the first teeth (Dupras 1999:48). It was also advised weaning should be completed by age three years, when enough teeth were erupted to consume solid foods (Dupras 1999:48). Soranus indicated that boiled honey or a mixture of honey and goat's milk constituted the first supplementary food of infants (Dupras et al. 2001). Bread was recommended as the first solid, which could be softened with animal milk. This transition to solid food was described as gradual; where breastmilk was slowly decreased and solid foods were increasingly introduced.

Isotopic evidence from Kellis 2 identifies infant and early childhood dietary patterns, namely the weaning transition. These data can be compared with the Roman period documentary evidence. Nitrogen isotopic values (δ^{15}N) indicate infants were exclusively breast fed until around six months of age. These values begin to decline at this age, while carbon isotopic values (δ^{13}C) begin to increase indicating the consumption of ^{13}C-enriched foods. By age three years δ^{15}N values have decreased to approximately adult levels, while δ^{13}C values are still elevated (Dupras 1999:250). As Dupras (1999:248) notes, the only source of food enriched ^{13}C that was likely fed to infants during this period was the milk of cows and goats. Therefore, it is probable that cow or goat's milk was consumed by infants around age six months (Dupras 1999:248). Both sources of animal's milk were recommended in the Roman period documentary evidence (Fildes 1986). Individuals were also weaned onto a solid food mixture of milk and millet (Dupras 1999). δ^{15}N values point to the completion of weaning by age three years; δ^{13}C values suggest infants were consuming adult food by about 3.5 years (Durpas 1999:250). The weaning transition is significant to early childhood dental disease patterns and to overall child health.

Following the weaning transition, a number of sources provide evidence regarding juvenile and adult diet at Kellis. There are no apparent shifts in diet after the weaning transition; by about age seven years isotopic values in children reflect adult values (Dupras 1999). The discovery of the *Kellis Agricultural Account Book* (KAB) provides documentary evidence of food production at the Dakhleh Oasis (Dupras 1999). The KAB is set of eight wooden tablets excavated in a house (House 2, Area A) at Kellis and date to approximately AD 350 (Hope 1987, 1988; Sharpe 1987). It contains an account, written in ancient Greek, of "all incomes and expenditures, including agricultural and animal goods that were coming in and out of an estate in the village of Kellis" (Dupras 1999:18). The KAB and isotopic evidence indicate a diet composed of C$_3$ foods, such as wheat, barley, fruit, cows and goats. However, isotopic values also identify millet, a C$_4$ plant, was a component of the diet (Dupras 1999:267). Millet was introduced during the Roman period (Dupras 1999:250). The diet at Kellis, therefore, was omnivorous with a considerable consumption of carbohydrates. Kellis 2 non-adults consumed an 'adult diet' beginning in early childhood, which remained consistent throughout adult life.

Methods

The following criteria were examined to assess the oral health of non-adults at Kellis: caries, periapical abscesses, antemortem trauma, enamel hypoplasia, attrition and antemortem tooth loss. These data were collected by Dr JE Molto of the University of Western Ontario over the past decade following Patterson (1984) with minor variations. The dental conditions were studied using both the naked eye and observed under a 10x magnification lens. Teeth were examined for presence, including complete eruption, partial eruption and no eruption. Absence of teeth was also classified as follows: postmortem absence, antemortem absence, congenital absence, and antemortem tooth loss, which included deciduous teeth replaced by permanent teeth. The observation of caries took into consideration its relationship with tooth status and other dental conditions, as dental caries is the main cause of tooth loss in children (Moynihan 2005). The detection of caries is concerned with all macroscopically observable caries. To increase the reliability of recording caries, the observation of caries is limited to cases that penetrate the enamel (Moore and Corbett 1971:157). According to Buikstra and Ubelaker (1994:55) these are observed as stained, irregularly walled cavities. Discolourations are recorded, but not included in caries prevalence. In addition to tooth loss, carious progression to the pulp chamber can result in a periapical abscess. Due to a time constraint for observation, Patterson's methods were simplified using recommendations in *Standards* (Buikstra and Ubelaker 1994:55). Abscesses often appear as circular lesions, which may be confused with circular defects in the alveolar bone that covers root surfaces, known as fenestrations (Hildebolt and Molnar 1991:227). These defects were observed, but not recorded. The analysis of antemortem tooth trauma was also limited to macroscopic observations; therefore, only chipping and fracturing were observed. Antemortem trauma and postmortem trauma were differentiated based on the surface features of rounded edges, scratching of the facets and shine on the enamel surface (Patterson 1984). All classes of hypoplastic developmental defects were considered, including furrow form, pit form and plane form (Hillson and Bond 1997:96). Although not a pathology, occlusal attrition was recorded as evidence of diet. A detailed outline of the scoring scheme can be found in Patterson (1984).

Cohort Approach
Although Patterson's (1984) dissertation included non-adults, the sample was not separated into cohorts. Patterson (1984:74) recommends that the age distribution of a population sample is indicated since dental disease (i.e. caries prevalence) is related to age. The non-adults at Kellis 2 were organized into the following four cohorts (Table 1), to assess the prevalence of dental pathology

throughout childhood growth and development: 1.0 to 3.5 years, 3.6 to 6.5 years, 6.6 to 9.5 years and 9.6 to 15.0 years. These cohorts reflect differences in diet and stages of dental development throughout infancy and childhood. For example, the first cohort (1.0 to 3.5 years) was established to assess the influence of a weaning diet on oral health, since children were weaned until approximately three years of age (Dupras et al. 2001). The second cohort (3.6 to 6.5 years) is representative of a post-weaning diet during which the entire deciduous dentition is exposed. Children in the third cohort have a mixed dentition, while children in the fourth cohort also have a mixed dentition, but have exfoliation of most of their deciduous teeth. Each cohort must have a small enough age range so that changes in pathology prevalence can be compared throughout childhood. On the other hand, the cohorts must be large enough so that the total tooth count in each is of sufficient size for statistical analysis.

Table 1. Cohorts (age categories).

Cohort	Age (years)	No. individuals	No. deciduous teeth
1	1.0-3.5	18	300
2	3.6-6.5	23	374
3	6.6-9.5	11	140
4	9.6-15.0	5	29
Total		57	843

The prevalence of dental pathology was calculated for each cohort at the individual and tooth level. The number of affected teeth was calculated as a proportion of the number of teeth remaining. The number of individuals with at least one affected deciduous tooth out of the number of individuals with deciduous teeth (n=57) was also calculated. The prevalence of pathological teeth and individuals in each cohort is compared by means of the G-statistic. The *G-test* will compare the cohort proportions of dental pathology. All statistical tests were performed using the SPSS statistical programme.

The significance level is set at $P \leq 0.05$, meaning that values falling below this alpha level are deemed significant, and the null hypothesis, that the prevalence of dental pathology between cohorts are equal, is rejected. These analytical and statistical procedures reveal the prevalence and distribution of dental disease throughout childhood during the Roman period of occupation at the Dakhleh Oasis.

Results

A summary of dental pathology prevalence per cohort is given in Tables 2 and 3. The total prevalence of non-adults with deciduous caries is 42%. The prevalence of individuals with at least one deciduous caries varies significantly among the cohorts (G=11.635, 3df, P=0.009). Cohort 3 has the highest proportion of individuals with caries (73%).

Most individuals in this age group have at least one carious tooth. Clearly, the number of carious teeth also varied markedly between the different age groups. The total prevalence of carious teeth in non-adults in this sample is 10.3%. The overall prevalence range among the cohorts is 3.3 to 19.3%. A breakdown of the number of caries according to tooth type is also shown in Table 3. Carious teeth increase with each successive cohort, excluding the last age group. The prevalence of carious teeth in the fourth cohort is an artefact of the normal loss of deciduous teeth and the eruption of permanent teeth. The overall prevalence of caries in the molars is much higher than the proportion of affected anterior teeth. Age and caries development in deciduous teeth are statistically significant (*G*=32.792, 3df, P=0.000).

Alveolar abscessing was scored by tooth site and by individual for all age cohorts. A summary of individuals with at least one periapical abscess is given in Table 2. The prevalence increases with age among the first and third cohorts. The prevalence of individuals with periapical abscessing is notably higher in Cohort 3 (64%). There is a significant difference among age groups (*G*=5.963, 3df, P=0.001). The total prevalence of periapical abscessing in deciduous tooth sites is 2%. Periapical abscessing of tooth sites also revealed an upward trend in prevalence, with a range between 0.3% and 6.5% (Table 3). Evidently, these proportions are significantly less when compared to the other pathological conditions examined in this study. An abscess develops from the progression of other dental diseases (i.e. caries, occlusal attrition, and traumatic injury

(Patterson 1984:76) and, therefore, has less time to develop in the deciduous dentition. Abscessing is absent in the fourth cohort. The prevalence is highest in the first molars (5%) followed by the second molars (2%). The calculations did not include permanent teeth associated with the condition; however, only one burial (burial 302, age 15 years) was excluded. The proportion of tooth sites with periapical abscessing is highly statistically significant among the cohorts (*G*=21.476, 3df, P=0.000).

The total prevalence of individuals with antemortem trauma is 28%. The prevalence of individuals with antemortem trauma among the cohorts is not significant (*G*=6.685, 3df, P=0.083). Again, the highest prevalence is observed in Cohort 3 (54.5%). The total prevalence of antemortem trauma in Kellis 2 deciduous teeth is 4.5%, which ranges between 0.7% and 9%. The prevalence of teeth with antemortem trauma increases with each successive cohort, excluding the last cohort. The highest prevalence of antemortem trauma is found in the third cohort (9%), while the first cohort experiences the lowest prevalence (0.7%). The total prevalence of antemortem trauma reveals it is the most common in the first molars (10%). The prevalence of antemortem trauma increases with age in all tooth types, excluding deciduous canines. A similar trend is evident in antemortem trauma prevalence to that observed in caries prevalence. Although the difference in antemortem trauma among the cohorts is not significant at the individual level, age and antemortem trauma are highly statistically significant (*G*=22.934, 3df, P=0.000).

Enamel hypoplasias are also reported by the prevalence of individuals and teeth affected in each cohort. The total prevalence of individuals with enamel hypoplasia is 14%, with Cohort 1 having the highest prevalence (22%) among the age groups. The prevalence of affected individuals in Cohort 3 is slightly less (18%). No statistical difference is found in enamel hypoplasia prevalence among the cohorts (*G*=3.148, 3df, P=0.369). Enamel defects occur on the following tooth types: canines (5%), second molars (3%), second incisors (1.4%), first molars (1%) and first incisors (0.7%). Enamel defects of the deciduous teeth include both pitting and localized hypoplasia of the deciduous canines (LHDC). Most defects are localized to the canine; however, one individual (burial 23) has 9 teeth with enamel pitting. This explains the higher prevalence of deciduous teeth with enamel hypoplasia in the first cohort (4%). No enamel pitting is found in the last two age cohorts. Dental caries can be an etiological factors in caries development; however, caries and enamel pitting is only observed on one tooth belonging to an individual in the second cohort (1/843 or 0.1%). Although the prevalence of enamel hypoplasia differs among cohorts, the difference is not significant (*G*=7.664, 3df, P=0.053).

Table 2. Cohort comparison of dental disease prevalence (individual count).

Cohort	No. individuals	Caries	Periapical abscess	AM trauma	Enamel hypoplasias	Attrition	AM tooth loss
		n (%)	*n (%)*	*n (%)*	*n (%)*	*n (%)*	*n (%)*
1	18	3 (17)	1 (6)	2 (11)	4 (22)	7 (39)	0 (0)
2	23	12 (52)	3 (13)	7 (30)	2 (9)	20 (87)	0 (0)
3	11	8 (73)	7 (64)	6 (54.5)	2 (18)	11 (100)	4 (36)
4	5	1 (20)	0 (0)	1 (20)	0 (0)	3 (60)	0 (0)
Total	57	24 (42)	11 (19)	16 (28)	8 (14)	41 (72)	4 (7)

n, number of affected individuals.

Table 3. Cohort comparison of dental disease prevalence (tooth count).

	First incisors		Second incisors		Canines		First molars		Second molars		Total	
Caries[1]												
Cohort	n	*n* (%)	n	*n* (%)	n	*n* (%)	n	*n* (%)	n	*n* (%)	n	*n* (%)
1	59	3 (5)	60	0 (0)	59	0 (0)	70	5 (7)	52	2 (4)	300	10 (33)
2	68	6 (9)	61	2 (3)	81	0 (0)	82	23 (28)	82	16 (19.5)	374	47 (13)
3	9	0 (0)	18	0 (0)	39	3 (8)	36	15 (42)	38	9 (24)	140	27 (19)
4	0	0 (0)	0	0 (0)	9	0 (0)	7	0 (0)	13	3 (23)	29	3 (10)
Total	136	9 (7)	139	2 (1)	188	3 (2)	195	43 (22)	185	30 (16)	843	87 (10)
Periapical Abscesses[2]												
Cohort	n	*n* (%)	n	*n* (%)	n	*n* (%)	n	*n* (%)	n	*n* (%)	n	*n* (%)
1	72	0 (0)	72	0 (0)	64	0 (0)	72	1 (1)	52	0 (0)	332	1 (0.3)
2	80	3 (4)	80	0 (0)	88	0 (0)	88	2 (2)	88	0 (0)	424	5 (1)
3	18	0 (0)	24	0 (0)	42	0 (0)	42	7 (17)	42	4 (9.5)	168	11 (6.5)
4	10	0 (0)	0	0 (0)	11	0 (0)	7	0 (0)	13	0 (0)	31	0 (0)
Total	170	3 (2)	176	0 (0)	205	0 (0)	209	10 (5)	195	4 (2)	955	17 (2)
Antemortem trauma[1]												
Cohort	n	*n* (%)	n	*n* (%)	n	*n* (%)	n	*n* (%)	n	*n* (%)	n	*n* (%)
1	59	0 (0)	60	0 (0)	59	0 (0)	70	4 (6)	52	0 (0)	300	2 (0.7)
2	68	4 (6)	61	6 (10)	81	2 (2.5)	82	8 (10)	82	2 (2)	374	21 (6)
3	9	2 (22)	18	4 (22)	39	0 (0)	36	8 (22)	38	4 (10.5)	140	13 (9)
4	0	0 (0)	0	0 (0)	9	0 (0)	7	0 (0)	13	4 (31)	29	2 (7)
Total	136	6 (4)	139	10 (7)	188	2 (1)	195	20 (10)	185	10 (5)	843	38 (4.5)
Enamel hypoplasia[1]												
Cohort	n	*n* (%)	n	*n* (%)	n	*n* (%)	n	*n* (%)	n	*n* (%)	n	*n* (%)
1	59	0 (0)	60	0 (0)	59	6 (10)	70	2 (3)	52	4 (8)	300	12 (4)
2	68	1 (1.5)	61	2 (3)	81	1 (1)	82	0 (0)	82	2 (2)	374	6 (2)
3	9	0 (0)	18	0 (0)	39	3 (8)	36	0 (0)	38	0 (0)	140	3 (2)
4	0	0 (0)	0	0 (0)	9	0 (0)	7	0 (0)	13	0 (0)	29	0 (0)
Total	136	1 (0.7)	139	2 (1)	188	10 (5)	195	2 (1)	185	6 (3)	843	21 (2.5)
Attrition[1]												
Cohort	n	*n* (%)	n	*n* (%)	n	*n* (%)	n	*n* (%)	n	*n* (%)	n	*n* (%)
1	59	16 (27)	60	14 (23)	59	11 (19)	70	12 (17)	52	5 (10)	300	58 (19)
2	68	52 (76.5)	61	40 (66)	81	52 (64)	82	43 (52)	82	33 (40)	374	220 (59)
3	9	9 (100)	18	15 (83)	39	36 (92)	36	27 (75)	38	31 (82)	140	118 (84)
4	0	0 (0)	0	0 (0)	9	5 (56)	7	3 (43)	13	8 (61.5)	29	16 (55)
Total	136	77 (57)	139	69 (50)	188	104 (55)	195	85 (44)	185	77 (42)	843	412 (49)
Antemortem tooth loss[2]												
Cohort	n	*n* (%)	n	*n* (%)	n	*n* (%)	n	*n* (%)	n	*n* (%)	n	*n* (%)
1	72	0 (0)	72	0 (0)	64	0 (0)	72	0 (0)	52	0 (0)	332	0 (0)
2	80	0 (0)	80	0 (0)	88	0 (0)	88	0 (0)	88	0 (0)	424	0 (0)
3	18	0 (0)	24	0 (0)	42	0 (0)	42	2 (5)	42	2 (5)	168	4 (2)
4	10	0 (0)	0	0 (0)	11	0 (0)	7	0 (0)	13	0 (0)	31	0 (0)
Total	170	0 (0)	176	0 (0)	205	0 (0)	209	2 (1)	195	2 (1)	955	4 (0.4)

[1] n, number of observable teeth; *n*, number of affected teeth.
[2] n, number of observable tooth sites; *n*, number of affected tooth sites.

The pattern and distribution of occlusal attrition on the deciduous teeth is positively correlated with age (G=19.073, 3df, P=0.000) (Table 3). Although the prevalence of attrition appears quite high in individuals and teeth, all levels of attrition are slight to moderate. Slight levels of attrition (i.e. enamel polishing) are observed in Cohort 1, with a somewhat higher degree of wear on the anterior teeth. Most deciduous teeth show some degree of attrition in Cohort 2, especially anterior teeth and attrition levels are slight to moderate in the deciduous teeth. Moderate levels of attrition are observed on most deciduous teeth of the third cohort, with some dentine exposure. Due to abnormal dental development, a high level of attrition was observed on one deciduous canine. Attrition was not typically observed in the deciduous dentition in Cohort 4; however, most teeth have been replaced by permanent teeth. Moderate attrition levels were limited to the posterior deciduous teeth in this age group. Three individuals retained their deciduous canines with the eruption of the permanent canine, showing a high degree of wear. The proportion of teeth with attrition is highly significantly different among the cohorts (G=205.176, 3df, P=0.000).

The prevalence of antemortem tooth loss due to pathology (rather than normal shredding) is relatively low in this sample compared to other dental conditions. The total prevalence of individuals with antemortem tooth loss is 36%, observed in the third cohort. The proportion of deciduous teeth lost antemortem is 2% and is limited to the deciduous molars. All AMTL is sequel to periapical abscessing, which is recorded for each tooth site. Large caries are observed in the third cohort in correlation with periapical abscessing. Therefore, caries is a likely source of AMTL in these individuals. The different in AMTL prevalence among the cohort is significant (G=13.981, 3df, P=0.003).

Discussion

Teeth provide a valuable source of physical evidence for studying health in antiquity. As they are composed of densely calcified tissue, teeth are particularly resistant to destructive natural taphonomic processes. Unlike bone, teeth do not remodel, providing an almost permanent record of dental health (Mayhall 2000:103). As oral health is associated with the rest of the body (Moynihan 2005), health status can be assessed by analyzing dental pathology in teeth. The age distribution of dental pathology reveals valuable information about the infants and children during the Roman period at Kellis 2, Dakhleh. In particular, this information sheds some light on the oral health throughout different stages of childhood. The results clearly indicate that that dental disease experience is different among the age groups.

The prevalence of carious teeth increases throughout childhood in this sample. Individuals in the third cohort experienced the highest rate of caries (19%). The inclusion of permanent teeth may reveal an increase in prevalence in the fourth cohort; however, the permanent teeth within this age category may not have had enough

time to develop caries as the deciduous dentition is not completely replaced until approximately twelve years of age (Langsjoen 1998). The fourth cohort is composed of individuals between the ages of 9.5 and 15.0 years; therefore, permanent teeth have had limited exposure in the oral cavity. Since caries is a progressive disease, it is unlikely that caries would be observed on most permanent teeth (i.e. canines, premolars and second molars). The first permanent molars are among the earliest teeth to erupt and may reveal time-dependent caries formation. Also notable is the relatively high prevalence of early childhood caries (ECC). Deciduous tooth types are at risk for developing caries at different times (Alvarez and Navia 1989:423). The caries data by tooth type appear to follow this trend. For example, there is a relatively high prevalence of first incisor (5%) and first molar caries (7%) in Cohort 1. Newly erupted deciduous teeth are especially prone to caries, since the roots are not fully developed and the enamel is thin (Drummond et al. 1997). Although the exposure of deciduous teeth to the oral cavity is limited, much less time is required for caries development compared to permanent teeth.

An analysis of these data must consider the role of diet in the development of certain dental diseases, since the types of food infants and young children eat impacts their health and survival. Diet is an important aetiological factor in dental caries, and nutritional status affects dental development and host resistance to oral conditions, such as periodontal disease (Moynihan 2005:571). The types of food consumed determine the micro-organisms in the oral cavity, and the condition of the dentition reflects food composition (Roberts and Manchester 2005:64). Depending on the type of food, some of the bacteria in the mouth produce an alkaline or acidic oral environment. The metabolization of protein and carbohydrates produces alkaline and lactic acid waste products, respectively (Caselitz 1998:204). The relative balance between oral acidity and alkalinity greatly influences the development of dental caries. Lactic acid produced by bacteria metabolizing carbohydrates results in the steady loss of tooth mineral. Eventually, the characteristic pit-like lesions will occur (Cook and Buikstra 1979). Therefore, an agriculturally-based diet is conducive to caries formation.

The diet at Kellis consisted of carbohydrates, such as wheat and millet, as indicated in the *Farm Accounts Book,* and confirmed isotopically (Dupras 1999). The prevalence of carious teeth increases with each age cohort, excluding the fourth cohort. Children in each successive cohort have been exposed to an 'adult diet' of carbohydrates for a longer period; therefore, it is expected that caries rates should increase with age.

The prevalence of dental pathology at a relatively young age in the first cohort may be due to specific Roman period child-rearing practices. As noted previously, it was recommended that boiled honey or a mixture of honey and goat's milk constituted the first supplementary food of infants (Dupras et al. 2001). Sugars are metabolized more rapidly than other carbohydrates, which result in lactic acid being produced more quickly (Hillson 1979:150). Isotopic evidence from Kellis 2 has confirmed that infants were introduced to supplementary foods after six months of age and were completely weaned by approximately 3.5 years of age (Dupras 1999:250). Children were also weaned onto a solid food mixture of milk and millet (Dupras 1999). This C_4-based 'gruel' was likely a factor in caries formation. Compared to breastmilk, this type of early childhood diet may influence nutritional levels in non-adults. Teeth that are developing are the most susceptible to nutritional insults as it reduces their resistance to caries attack (Alvarez and Navia 1989:422). Malnutrition likely has the greatest impact on deciduous teeth that are still developing. During this time children are growing rapidly so that even minor changes in nutrient availability are significant (Alvarez and Navia 1989:423). Also, the environment at Dakhleh was ideal for producing high quality dates (Dupras 1999:24). The relationship between caries and diet is investigated in a sample from the late Iron Age of Oman from the Samad Oasis. Nelson and colleagues (1999:340-341) suggest that the number of young individuals with large caries in this population could result from the consumption of dates as snacks. Clinical data identify a typical weaning age of about 5-6 months in poor, less developed countries, which results in an increased risk of infant malnutrition, diarrhea and other infectious diseases (Alvarez and Navia 1989:423). Based on the type of diet during early childhood, it appears that weaning and the transition to solid foods at Kellis 2 resulted in a higher than expected caries rate in non-adults.

The high prevalence of caries in individuals in the first cohort may be due to the fact that individuals are immuno-compromised during this period. The host defense systems and bacterial flora in young children are in the process of developing (Harris et al. 2004:71). Immunity is provided to infants by breastmilk, as it is known to contain T and B lymphocytes, immunogloblins and antistaphlococcal factor (Katzenberg et al. 1996). Colostrum contains the highest concentration of immunoglobulins; however, the presence of these defense factors is maintained throughout lactation (Lawrence 1994 cited in Katzenberg et al. 1996:39). The transfer of immunoglobins is extremely beneficial because the immune system of an infant is immature (Katzenberg et al. 1996:39). The isotope data indicated that infants were breastfed for six months and then introduced to supplementary foods and liquids (Dupras 1999). During this period individuals lack immunological protection from their mother's antibodies and have yet to produce their own.

Burial 146 is a noteworthy case of a 3-year-old individual with extensive cemento-enamel junction (CEJ) caries on both the maxillary and mandibular teeth (see Figures 1ab). CEJ caries develop when the gingival recedes most commonly due to inflammation and periodontitis. This unusual state in a young child probably reflects a person with a compromised immune system. The immunological

effects in combination with a cariogenic weaning diet of millet gruel may have created nutritional stress and compromised health, probably accounting for prevalence of caries in this young individual. Of note is the fact that the only osseous lesions present on this well-preserved skeleton are slight healed porotic hyperostosis in both orbits (JE Molto pers. comm. 2008). This 'absence of infracranial bone lesions' may be an example of the 'healthy but dead' phenomenon outlined in the 'Osteological Paradox' (Wood et al. 1992).

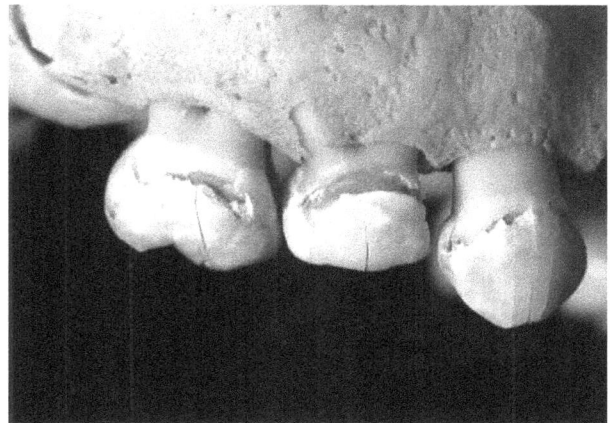

Figure 1a SK146, cemento-enamel junction caries, buccal view of maxillary right canine and molars.

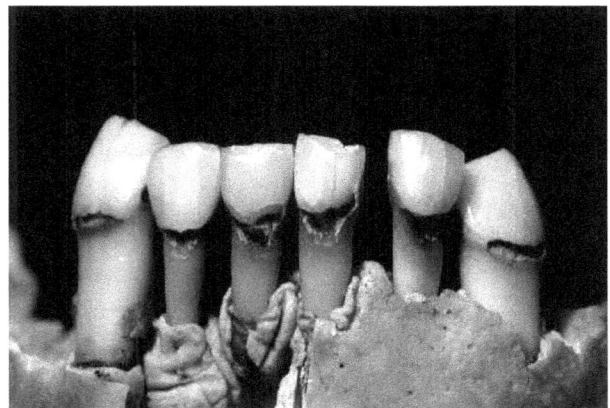

Figure 1b SK146, cemento-enamel junction caries, labial view of mandibular incisors and canines.

The analysis of antemortem trauma includes both the fracturing and chipping of teeth, which are characterized as varying degrees of tooth damage. Generally, chipping is a minor injury to dental structure, while fracturing results in a greater extent of damage (Patterson 1984). Small-scale dental damage is usually due to dietary inclusions. This type of damage can occur throughout the dentition and does not differentially affect a specific tooth class (Lukacs 2007:169). Large-scale trauma is more prevalent in the anterior dentition and is usually not of dietary origin. Rather, these types of fractures are the result of occupational use of teeth as tools, accidental falls or unanticipated encounters with objects, and violent interpersonal interactions (Pindborg 1970; Andraesen 1982 cited in Lukacs 2007:168). Although fractures were observed, none were highly destructive and likely resulted from dietary origins. The first molars and second incisors have the highest overall prevalence of antemortem trauma. However, the distribution does not significantly affect one tooth class. Trauma that does occur in the anterior teeth is usually the result of chipping, but based on the distribution of antemortem trauma in the Kellis 2 dentitions the main aetiology is likely to be dietary. Excluding the first molars, antemortem trauma is absent in the first cohort followed by an increase in the second cohort. The transition from a soft weaning diet to more abrasive solid foods may explain this observation. The posterior teeth are exposed to the oral cavity for a longer period and responsible for the mastication of food. The prevalence of antemortem trauma is the highest in the third category for all tooth types, excluding the second molar. The prevalence of second molars affected increases significantly in the fourth cohort. Therefore, these teeth are more susceptible to trauma, especially when subjected to an abrasive diet for an extended interval of time.

The relationship between attrition and age is also highly statistically significant. Although the proportions of individuals and teeth affected appear extremely high, the levels of attrition are slight to moderate. The pattern and amount of attrition in the deciduous dentition is expected as all human dentitions will experience some degree of enamel and dentine loss due to functional wear (Langsjoen 1998). However, wear tends to occur at a faster rate in younger individuals (Spinage 1973 cited in Hillson 2005:216). Isotopic values in children reflect adult values at about age seven years, indicating that after weaning there are no apparent dietary shifts (Dupras 1999). The noticeable increase in attrition prevalence in Cohort 2 may be a result of the transition from a softer weaning diet to more abrasive solid foods. Occlusal attrition can result from the physical and physiological processes of masticating food, during which the abrasive elements of food produce wear facets where teeth occlude (Patterson 1984:56). Abrasive substances, such as sand or grit that are introduced into food during its collection or preparation can cause attrition (Cross et al. 1986:101). Due to an extended exposure to these substances, the prevalence of occlusal attrition increases in older non-adults.

Periapical abscessing is a pathological condition that is sequel to an infection of a diseased tooth in which the pulp has been exposed (Langsjoen 1998). An exposed pulp chamber can lead to systemic infection, causing morbidity and mortality. Both antemortem trauma and caries can result in pulp exposure. A number of the dentitions (i.e. Burials 24, 163, 360 and 454 and 510) show evidence of abscesses that are concomitant with caries formation (Figure 2).

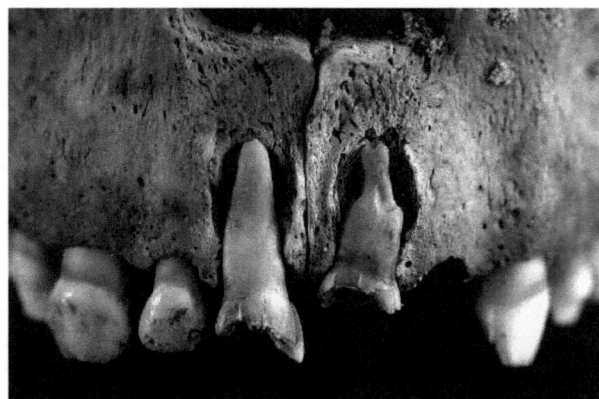

Figure 2. Example of periapical abscessing of maxillary first incisors as a result of caries.

Both antemortem trauma and caries are found in Burials 24 (lower left first molar) and 163 (upper right first incisor). The individuals suffering from both caries and abscessing are relatively young, all between the ages of five and eight years. The individuals with dental conditions associated with one another also fall within this age range. Since periapical abscessing is sequel to an infection of a diseased tooth, time is a factor in its development. The prevalence of each dental pathology increases with age; however, a noticeable increase in abscessing occurs in the third cohort. Teeth belonging to individuals in the third cohort have had sufficient time to develop abscesses. It is known that exposure of the pulp can be quite painful (Papageorge and Kronman 1986) and a chronic dental abscess can lead to systemic infection (Kieser et al. 2001:290). Abscessing produces the unpleasant experience of a toothache and can lead to septicemia. The relationship of antemortem trauma, caries and abscess formation is a notable source of morbidity and possible mortality.

Relative to the number of studies that report linear enamel hypoplasia of the permanent teeth, enamel hypoplasia of the deciduous teeth is not often observed or recorded (Lovell and Whyte 2001; Halcrow and Tayles 2008). Deciduous enamel defects are not a health risk per se; however, these defects are useful indicators of morbidity in non-adults. The prevalence of enamel hypoplasia at Kellis includes pitted enamel defects and LHDC. Localized hypoplasia of the deciduous canine represents a disproportionate number of dental enamel defects of the deciduous teeth in bioarchaeological studies (Halcrow and Tayles 2008). Hypoplasias were also present in the deciduous dentition of Kellis 2 non-adults as pits, which result from unspecific physiological disturbances (Blakey et al. 1994:372). The prevalence of individuals and teeth affected by enamel hypoplasia is the highest in the first cohort, and this inverse relationship between age at death for individuals with and without enamel defects is commonly observed (Cook and Buikstra 1979; Blakely 1988; Cook 1990; Stodder 1997; Duray 1990). These results may indicate that individuals who experienced stress during early childhood were predisposed to a premature death (Larsen 1997).

Antemortem tooth loss (AMTL) is a complex and multifaceted process as it is the result of a number of factors. Abscessing is a significant source of antemortem tooth loss due to the destruction of the alveolar bone. Periapical abscessing is concomitant to tooth loss in Burials 195, 454 and 505. Each of theses burials is assigned to cohort three, which reinforces the time-dependence of dental disease in childhood. Therefore, a greater consumption and exposure to the adult carbohydrate diet at Kellis likely caused tooth loss through abcessing, in older individuals.

Conclusions and future directions

Oral health is often viewed as separate from the rest of the body (Moynihan 2005). Dental pathology in non-adults is a source of morbidity and mortality data, which draws from the assumption that oral health is associated with general health. Nutrition and diet influence the oral cavity and impact the health and survival of non-adults. Dietary factors are expressed in the oral cavity in a number of ways and as such, this study examined caries, abscessing, antemortem trauma, and attrition in its analysis of non-adult dentitions. Each of these pathological conditions was also considered in association with antemortem tooth loss. However, this is complicated by the fact that many deciduous teeth are in the process of being replaced or have been replaced.

This study has shown that the prevalence of dental disease in each cohort increased throughout childhood. The high prevalence of dental caries in non-adults at Kellis 2 is characteristic of an agriculturally-based economy. Carbohydrates are conducive to caries formation due to an increased production of lactic acid. Children consuming an adult carbohydrate diet for a longer period of time (i.e. older individuals) experience a higher caries rate. Therefore, caries prevalence increases with age throughout childhood development. In addition, a Roman period weaning diet appears to have resulted in a relatively high prevalence of caries in those individuals between ages 1.0 and 3.5 years. During this period individuals lack immunological protection from their mother's antibodies and have yet to produce their own, which would also account for the high prevalence of caries. Caries is observed as concomitant of abscessing in a number of burials, influencing the morbidity and possibility the mortality of the population if septicemia resulted. Dental caries is caused by a number of interacting factors, including a susceptible tooth and host, the presence of cariogenic bacteria and fermentable carbohydrates (Patterson 1984:62). Caries experience was also associated with antemortem trauma. Caries development during childhood is evidently a result of a number of interrelated factors. Based on the interrelationship among oral dental disease it is not surprising to find a similar trend in the prevalence of caries, antemortem trauma and periapical abscessing. The presence of extensive lesions in the deciduous dentition may be symptomatic of an underlying medical disorder

(Aldred et al. 1997:143). Therefore, dental pathology is a valid indicator of morbidity and mortality and can be used to assess changes in health status throughout childhood.

Studies that include non-adult remains often treat children as one expansive category, for instance ages 2 to 16 years (Patterson 1984; Whittaker and Molleson 1996; Delgado-Darias et al. 2005). Although various factors preclude further division, the amalgamation of all infants and children assumes a consistent experience of dental disease throughout childhood. The dental health of children can change throughout growth and development, especially considering that most dental disease is age-progressive (Hillson 2005). Infants and children are not affected by dental pathology in certain populations; however, this observation should not be assumed for all investigations and may be influenced by preservation issues. The expression of pathology usually differs between adults and children as lesions can change in appearance and severity with growth (Aldred et al. 1997:143). A cohort analysis allows for the health experience of non-adults to be accurately assessed at different ages. For example, the impact of weaning is analyzed, which occurs at an age that is culturally specific. Overall, non-adult health at Kellis 2 appears to be compromised due the relatively high prevalence of dental disease.

The analysis of childhood dental disease at Kellis 2 was challenging as few comparative studies were available. Further analysis of the dental data from the current study sample will allow us to evaluate the interplay between cultural, genetic and dietary factors, as well as their influence on dental pathology and the resulting morbidity. The 2007 field season has increased the sample size to over 94 dentitions, of which 20 were re-analyzed to account for interobserver error. Future research on non-adult dental pathology at Kellis 2 will hopefully help to negate the isolation that is perceived between oral health and general health.

Acknowledgements

This paper is part of an MA thesis under the supervision of Dr JE Molto at The University of Western Ontario in London, ON. I am grateful to members of my thesis committee, Dr JE Molto and Dr Christine White. I would like to thank Sandra Wheeler and Lana Williams for all their guidance and support. Thanks also goes to Lindsay Foreman for editing and Dr Peter Sheldrick for photography. In addition, I would thank to thank two anonymous reviewers for their invaluable comments and criticisms on an earlier version of this paper. This work was supported by the Office of the Dean, Faculty of Social Science, The University of Western Ontario through a Graduate Thesis Research Award. This research is also supported by a Social Sciences and Humanities Research Council of Canada (SSHRC) grant (No: 50-1603-0500) awarded to Dr JE Molto, 2002-2005.

Literature cited

Aldred, M, Hall, R and Cameron A. 1997. Pediatric Oral Pathology. In: Cameron, AC and Widmer, RP (eds.) *Handbook of Pediatric Dentistry*. London: Mosby International, 143-178.

Alvarez JO and Navia, JM. 1989. Nutritional status, tooth eruption, and dental caries: a review. *The American Journal of Clinical Nutrition* 49:417-426.

Andraesen, J.O. 1982. *Traumatic Injuries to the Teeth*. Copenhagen: Munksgaard.

Blakely, RL. 1988. The life cycle and social organization. In: Blakely, RL (ed.) *The King Site: Continuity and Contact in Sixteenth-century Georgia*. Athens: University of Georgia Press, 17-34.

Blakey, ML and Armelagos, GJ. 1985. Deciduous enamel defects in prehistoric Americans from Dickson Mounds: prenatal and postnatal stress. *American Journal of Physical Anthropology* 66: 371-380.

Blakey, ML, Leslie, TE and Reidy, JP. 1994. Frequency and chronological distribution of dental enamel hypoplasia in enslaved African Americans: a test of the weaning hypothesis. *American Journal of Physical Anthropology* 95: 371-383.

Boldsen, JL. 2007. Early childhood stress and adult age mortality – a study of dental enamel hypoplasia in the medieval Danish village of Tirup. *American Journal of Physical Anthropology* 132: 59-66.

Buikstra, JE and Ubelaker, DH. 1994. *Standards for Data Collection from Human Skeletal Remains*. Fayetteville: Arkansas Archaeological Survey.

Caselitz, P. 1998. Caries – Ancient Plague of Humankind. In: Alt, KA, Rosing, FR and Techler-Nicola, M (eds.) *Dental Anthropology: Fundamentals, Limits and Prospects*. New York: Springer, 203-226.

Cook, DC. 1990. Epidemiology of circular caries: a perspective from prehistoric skeletons. In: Buikstra, JE (ed.) *A Life of Science: Papers in Honor of L. Lawrence Angel*. Center for American Archaeology, Scientific Papers, 6. 64-86.

Cook, DC and Buikstra, JE. 1979. Health and differential survival in prehistoric populations: prenatal dental defects. *American Journal of Physical Anthropology* 51 (4): 649-664.

Corbett, ME and WJ, Moore. 1976. Distribution of dental caries in ancient British populations. 4. The 19th century. *Caries Research* 10:104-114.

Cross, JF, Kerr, NW and Bruce, MF. 1986. An evaluation of Scott's method for scoring dental wear. In: Cruwys, E and Foley, RA (eds.) *Teeth and Anthropology*. Oxford: British Archaeological Reports, International Series, 291. 101-108.

Delgado-Darias, T, Velasco-Vázquez, J, Arnay-de-la-Rosa, M, Martín-Rodríguez, E and González-Reimer, E. 2005. Dental caries among the prehispanic population from Gran Canaria. *American Journal of Physical Anthropology* 128 (3): 560-568.

Drummond, B, Kilpatrick, N, Bryant, R, Lucas, J, Hallet, K, Silva, M, Johnston, T, Verco J and Messer, LB. 1997. Dental caries and restorative pediatric dentistry. In: Cameron, AC and Widmer, RP (eds.) *Handbook of Pediatric Dentistry*. London: Mosby, 55-82.

Dupras, TL. 1999. Dining in the Dakhleh Oasis, Egypt: Determination of diet using document and stable isotope analysis. PhD. dissertation. Department of Anthropology, McMaster University.

Dupras, TL, Schwarz, HP and Fairgrieve, SI. 2001. Infant feeding and weaning practices in Roman Egypt. *American Journal of Physical Anthropology* 115 (3): 204-212.

Duray, SM. 1990. Deciduous enamel defects and caries susceptibility in a prehistoric Ohio population. *American Journal of Physical Anthropology* 81: 27-34.

Fildes VA. 1986. *Breasts, Bottles and Babies: A History of Infant Feeding*. Edinburgh: Edinburgh University Press.

Goodman, AH, Armelagos, GJ and Rose, JC. 1980. Enamel hypoplasias as indicators of stress in three prehistoric populations from Illinois. *Human Biology* 52: 515-528.

Gottlieb, A. 2000. Where have all the babies gone? Toward an anthropology of infants (and their caretakers). *Anthropological Quarterly* 73(3):121-132.

Green, RM, translator. 1951. *Hygiene (De sanitate tunenda)*. Galen. Springfield, Illinois: Thomas.

Halcrow, SE and Tayles, N. 2008. Stress near the start of life? Localized enamel hypoplasia of the primary canine in late prehistoric mainland Southeast Asia. *Journal of Archaeological Science* xx: 1-8.

Harris, R, Nicoll, AD, Adair, PM, Pine, CM. 2004. Risk factors for dental caries in young children: a systematic review of the literature. *Community Dental Health* 21 (Supplement): 71-85.

Hildebolt, F and Molnar, S. 1991. Measurement and description of periodontal disease in anthropology studies. In: Kelley, MA and Larsen, CS (eds.) *Advances in Dental Anthropology*. New York: Wiley-Liss Inc., 225-240.

Hillson, S. 1979. Diet and dental disease. *World Archaeology* 11 (2): 147-162.

Hillson, S. 2005. *Teeth*. Second Edition. Cambridge: Cambridge University Press.

Hillson, S and Bond, S. 1997. Relationship of enamel hypoplasia to the pattern of tooth crown development: a discussion. *American Journal of Physical Anthropology* 104: 89-103.

Hope, CA. 1987. The Dakhleh Oasis Project: Ismant el-Kharab 1988-90. *Journal of the Society for the Study of Egyptian Antiquities* XVII (4): 192-197.

Hope, CA. 1988. Three seasons of excavation at Ismant el-Gharab in Dakhleh Oasis, Egypt. *Mediterranean Archaeology* 1: 160-178.

James, PMC and Miller, A. 1970. Dental conditions in a group of Medieval English children. *British Dental Journal* 128: 391-396.

Katzenberg, AM, Herring DA and Saunders, SR. 1996. Weaning and infant mortality: evaluating the skeletal evidence. *Yearbook of Physical Anthropology* 39: 177-199.

Kieser, JA, Kelsen, A, Love, R, Herbison PGP, and Dennison, KJ. 2001. Periapical lesions and dental wear in the early Maori. *International Journal of Osteoarchaeology.* 11 (4): 290-297.

Langsjoen, OM. 1998. Diseases of the dentition. In: Auferheide AC and Rodriquez, C (eds.) *The Cambridge Encyclopedia of Human Palaeopathology*. Cambridge: Cambridge University Press, 393-412.

Larsen, CS. 1997. *Bioarchaeology: Interpreting Behaviour from the Human Skeleton*. Cambridge: Cambridge University Press.

Lawrence, RA. 1994. *Breastfeeding: A Guide for the Medical Profession*, 4th Edition. St. Louis: Mosbey.

Lovell, NC and Whyte, I. 1999. Patterns of dental enamel defects at Ancient Mendes, Egypt. *American Journal of Physical Anthropology* 110: 69-80.

Lukacs, JR. 1989. Dental paleopathology: methods of reconstructing dietary patterns. In: Iscan, MY and Kennedy, KAR (eds.) *Reconstructing life from the human skeleton*. New York: Alan R. Liss. 261-286.

Lukacs, JR. 2007. Dental trauma and antemortem tooth loss in prehistoric Canary Islanders: prevalence and contributing factors. *International Journal of Osteoarchaoelogy.* 17 (2): 157-173.

Lunt, DA. 1972. The dentition in a group of Medieval Scottish children. *British Dental Journal* 132: 443-446.

Lunt, DA. 1974. The prevalence of dental caries in the permanent dentition of Scottish prehistoric and medieval populations. *Archives of Oral Biology* 19: 431-437.

Mayhall, JT. 2000. Dental Morphology: Techniques and Strategies. *In*. Katzenberg, MA andSaunders, SR (eds.) *Biological Anthropology of the Human Skeleton*. New York: Wiley-Liss, Inc.,103-134.

Moore, WJ and Corbett, ME. 1971. The distribution of dental caries in ancient British populations. 1. Anglo-Saxon period. *Caries Research* 5: 151-168.

Moore, WJ and Corbett, ME. 1973. The distribution of dental caries in ancient British populations. 2. Iron Age, Romano-British and medieval periods. *Caries Research* 7: 139-153.

Moore, WJ and Corbett, ME. 1975. The distribution of dental caries in ancient British populations. 3. The 17th century. *Caries Research* 9:163-175.

Moynihan, P. 2005. The interrelationship between diet and oral health. *Proceedings of the Nutrition Society* 64: 571-580.

Nelson, GC, Lukacs, JR and Yule, P. 1999. Dates, caries and early tooth loss during the Iron Age of Oman. *American Journal of Physical Anthropology* 108: 333-343.

O'Sullivan EA, Williams SA, Wakefield RC, Cape JE, and Curzon MEJ. 1993. Prevalence and site characteristics of dental caries in primary molar teeth from prehistoric time to the 18th century in England. *Caries Research* 27: 147-153.

Oyamada, J, Igawa, K, Yitagawa, Y, Manabe, Y, Kato, K, Matsushita, T and Rokutanda, A. 2008. Pathology of deciduous teeth in the samurai and commoner children of early modern Japan. *Anthropological Science* 166: 9-15.

Papageorge, MB and Kronman, JH. 1986. Referral symptoms from the trigeminal to the facial nerve as a sequel to dental infection. *Oral surgery, Oral Medicine and Oral Pathology* 62: 643-645.

Papathanasiou, A. 2005. Health status of the Neolithic population of Alepotrypa cave, Greece. *American Journal of Physical Anthropology* 126: 377-390.

Patterson, DK. 1984. A diachronic study of dental paleopathology and attritional status of prehistoric Ontario pre-Iroquois and Iroquois populations. *National Museum of Man Mercury Series, Archaeological Survey of Canada*. Paper No. 122.

Pindborg, JJ. 1970. *Pathology of the Dental Hard Tissues*. Philadephia: WB Saunders.

Roberts, C and Manchester, K. 2005. Dental disease. In: *The Archaeology of Disease*, Third Edition. New York: Cornell University Press, 63-83.

Schulz, PD. 1992. Turner teeth and childhood cares in a Protohistoric California Indian population. *International Journal of Osteoarchaeology* 2:263-270.

Seidemann, RM and McKillop, H. 2007. Dental indicators of diet and health for the Postclassic Maya on Wild Cane Cay, Belize. *Ancient Mesoamerica* 18: 303-313.

Sharpe, JL. 1987. The Kellis Codices. *Journal of the Society for the Study of Egyptian Antiquities* XVII (4): 192-197.

Spinage, CA. 1973. A review of the age determination of mammals by means of teeth, with especial reference to Africa. *East African Wildlife Journal* 11: 165-187.

Stodder, ALW. 1997. Subadult stress, morbidity and longevity in Latte Period populations on Guam, Mariana Islands. *American Journal of Physical Anthropology* 104: 363-380.

Tempkin, O., translator. 1956. *Gynecology. Soranus and Ephesus*. Baltimore: John Hopkins Press.

Tocheri, MW, Dupras, TL, Sheldrick, P and Molto, JE. 2005. Roman period fetal skeletons from the east cemetery (Kellis 2) of Kellis, Egypt. *International Journal of Osteoarchaeology*. 15 (5): 326-341.

Varrela, TM. 1991. Prevalence and distribution of dental caries in a late medieval population in Finland. *Archives of Oral Biology* 36: 553-559.

Watt, ME, Lunt, DA and Gilmour, WH. 1997. Caries prevalence in the deciduous dentition of a mediaeval population from the southwest of Scotland. *Archives of Oral Biology* 12: 811-820.

Whittaker, DK and Molleson, T. 1996. Caries prevalence in the dentition of a late eighteenth century population. *Archives of Oral Biology*. 41 (1): 55-61.

Williams, SA and Curzon, MEJ. 1985. Dental caries in a Scottish medieval child population. *Caries Research* 19: 162.

Wood, JW, Mitner, GR, Harpending, HC and Weiss, KM. 1992. The osteological paradox, problems of inferring prehistoric health from skeletal samples. *Current Anthropology* 33: 343-370

Skeletal Manifestation of Non-Adult Scurvy from Early Medieval Northumbria: The Black Gate Cemetery, Newcastle-upon-Tyne.

Diana Mahoney-Swales and Pia Nystrom

Department of Archaeology, University of Sheffield, Northgate House, West Street, Sheffield,

South Yorkshire, S1 4ET

D.Swales@sheffield.ac.uk

Abstract

Several authors have identified the paucity of evidence for scurvy throughout the British archaeological record, including the early medieval period. Such absence has been ascribed to under-diagnosis of the condition in archaeological material, under-representation of non-adult remains, or simply to the fact that few people in pre-industrial Britain were affected by vitamin C deficiency.

The skeletal remains of two young children aged between 1 and 2 years, from the Black Gate cemetery, Newcastle-upon-Tyne (ca. AD 800-1100), exhibited lesions consistent with descriptions of infantile scurvy in the palaeopathological literature. The exellent preservation of these skeletal remains enabled post-cranial manifestations of scurvy to be observed in greater detail. Consequent observations of increased porosity on the dorsal rib surfaces, expressed solely in the scorbutic individuals, suggest the aetiology of these lesions to be vitamin C deficiency. The occurrence of only two individuals exhibiting the specific combination of lesions suggestive of scurvy from this assemblage of 194 non-adults (1%), suggests the diagnostic criteria are an accurate resource from which to distinguish scurvy from other metabolic conditions. The low prevalence within this well-preserved assemblage supports the hypothesis that scurvy was a rare condition in pre-industrial Britain.

Keywords: Non-adult; early medieval; Anglo-Saxon; scurvy; metabolic disease; Northumbria

Introduction

Scurvy is a disease of dietary deficiency of ascorbic acid (vitamin C). It is one of a number of specific metabolic afflictions identifiable in the palaeopathological record, in addition to rickets and anaemia. Humans are unable to synthesise ascorbic acid and are therefore dependant on a dietary source of vitamin C. This is a trait shared with guinea pigs and some non-human primates (Kipp et al. 1996). The anti-scorbutic effects of citrus fruits, such as oranges and lemons, are well known from Lind's 1747 trials (Carpenter 1986). However, there are a wide range of foods, especially vegetables such as cabbages, which are rich in vitamin C. A varied diet is conducive to the prevention of scurvy, a fact demonstrated by Holst and Frolich in 1907 (cited in Pimentel 2003), who documented the stimulation and subsequent cure of vitamin C deficiency in guinea pigs using fresh fruit and vegetables.

Vitamin C is a vital component in the synthesis of collagen, the structural protein for blood capillaries and bone matrix (Aufdeheide and Rodriguez-Martin 1998). A deficiency of vitamin C disrupts the proline hydroxylation step of collagen synthesis, resulting in tissue and capillary fragility. This causes endofractures, sub-periosteal haemorrhage and blood clots when the capillaries are subjected to direct stress or indirect stress from muscle activity (Ortner et al. 1999, 2001; Maat 2004).

Clinical studies estimate that the symptoms of scurvy appear within 2-4 months of insufficient ascorbic acid intake (Hodges et al. 1971). However, for non-adults the increased turnover of connective tissue due to the demands of growth and development can result in a more rapid expression of the symptoms (Brickley 2000; Mays 2007). Ortner (2003) identifies that scurvy is manifest once birth stores have been depleted, resulting in a higher prevalence in individuals aged between 6 months and 2 years of age. Today, it is calculated that 60mg/day is the quantity of vitamin C required to cure or prevent scurvy. However, the amount required increases during periods of stress, illness, infection or trauma (Pimentel 2003).

Scurvy is rarely mentioned in studies of the early medieval period in Britain (AD 410-1066). Roberts and Cox (2003:189) cite only three known cases of non-adult scurvy, and no adult cases, in their study of osteological reports available for this period. Roberts and Cox (2003) suggest adequate levels of vitamin C account for the low prevalence of scurvy in the early medieval period. This view is supported by others (Melikian and Waldron 2003; Mays 2007). Alternatively, the near absence of vitamin C deficiency in the archaeological record may be a consequence of either under- or misdiagnosis, or the under-representation of non-adult remains (Lewis 2002ab; Loe and Robson-Brown 2005; Brickley and Ives 2006; Mays 2007).

In this paper we describe cases of vitamin C deficiency in the Black Gate assemblage following the diagnostic criteria proposed by Ortner and associates (Ortner and Ericksen 1997; Ortner and Mays 1998; Ortner et al. 1999, 2001) and Brickley and Ives (2006). Detailed descriptions of all the skeletal lesions observed are provided within the Results section below.

Background to early medieval infantile scurvy

There are several reasons proposed for the low prevalence of infantile scurvy in the archaeological record. Malnutrition or under-nutrition is often a common underlying cause of metabolic diseases. An inadequate diet is likely to be deficient in more than one nutritional requirement, predisposing an individual to multiple deficiency diseases (Ortner and Mays 1998:45). Several underlying metabolic conditions can cause a single pathological lesion, and it may not be possible to associate a specific skeletal irregularity with a particular dietary deficiency (Ortner et al. 2001). Therefore, ascribing a specific disease is problematic. A prime example of the similarity and multiple aetiologies of some lesions is the presence of abnormal porosity of the orbits recorded in cases of scurvy, rickets and anaemia (Mays 2007). Such porous lesions and hypertrophic new bone growth within the orbits may have been recorded as iron deficiency anaemia in archaeological assemblages without adequate consideration of other skeletal lesions, which may have provided a differential diagnosis of scurvy. This is most likely to have occurred prior to the publication of the work by Ortner and associates describing the dry-bone manifestations of scurvy. Before Ortner and Ericksen's (1997) publication, osteologists and palaeopathologists may have identified scurvy but been hesitant to ascribe a definite diagnosis, a predicament noted for the post-medieval Cross Bones burial ground in London (Brickley and Buteux 2006:130).

Multiple aetiologies of a single dry bone lesion complicate clinical examples of metabolic disease often used as the basis for palaeopathological diagnosis. The clinical examples in the literature are often extreme cases selected for their unique representation of advanced stages of the specific condition. Therefore, dry bone manifestations of metabolic conditions observed in archaeological remains often differ from the clinical example. In addition, it cannot be assumed that the clinical diagnosis is correct or that the lesions of a clinical case result exclusively from the listed pathology (Ortner et al. 2001). Historical studies of infantile scurvy highlight the problems arising from the probability that clinical cases display the symptoms of more than one underlying condition (Pimentel 2003:330; Rajakumar 2001). Such co-expression of scurvy and rickets may have resulted in the under-diagnosis of scurvy in the archaeological record, as the skeletal manifestations of scurvy are less prominent than those of rickets. Several studies following Ortner and Ericksen's (1997) guidelines have still failed to identify any cases of infantile scurvy from the early medieval period (Loe and Robson-Brown 2005; Mays 2007). Due to the near-absence of infantile scurvy in the archaeological record it has been proposed

that scurvy may have been a genuinely rare condition in early medieval Britain (Roberts and Cox 2003:189). Documentary sources indicate that diets during the medieval period tended to be deficient in protein rather than fruit and vegetables (Dyer 1993:154-159). Prolonged breast-feeding and weaning using vegetable-based foods may also have had a protective effect (Mays 2007:6).

Materials and methods

During two phases of excavation at the Black Gate cemetery associated with the Keep of Newcastle Castle (1979-80 and 1990-92), the skeletal remains of 660 individuals were recovered. Of these, 194 (29%) were non-adults aged from 0-17 years. The assemblage dates to approximately AD 800-1100.

As part of a larger project examining health status and life histories within this population, macroscopic analysis of the non-adult remains was undertaken, during which the proposed cases of infantile scurvy were observed. The non-adult skeletons were aged by dental development (Moorrees et al. 1963), epiphyseal fusion (Bass 1987; Schwarz 1995) and diaphyseal long bone length (Scheuer et al. 1980; Hoppa 1992). No attempt was made to determine sex, in accordance with current osteological practice.

Only macroscopic analysis of the skeletal assemblage has been undertaken, with occasional use of light microscopy, to enable comparisons with contemporary assemblages. The diagnoses of infantile scurvy observed within Black Gate were made following the distribution pattern of porous and hypertrophic lesions of the skull and post-cranial remains, proposed to result from scurvy (Ortner and Ericksen 1997; Ortner et al. 1999, 2001; Maat 2004; Brickley and Ives 2006).

A deficiency of vitamin C results in weakened bone tissue and capillary fragility (Maat 2004). Slight direct stress, such as trauma, or indirect stress from muscle activity may result in endofractures, capillary bleeding and sub-periosteal haemorrhage (Ortner and Ericksen 1997; Maat 2004). The vascular inflammatory response to scorbutic bleeding includes the formation of additional defective blood vessels and increased vascular pathways through the bone to remove the excess blood (Ortner et al. 2001). This inflammatory response can manifest skeletally as abnormal increased porosity. Sub-periosteal bleeding can also stimulate the periosteum, causing it to detach from the underlying bone in non-adults, activating new bone formation, although this is a relatively uncommon occurrence (Ortner et al. 1999). Therefore, increased porosity sometimes occurs in conjunction with bone hyperplasia, but this is less common than the presence of porosity alone (Ortner et al. 1999).

To identify scurvy in the Black Gate assemblage we followed the definition of porosity as 'a localised, abnormal condition in which fine holes, visible without magnification but typically less than 1mm in diameter, penetrate a lamellar surface. The lamellar bone may be normal or the result of abnormal (hypertrophic) bone formation' (Ortner and Ericksen 1997:212). To distinguish such porosity from normal variation such pores had to be 'finer, greater in number and ... enter the bone at more vertical angles' (Mays 2007:3). To identify porosity as pathological in the maxillary and mandibular alveolar bone, the area of porosity had to extend well beyond the alveolar processes surrounding an erupting molar (Ortner et al. 1999:327).

Haemorrhage and inflammatory response resulting from muscle activity is more likely to occur in areas where the blood vessels supplying the muscle are located between the muscle and underlying bone. Lesions on the skull associated with scurvy follow a pattern consistent with trauma to the branches of the maxillary and deep temporal arteries supplying the temporalis muscle, a major muscle employed in mastication (Ortner and Ericksen 1997). The temporal arteries lie deep to the temporalis muscle upon the periosteum covering the greater wing of the sphenoids and temporal squama. Any haemorrhage of the deep temporal arteries, in response to the stresses of mastication, would occur between muscle and bone causing inflammatory response in both (Ortner and Ericksen 1997:215). Such inflammatory response is expressed as abnormal porosity and, in some cases, new bone growth upon the skeletal elements directly involved with temporalis and the temporal arteries, such as the greater wing of the sphenoids, posterior maxilla, infraorbital foramen, the posterior zygomatic bone, medial coronoid process and temporal bones. Haemorrhage of the palatine branches of the maxillary artery that supply the soft palate, gingival and mucous membranes, and bone of the hard palate, results in porosity of the hard palate and palatine bones (Ortner and Ericksen 1997). The anterior deep temporal artery anastomoses with the lacrimal branch of the ophthalmic artery (Ortner and Ericksen 1997). Therefore, new-bone formation and abnormal porosity in the orbital roofs could be an indirect inflammatory response to the stresses imposed upon the deep temporal artery during mastication. However, it is possible that orbital lesions result from haemorrhage of the fragile capillaries by normal movement of the eye (Brickley and Ives 2006).

Several studies of possible archaeological cases of scurvy describe endocranial vascularity and plaques of new bone on the occipital (Lewis 2004) and parietal (Mays 2007) bones. However, their aetiology is under much debate (Lewis 2004; Brickley and Ives 2006) and it is not conclusive that they are uniquely associated with scurvy. Many of the recorded cases of probable scurvy in the palaeopathological literature lack post-cranial remains. However, the relevant papers have determined the post-cranial lesions one would expect on a scorbutic individual from clinical studies and the anatomy of the musculo-skeletal and vascular systems (Ortner et al. 1997; 1999; Mays 2007). The few papers that do provide descriptions of both cranial and post-cranial lesions observed on

scorbutic non-adults confirm these predictions (Ortner et al. 2001; Brickley and Ives 2006).

Ortner and Erickson (1997:219) state that the presence of lesions on the scapula is helpful in confirming the presence of scurvy in skeletal remains if associated with other more pathognomonic lesions. As with the sphenoid, the blood vessels supplying the supraspinous and infraspinous muscles lie between the muscles and the underlying bone (Ortner et al. 2001:346-7). Contraction of these muscles can easily traumatise defective blood vessels instigating chronic bleeding and an inflammatory response. Any movement of supraspinatus, predominantly involved in the initiation of abduction of the arm (Lieber 2002), may damage these underlying blood vessels. The inflammatory response to such mechanical stress is visible as increased porosity in the suprascapular fossa and the posterior surface of the blade of the scapula (Ortner et al. 2001:348).

In clinical cases of scurvy chronic bleeding in the metaphyseal areas of long bones, particularly the knees, is well documented (Hirsch et al. 1976). Primary bone changes are mainly manifest in the region of the growth plate. These changes manifest because both the calcified cartilage and the early trabecular bone near the growth plate is defective and has poor mechanical strength. In severe cases, this results in a compression fracture in which the trabeculae are broken and compressed. This creates a dense band of increased radiographic density, known as the 'scurvy line' or 'Truemmerfeld (trauma) zone' (Tamura et al. 2000; Burgener and Kormano 1991). Consequently, endofractures are commonly found at the metaphyses of weight bearing long bones (Brickley 2000; Ortner et al. 2001). Evidence of the inflammatory response to chronic bleeding in the metaphyses of long bones is manifest skeletally as areas of abnormal porosity or extensive periosteal bone growth (Tamura 2000). However, only porosity extending beyond approximately 10 mm on long bones can be determined as pathological, because normal developmental cortical porosity can extend 5-10 mm from the growing end of the metaphysis in non-adults (Ortner et al. 2001:348). Metaphyseal fractures can also manifest in cases of vitamin D deficiency. Deficient mineralization of osteoid also results in poor mechanical strength, especially near the growth plate where the rapid turnover of bone enables it to accumulate (Ortner and Mays 1998). Therefore, metaphyseal fractures alone are not pathognomonic of vitamin C deficiency.

Ortner et al. (2001:348) allude to cortical porosity of the ribs as a further indicator of scurvy in association with porotic lesions of the long bones and skull seen in a Native American child aged about 12 months of age at the time of death (NMNH382489). However, no description or photograph is provided of these rib lesions. The only pathological lesions of the ribs associated with scurvy described in the palaeopathological literature is widening of the costo-cartilage junctions in response to chronic bleeding, as seen at the long-bone metaphyses (Aufderheide and Rodriguez-Martin 1998:311; Brickley and Ives 2006:8). Although Brickley and Ives (2006) cite Aufderheide and Rodriguez-Martin in their literature review, they describe no cases of costo-cartilage expansion or cortical porosity in their post-medieval assemblage. Increased porosity is documented for cases of vitamin D deficiency, and it is possible that the lesions observed here represent defective osteoid production during the early stages of rickets. However, the porosity observed in cases of rickets are localised to the costo-chondral ends of the ribs (Ortner and Mays 1998). In addition, the two individuals reported upon herein are the only two individuals expressing porosity along the majority of the rib shaft, suggesting it is a characteristic of vitamin C deficiency.

Results

Two individuals (BG281 and BG521) exhibit substantial evidence for scurvy. A summary of the sites of porous and hypertrophic lesions observed in the two cases of scurvy is provided in Table 1. Composite photographs of the lesions expressed in individuals BG281 and BG521 are displayed in Figures 1a-j and 2a-f, respectively.

Table 1 Anatomical sites of abnormal porosity and hypoplastic new bone growth associated with Vitamin C deficiency. Adapted from Ortner and Ericksen (1997), Ortner et al. (1999), Melikian and Waldron (2003) and Brickley and Ives (2006).

Anatomic site of scorbutic lesion	Skeleton BG281	Skeleton BG521
Cranium		
Greater wing of sphenoid	P	P
Orbit, frontal (roof)	P	P
Orbit, zygomatic (lateral)	P	P
Cranial vault	P	P
Maxilla, posterior surface	P	P
Zygomatic bone, posterior surface	P	P
Infraorbital foramen	P	P
Hard Palate	P	P
Mandible		
Coronoid process, medial surface	P	P
Alveolar process	P	P
Alveolar sockets	P	P
Post-cranial skeleton		
Scapula, supraspinous fossa	P	A
Scapula, infraspinous fossa	P	A
Long bones, metaphysis *	P	A

(P=pathological lesion present; NP=pathological lesion not present; A=skeletal element not present or unobservable; *= long bone metaphyses recorded as present only if distal femora are present).

Skeleton BG281

BG281, recovered from an earth-cut grave, is aged approximately 1-2 years of age. The skeleton is 50-74% complete from the skull to the knees, but the bones inferior to the knee are missing. The skeleton is in good condition with limited post-depositional cortical erosion corresponding with grades 1 and 2 following the scoring criteria proposed by Brickley and McKinley (2004:17).

BG281 exhibits a greater density of abnormal porosity on the greater wing of the sphenoids (Fig. 1a). The posterior maxilla, posterior surface of the zygomatic bone, and anterior maxilla, surrounding the infraorbital foramen, and hard palate all express a high density of porosity (Figs. 1b-d). Abnormal porosity is expressed bilaterally on the posterior maxilla extending onto the internal zygomatic bone beyond the alveolar bone surrounding the erupting first permanent molars (Fig. 1c). This distinguishes the porosity from developmental porosity associated with dental eruption. The increased density of porosity on the hard palate extends beyond the anterior surface onto the posterior surface of the palate (Fig. 1d).

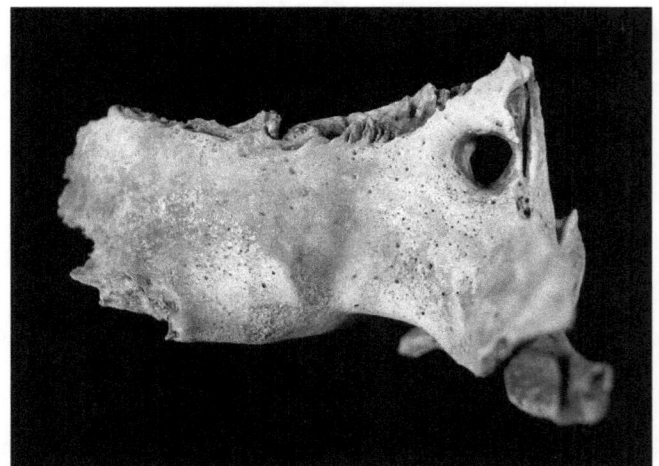

Figure 1a. Anterior surface of greater wing of sphenoid exhibiting abnormal porosity.

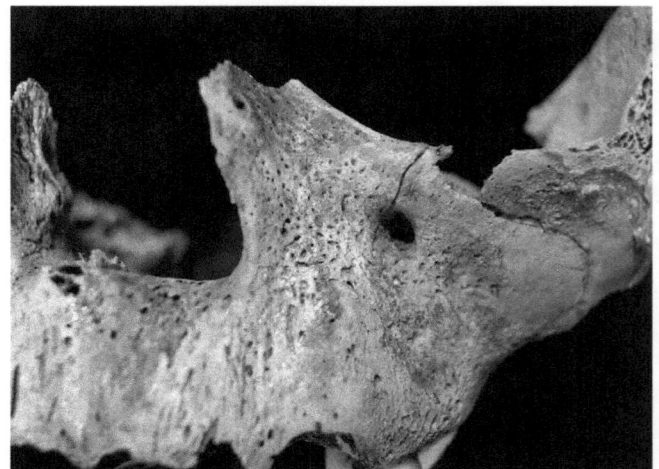

Figure 1b. Anterior view of maxilla showing increased porosity surrounding infraorbital foramen.

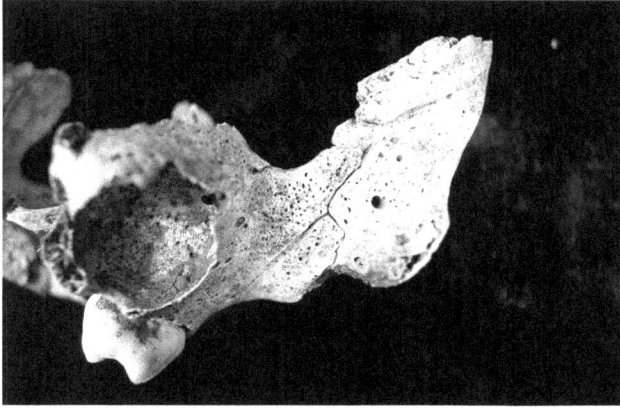

Figure 1c. Inferior view of mandible and zygomatic bone showing abnormal porosity extending beyond the erupting first permanent molar, onto the posterior surface of zygomatic bone.

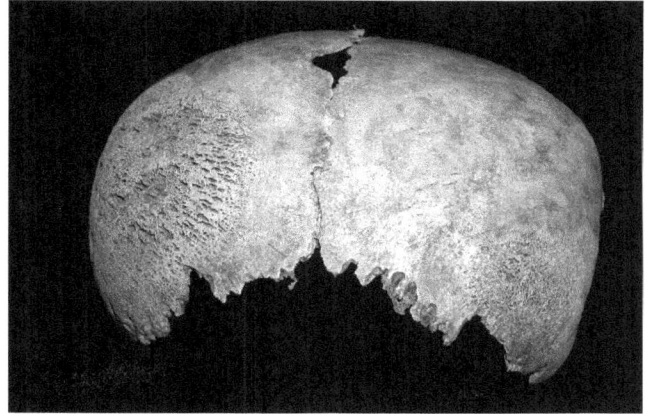

Figure 1e. Posterior view of cranial vault showing abnormal porosity and hypertrophic bone growth on both parietals.

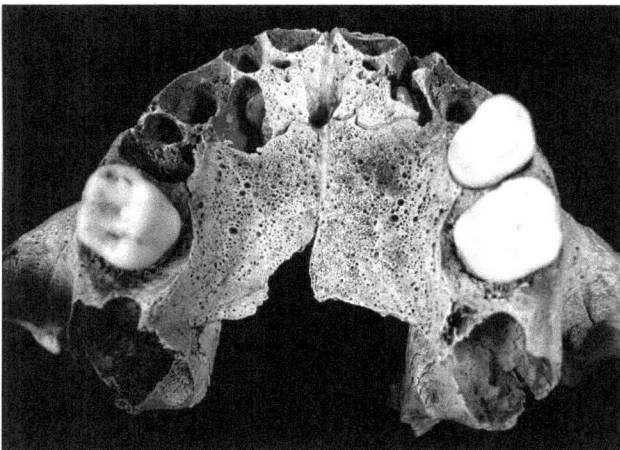

Figure 1d. Hard palate exhibiting abnormal porosity extending posteriorly onto the palatine process.

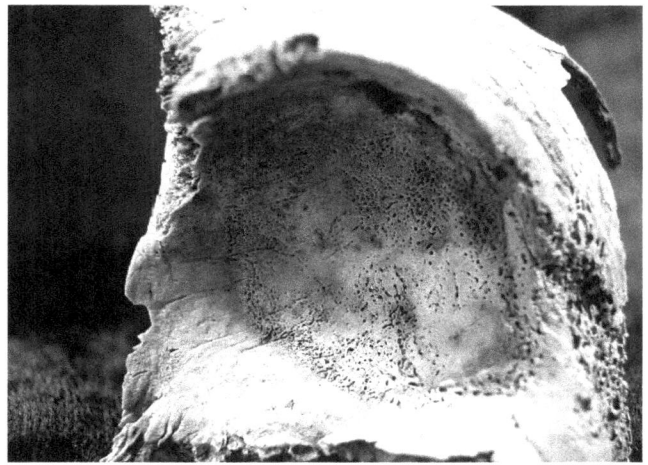

Figure 1f. Frontal bone of right orbit exhibiting abnormal porosity and slight deposits of porous, hypertrophic bone with small channels indicating the course of minor blood vessels.

The right temporal bone exhibits increased porosity upon the squama and zygomatic process. There is an area of increased porosity lateral to the right orbit, localised upon the temporal ridge of the parietal bone. No left temporal was recovered. There is a proliferation of new bone on the surviving parietal and occipital fragments (Fig. 1e). Porous enlargement and hypertrophic bone growth covers over half of the left parietal extending from the parietal eminence to slightly superior to the left lambdoid suture. These lesions continue approximately 2cm across the lambdoid suture onto the occipital, and are replicated on the right half of the occipital. The frontal bone of both orbits exhibits porosity and slight deposits of porous, hypertrophic bone (Fig. 1f). These bony deposits on the superior roof of the orbits exhibit small channels indicating the course of minor blood vessels, as observed in May's (2007) Bronze Age scorbutic infant. Plaques of new bone deposition with vascular channels are present within the internal occipital protuberance, centering in the confluence of sinus. There is abnormal porosity on the medial surface of the mandible superior to the mandibular foramen and extending onto the base of the coronoid and condyloid processes (Fig. 1g).

Figure 1g. Medial view of mandible showing abnormal porosity superior to the mandibular foramen, extending onto base of coronoid and condyloid processes.

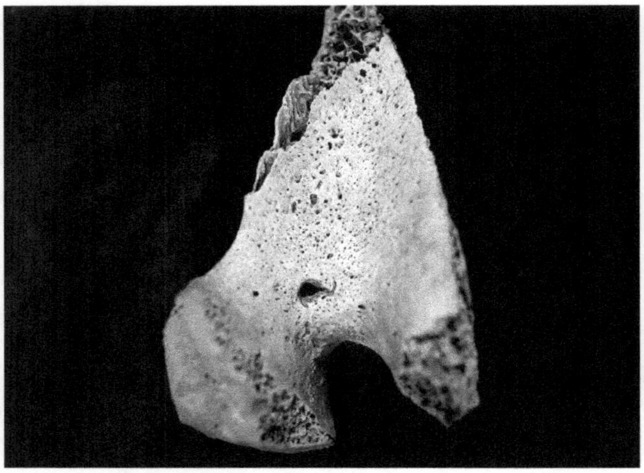

Figure 1h. Superior view of scapula showing abnormal porosity within suprascapular fossa.

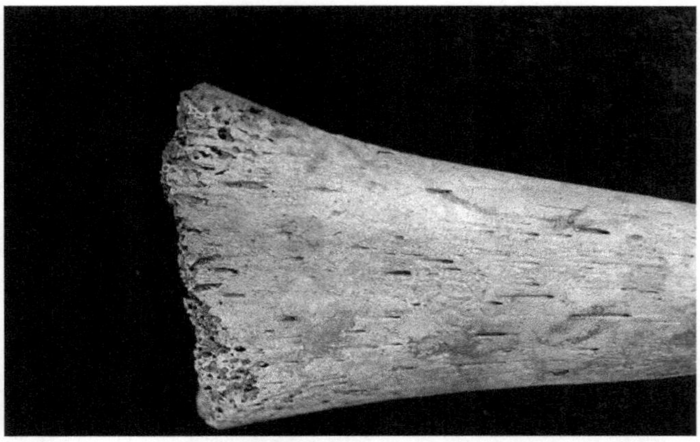

The supraspinous fossa of the left scapula exhibits a high density of macroscopic porous lesions (Fig. 1h). There is a slightly increased presence of porosity upon the posterior surface of the blade of the left scapula, but it is possible that this porosity is within normal variation. There is no evidence for endofractures in BG281. However, there is new bone growth at the metaphyses and abnormal porosity extending beyond 1cm from the growth plate of the distal femora (Fig. 1i). Such lesions correspond with scorbutic cases from North America (Ortner et al. 2001). A high density of porosity is present on the lateral surface of two left and four right rib shafts, extending anteriorly from the angle of the neck and ceasing approximately 1cm from the costo-chondral end (Fig. 1j). The costo-chondral ends of six unsided true ribs exhibit cortical porosity and slight metaphyseal flaring.

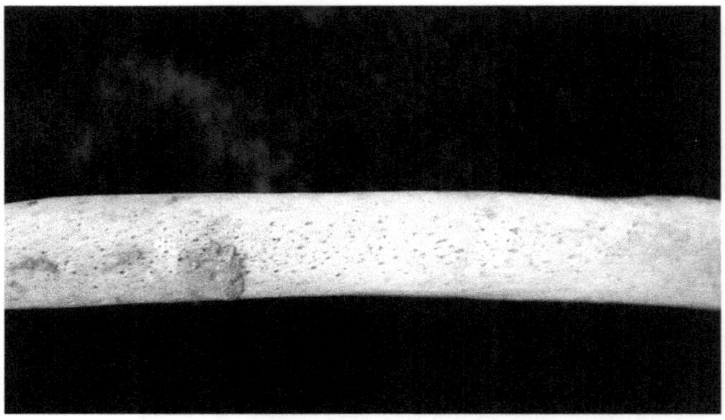

Skeleton BG521
BG521, recovered from an earth-cut grave containing remnants of coffin wood, is aged approximately 1-2 years of age. The skeleton is 25-50% complete, truncated from below the mid-thorax, consisting of cranial fragments, maxilla, mandible, bilateral clavicles, ribs, cervical vertebrae and right humerus. This skeleton is in good condition exhibiting Grade 2 cortical erosion (Brickley and McKinley 2004:17).

The anterior surfaces of the greater wing of the sphenoids exhibit increased porosity and porous new woven bone, but are largely obscured by post-mortem damage and cortical erosion, preventing observation of cortical porosity on approximately 50% of their surfaces (Fig. 2a). The bilateral anterior and lateral maxilla exhibit increased porosity (Fig. 2b), which is also visible on the anterior and posterior surfaces of the right zygomatic (Fig. 2c), and the palatine processes of the hard palate.

The right temporal bone exhibits increased porosity on the anterior-superior squamosal surface consistent with the overlying temporalis muscle. The left temporal bone has not survived. Porous lesions are visible on the parietal and occipital bones without hypertrophic bone growth.

Figure 1i. View of anterior distal end of femoral shaft showing abnormal porosity and slight new bone formation.

Figure 1j. Lateral view of rib shaft showing abnormal porosity.

Even though these lesions are not as severe or extensive as seen in BG281, they are clearly visible and recognisable.

Figure 2a. Abnormal porosity and new bone formation on greater wing of sphenoid. Partially obscured by post-mortem damage and erosion.

Figure 2b. Lateral view of maxilla showing abnormal porosity surrounding the infraorbital foramen, extending posteriorly.

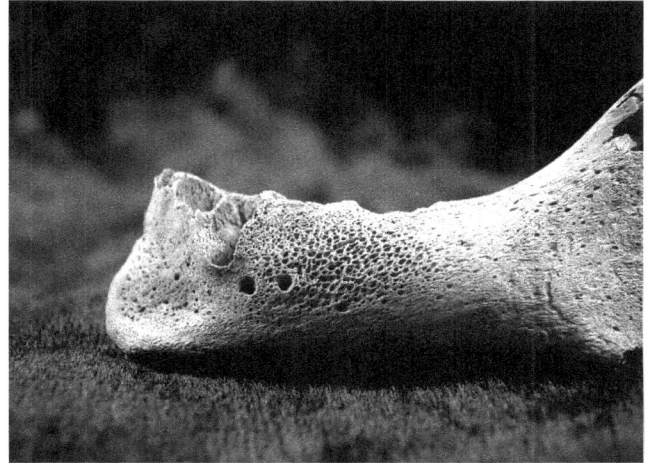

Figure 2e: Lateral surface of mandible exhibiting abnormal porosity associated with mental foramina.

Figure 2c. Posterior view of zygomatic bone showing abnormal porosity.

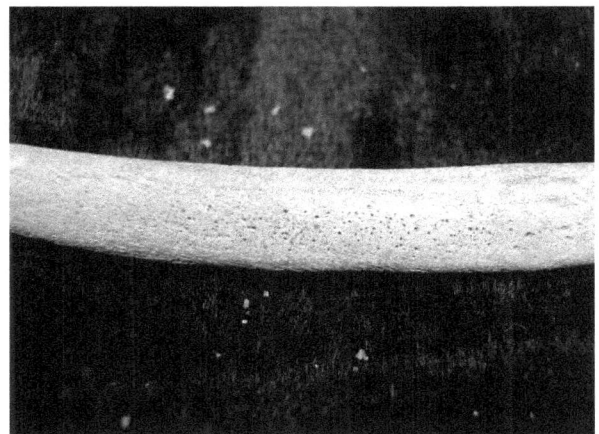

Figure 2f: Lateral view of rib shaft showing abnormal porosity.

There is abnormal porosity on the medial surface of the left mandible, superior to the mandibular foramen, extending onto the base of the coronoid process (Fig. 2d). Porous lesions are present on the lateral surface of the left mandible, inferior to the erupting deciduous molars and posterior to the mental foramina (Fig. 2e). The mental foramen in this individual is duplicated, resulting in two foramina. Porosity on the lateral mandible is not documented in the palaeopathological literature associated with scurvy but the porosity is consistent with what one would expect from the presence of chronic bleeding. It is possible that the blood derives from stresses to the inferior alveolar neurovascular bundle that passes through the mental foramen. This may be a similar occurrence to the inflammatory response observed on the anterior maxilla surrounding the infraorbital foramen.

Figure 2d. Medial view of mandible showing abnormal porosity superior to the mandibular foramen, extending onto base of coronoid and condyloid processes.

The surviving frontal bone of the right orbit exhibits new woven bone growth upon the cortical surface. There is no porosity, indicating an inflammatory response associated with haemorrhaging rather than marrow expansion associated with anaemia. BG521 exhibits plaques of new bone deposition with vascular channels within the internal occipital protuberance, centering in the confluence of sinus.

One right true rib in BG521 appears to have the remnants of a healed endofracture at the costo-chondral end, which may be associated with tissue fragility. All five surviving costo-chondral rib ends exhibit widening of the costo-cartilage junction. A high density of porosity is present on the lateral surface of three out of six right rib shafts, extending anteriorly from the angle of the neck and ceasing approximately 1cm from the costo-chondral end (Fig. 2f). Only the right distal humerus survives, the distal metaphyseal area of which displays neither abnormal porosity nor new bone growth. No scapulae were recovered.

Discussion

The presence of these two cases, which show clear evidence of infantile scurvy, has doubled the number of known cases from the early medieval period. Therefore, it is possible that instances of under- or misdiagnosis of scurvy occur within analyses of archaeological human remains. More careful examination following the diagnostic criteria of Ortner and associates may reveal additional cases of scurvy, especially in collections analysed prior to Ortner and Ericksen's (1997) publication.

The problem of under-representation of non-adults in the British archaeological material may be due to differential burial practices, excluding non-adult remains from the archaeological osteological assemblage (Mays 2007:6; Pearson 1997), or poor preservation of fragile infant and young child bones in the early medieval period (Buckberry 2000; Loe and Robson-Brown 2005). Poor preservation can be exaggerated further by the friable nature of the bones of non-adults with rickets and scurvy, which may also account for under-diagnosis if bones are very fragmentary and appear badly preserved (Lewis 2002a). However, the good condition of the Black Gate assemblage, and high percentage of non-adults (29%) means the low prevalence of infantile scurvy is not a consequence of under-representation of non-adult remains at Black Gate. The good level of preservation may explain the higher prevalence observed here than at sites such as Raunds Furnells and St Helen-on- the-Walls (Lewis 2002ab).

The occurrence of only two out of 194 (1%) non-adults displaying evidence of scorbutic lesions is consistent with the findings of several authors who have undertaken analysis of early medieval skeletal assemblages following the diagnostic criteria of Ortner and associates (Lewis 2002ab; Melikian and Waldron 2003; Loe and Robson-Brown 2005; Mays 2007). This suggests that scurvy was rarely manifested within the early medieval non-adult skeleton at time of death, and that the low prevalence in the archaeological record is not exclusively a consequence of under-diagnosis. This hypothesis is supported by the inclusion of antiscorbutic fruit and vegetables in place names dating back to the medieval period. Examples of such are Peasenhall, Suffolk (peas); Colworth, Bedfordshire (cabbage); and Appledore, Kent (apples) (Lester 1976:28-9).

It is possible that scurvy was a common disease, but one that infants and children regularly survived, with complete healing and remodelling of skeletal lesions (Ortner and Mays 1998:54). Melikian and Waldron (2003:211) state that scurvy was likely to have shown considerable seasonal variation in the past, being most prevalent in the seasons when fresh fruit and vegetables were least available. In Northern Europe during the medieval period, scurvy was endemic during the winter months when fresh fruit and vegetables were unobtainable (Waldron 1989:57). Pearson (1997:30) ascribes fluctuations in the availability of fresh fruit and vegetables to droughts and floods. Maybe the scorbutic individuals observed here died during the late winter or early spring, or after a natural event such as flooding, before they had time to recuperate from the skeletal effects of vitamin C deficiency. It is also possible that the vitamin C within their diet was destroyed by a preparatory process, as vitamin C is easily destroyed by heat.

Both probable cases of scurvy observed were aged between 1 and 2 years. Brickley and Ives (2006:165) observe that the individuals in their study, as with these individuals recovered from Black Gate, were too young to have been chewing solid foods. They suggest that the actions of the muscles used when suckling and swallowing during breast-feeding and ingestion of soft weaning foods would have been sufficient mechanical stress to cause bleeding and the consequent inflammatory response. Ortner and Mays (1998:52) ascribe rachitic deformities of the mandibular ramus in two individuals aged 12 and 4-6 months from Wharram Percy to muscle action during the habitual chewing of hard non-food objects during teething. It is possible that such stress could cause the facial lesions observed in the two scorbutic cases observed amongst the Black Gate non-adult assemblage.

Cribra orbitalia is expressed in 64 non-adults within the Black Gate assemblage (Crude Prevalence Rate=33%; True Prevalence Rate=54%). However, BG281 and BG521 are the only individuals who exhibit orbital lesions alongside the cranial and post-cranial lesions associated with scurvy. It is possible that these orbital lesions are associated with an underlying anaemic condition, co-existing with scurvy. However, it is only the combination and pattern of lesions observed which can allow macroscopic identification of possible scurvy. If only the orbits survived from these three individuals, such diagnosis would not be possible. The majority of individuals exhibiting cribra orbitalia within Black Gate are, like the two scorbutic individuals, within the Young Child age category. It is probable that these individuals were undergoing weaning and, therefore, being exposed to inadequate dietary replacement foods, and increasing numbers of diarrhoea causing bacterial and parasitic infections (weanling's dilemma) (Kamp 2001; Lewis

2007). The consequent diarrhoea would cause undernutrition, typically associated with iron deficiency. Such malnourishment could be responsible for the occurrence of other metabolic conditions such as the two cases presented here. The probability that the Black Gate non-adults were weaned around the first year of life is supported by a decrease in oxygen and nitrogen values in the mandibular first permanent molars observed by MacPherson et al. (2007). Oxygen isotopes suggested that non-adults from Black Gate received their nutritional requirement from breastmilk for at least the first six to nine months of their lives (MacPherson et al. 2007:42).

The high prevalence of endocranial lesions within the Black Gate non-adult assemblage (CPR=19%; TPR=26%) indicates their aetiology is not uniquely pathological, and may, in some cases, be developmental. Further research is being undertaken to determine the form and distribution of endocranial lesions within the Black Gate non-adult assemblage (Mahoney-Swales, in prep). The inflammatory porosity present bilaterally on the lateral surfaces of the rib shafts may be caused by handling or swaddling of the young child inflicting enough stress to rupture the delicate overlying blood vessels. The sub-cutaneous nature of the external rib shafts would increase the likelihood of stresses from such activities bruising the periosteum.

Conclusions

The main conclusion of this research is that infantile scurvy was an affliction of young children in the early medieval period, but is rarely manifested skeletally. The study of infantile scurvy over the last decade has provided a vital resource to identify possible cases of scurvy within archaeological skeletal assemblages. However, diagnosis is complicated by the poor preservation of many archaeological assemblages, problems with distinguishing scorbutic lesions from normal developmental porosity and new bone growth, and underlying conditions such as anaemia. The more cases of infantile scurvy that are identified, the greater our understanding of this metabolic disease will become. One has to be careful to not ascribe too much importance to one element to identify scurvy. Ortner et al. (2001:347-8) have identified cases lacking sphenoid porosity, which was initially thought to be almost pathognomonic of scurvy. Therefore, researchers are not to be constrained by the guidelines proposed, ignoring other lesions, which may be related to the capillary fragility. Only BG521 and BG281, out of the entire Black Gate assemblage, display extensive abnormal porosity on the lateral rib surfaces, an area rarely surviving in the archaeological record. This is possibly a further manifestation of scurvy, due to the anatomy of the blood vessels, muscles and sub-cutaneous nature of this area being likely to cause capillary damage and sub-periosteal haemorrhage. However, it is scarcely mentioned in the literature.

To support the identification of scurvy, and to identify any underlying conditions it is paramount that high-resolution microscope examination is undertaken on the porous lesions observed to determine if they are in fact vascular responses to scorbutic capillary fragility and associated blood loss, not the consequence of other pathological conditions or normal developmental processes. In addition, radiographs of the distal femora and proximal tibiae of all the individuals aged 6-12 months, which are the most susceptible to vitamin C deficiency, should assist in detection of changes to the epiphyses. The skeletal changes which can be observed radiographically are often still present some years after the other signs of the condition have been remodelled, therefore, a radiographic study is proposed for further study of the Black Gate non-adult skeletal collection, to identify the true prevalence of death and survival rates from vitamin C deficiency.

Acknowledgements

The data included within this report derives from PhD research being undertaken by the first author at the Department of Archaeology, University of Sheffield. Supervision for the PhD is provided by Dr Pia Nystrom and Dr Dawn Hadley, Department of Archaeology, University of Sheffield. The University of Sheffield provided a PhD studentship enabling this research.

Literature cited

Aufdeheide, AC and Rodriguez-Martin, C. 1998. *The Cambridge Encyclopedia of Human Paleopathology.* Cambridge: Cambridge University Press.

Bass, WM. 1987. *Human Osteology: A Laboratory and Field Manual.* 3rd Edition Missouri Archaeological Society Special Publication, no. 2: Columbia.

Brickley, M. 2000. The diagnosis of metabolic disease in archaeological bone. In: Cox, M and Mays, S (eds.) *Human Osteology in Archaeology and Forensic Science.* London: Greenwich Medical Media Ltd. 183-197

Brickley, M and McKinley, J (eds.) 2004. *Guidelines to the standards for recording human remains.* Institute of Field Archaeologists, Paper No. 7. Southampton: BABAO.

Brickley, M and Buteux, S. 2006. *St Martin's Uncovered: Investigations in the Churchyard of St. Martin's-in-the-Bull-Ring, Birmingham.* Oxford: Oxbow Books.

Brickley M and Ives R. 2006. Skeletal manifestations of infantile scurvy. *American Journal of Physical Anthropology* 129:163-172.

Buckberry, J. 2000. Missing, presumed buried? Bone diagenesis and under-representation of Anglo-Saxon children. *Assemblage* 5:1-14.

Burgener, FA. and Kormano, M. 1991. *Differential Diagnosis in Conventional Radiology.* Thieme Publishing Group.

Carpenter, KJ. 1986. *The History of Scurvy and Vitamin C*. Cambridge: Cambridge University Press.

Dyer, C. 1993. *Standards of Living in the Later Middle Ages: Social Change in England c. 1200-1520*. Cambridge Medieval Textbooks. Cambridge University Press.

Hirsch, M, Mogle, P and Barkli, Y. 1976. Neonatal scurvy: report of a case. *Pediatric Radiology* 4:251-253.

Hodges, RE, Hood, J, Canham, JE, Sauberlich, HE and Baker, EM. 1971. Clinical manifestations of ascorbic acid deficiency in man. *American Journal of Clinical Nutrition* 24:432-443.

Holst, A and Frolich, T. 1907. Experimental studies relating to ship-beriberi and scurvy: II On the etiology of scurvy. *Journal of Hygiene* 7: 634-671.

Hoppa, RD. 1992. Evaluating human skeletal growth: An Anglo-Saxon example. *International Journal of Osteoarchaeology* 2: 275-288.

Kamp, KA. 2001. Where have all the children gone?: The archaeology of childhood. *Journal of Archaeological Method and Theory* 8(1):1-34.

Kipp, DE, McElvain, M, Kimmel, DB, Akhter, MP, Robinson, RG and Lukert, BP. 1996. Scurvy results in decreased collagen synthesis and bone density in the guinea pig animal model. *Bone* 18 (3): 281-288.

Lester, G. 1976. *The Anglo-Saxons: How They Lived and Worked*. England: Dufour Editions.

Lewis, M. 2002a. *Urbanisation and Child Health in Medieval and Post-Medieval England*. BAR British Series 339.

Lewis, M. 2002b. Impact of industrialization: Comparative study of child health in four sites from medieval and post medieval England (A.D. 850-1859). *American Journal of Physical Anthropology* 119:211-223.

Lewis, M. 2004. Endocranial lesions in non-adult skeletons: Understanding their aetiology. *International Journal of Osteoarchaeology* 14(2):82-97.

Lewis, M. 2007. *The Bioarchaeology of Children: Perspectives from Biological and Forensic Anthropology*. Cambridge: Cambridge University Press.

Lieber, RL. 2002. *Skeletal Muscle Structure, Function and Plasticity: The Physiological Basis of Rehabilitation*. 2nd Edition. Philadelphia: Lippincott Williams and Wilkins.

Loe, L and Robson-Brown, K. 2005. Summary report on the human skeletons. In: Holbrook, N and Thomas, A. An early monastic cemetery at Llandough, Glamorghan: Excavations in 1994. *Medieval Archaeology* 49:42-52.

Maat, GJR. 2004. Scurvy in adults and youngsters: The Dutch experience. A review of the history and pathology of a disregarded disease. *International Journal of Osteoarchaeology* 14(2):77-81.

MacPherson, P, Chenery, CA and Chamberlain, AT. 2007. Tracing change: Childhood diet at the Anglo-Saxon Black Gate cemetery, Newcastle upon Tyne, England. In: Robson-Brown, K and Roberts, AM (eds.) *BABAO 2004: Proceedings of the 6th Annual Conference of the British Association for Biological Anthropology and Osteoarchaeology, University of Bristol*. BAR International Series 1623. Oxford: BAR Publishing, pp 37-44.

Mays, S. 2007. A likely case of scurvy from early Bronze Age Britain. *International Journal of Osteoarchaeology* Early View. www.interscience.wiley.com/journal/oa. 02/01/08.

Melikian, M and Waldron, T. 2003. An examination of skulls from two British sites for possible evidence of scurvy. *International Journal of Osteoarchaeology* 13:207-212.

Moorees, CFA, Fanning, EA and Hunt, EE. 1963. Age variation of formation stages for ten permanent teeth. *Journal of Dental Research* 42: 1490-1502.

Ortner, D. 2003. *Identification of Pathological Conditions in Human Skeletal Remains*. New York: Academic Press.

Ortner, DJ and Ericksen, MF. 1997. Bone changes in the human skull probably resulting from scurvy in infancy and childhood. *International Journal of Osteoarchaeology* 7:212-220.

Ortner, DJ and Mays, S. 1998. Dry-bone manifestations of rickets in infancy and early childhood. *International Journal of Osteoarchaeology* 8:45-55.

Ortner, DJ, Butler, W, Cafarella, J and Milligan, L. 2001. Evidence of probable scurvy in subadults from archaeological sites in North America *American Journal of Physical Anthropology* 114:343-351.

Ortner, DJ, Kimmerle, E and Diez, M. 1999. Skeletal evidence of scurvy in archaeological skeletal samples from Peru. *American Journal of Physical Anthropology* 108:321-331.

Pearson, KL. 1997. Nutrition and the early-medieval diet. *Speculum* 72(1):1-32.

Pimentel, L. 2003. Scurvy: Historical review and current diagnostic approach. *American Journal of Emergency Medicine* 21:328-332.

Rajakumar, K. 2001. Infantile scurvy: A historical perspective. *Pediatrics* 108:76-78.

Roberts, C and Cox, M. 2003. *Health and Disease in Britain: From Prehistory to the Present Day.* Stroud: Sutton Publishing Ltd.

Scheuer, JL, Musgrave, JH and Evans, SP. 1980. The estimation of late foetal and perinatal age from limb bone length by linear and logarithmic regression. *Annals of Human Biology* 7 (3): 257-265.

Schwarz, J. 1995. *Skeleton Keys*. USA: Routledge.

Tamura, Y, Welch, DC, Zic AJ, Cooper, WO, Stein, SM and Hummel, DS. 2000. Scurvy presenting as a painful gait with bruising in a young boy. *Archives of Pediatric and Adolescent Medicine* 154:732–735.

Waldron, T. 1989. The effects of urbanisation on human health: The evidence from skeletal remains. In: Serjeantson, D and Waldron, T (eds.) *Diet and Crafts in Towns: The Evidence of Animal Remains from the Roman to the Post-Medieval Periods.* Oxford: BAR British Series 199, pp55-73.

Infantile Cortical Hyperostosis: Cases, Causes and Contradictions

Mary Lewis,[1] and Rebecca Gowland[2]

[1]Department of Archaeology, University of Reading, Whiteknights, Reading RG6 6AB.
[2]Department of Archaeology, University of Durham, South Road, Durham, DH1 3LE

m.e.lewis@reading.ac.uk

Abstract

The inhumation burial of a 1.5-year old child, excavated from a 1st century AD cremation cemetery at Stanton Field, Newton St Loe, Bath, prompted research into the identification of the pathological lesions it displayed, and a review of infantile cortical hyperostosis (ICH). Also known as Caffey's disease, ICH was first described in 1945 and denotes a triad of lesions comprising soft tissue swelling, irritability and cortical bone lesions. The condition has both a familial and sporadic aetiology, heals spontaneously and has its onset and resolution in infancy. Skeletal lesions include layers of subperiosteal bone formation and cortical thickening of the long bones, especially the tibia and ulna, with the mandible most commonly affected in the sporadic form of the disease. Several cases of ICH have been reported in the palaeopathological literature, but the aetiology of this condition is still unknown. Modern cases are thought to result from a latent infection, genetic defect, arterial abnormality or an allergic reaction.

This paper discusses the diagnostic criteria and differential diagnoses for ICH in light of several cases from Roman Britain. The confusion surrounding the aetiology and manifestation of ICH in the medical literature seems to be reflected in palaeopathology, with ICH used as a 'catch-all' to describe widespread lesions on infant remains. It is perhaps prudent to consider infantile cortical hyperostosis as descriptive of a series of lesions, rather than as a particular disease entity.

Keywords: Infantile cortical hyperostosis, histology, Roman Britain, non-adult palaeopathology

Introduction

Excavations at Stanton Field, Bath, England, were carried out by Bath Archaeological Trust between 1999 and 2000. Stanton Field is situated below Stantonbury Hillfort, near a natural spring. Material excavated from the site revealed activity dating as far back as the Neolithic, although the majority of the human remains dated from the Bronze Age through to the Roman period. Among the finds were the remains of several cremated individuals along with five inhumation burials (two adult females and three non-adults), and the disarticulated bone fragments of a further four individuals (two adults, one infant and one neonate). While use of the site for burial was by no means contiguous, its ritual significance appears to have persisted over millennia, and this may be related to its proximity to the natural spring (Moore 2003). The normal mode of burial at this time, and in this area, was cremation making the presence of inhumations notable. Two of the inhumations were of particular interest and may help to shed light on the significance of the site itself. The first was a male (burial 132) aged 25-35 years, radiocarbon dated to the first half of the 3rd century AD. The skeleton of this individual exhibited profuse new bone formation and lytic lesions on four lower right ribs, indicative of tuberculosis or a chronic pulmonary infection (Gowland et al. 2003). If this individual was suffering from tuberculosis, then it is an early example of this disease in the UK (although not the earliest, see Mays and Michael Taylor 2003).

The burial that forms the focus of this study, however, is a child (burial 107) whose skeleton exhibited pathological changes throughout, and whose grave had been covered with limestone blocks. Radiocarbon dates placed the burial of this child earlier than the adult male, to the second half of the first century AD (Moore 2003: 15). Attempts to understand the nature of the lesions in this child prompted a review of the clinical diagnostic features of infantile cortical hyperostosis (ICH), and a re-assessment of previously reported archaeological cases of ICH from Roman Britain.

Burial 107: macroscopic description

Figure 1 illustrates the preservation of the skeleton and distribution of pathological lesions. The age of the skeleton was estimated from the dentition (Moorrees et al. 1963). The deciduous molars were not fully occluded and the extent of root formation of the second deciduous molar showed the child to be around 1.5 years of age. Almost all of the surviving bones exhibit some pathological change. Hypertrophy and a mixture of healing and active new bone lesions are evident on the right and left orbits, the frontal and occipital bones, and the right and left parietals.

In some areas on the parietals and frontal bone, the new bone formation has a stellate arrangement (Fig 2), and the pitted lesions are rounded, suggesting healing. The mandibular body (Fig 3) and both greater wings of the sphenoid also exhibit pitting. The pathological changes are not uniform throughout the cranial vault, with the left orbit and frontal being thickened. In cross-section, successive episodes of new bone formation followed by remodelling can be observed, giving the appearance of a series of concentric rings (Figs 4ab). On the endocranial surface, vascular woven bone is present on the occipital bones near the cruciate eminence, and there is a crest of lamellar bone along the central aspect of the frontal bone, in the location of the crista frontalis (Fig 5). This feature is unusually marked in a child where, normally, the metopic suture would have only just fused (between 2-4 years, Scheuer and Black 2004). All of the lesions suggest a long-term chronic condition with periods of healing and recurrence. Although no enamel hypoplasias are evident, the roots of the mandibular and maxillary deciduous central incisors appear constricted towards the apex, in a location that corresponds to 12 months of development. This perhaps suggests an age of onset for the condition. The postcranial bones are very fragmentary; however, inflammatory pitting is evident on the right tibial shaft and scapulae.

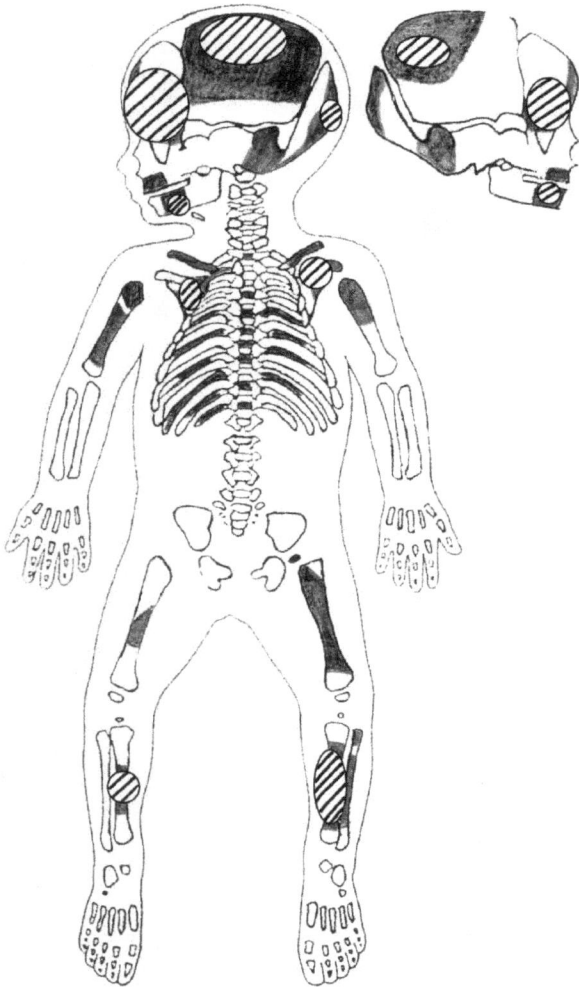

Figure 2. Left parietal bone showing new bone formation with vascular channels, pitting and a stellate appearance.

Figure 3. Fragment of the left mandibular body with inflammatory pitting and new bone formation.

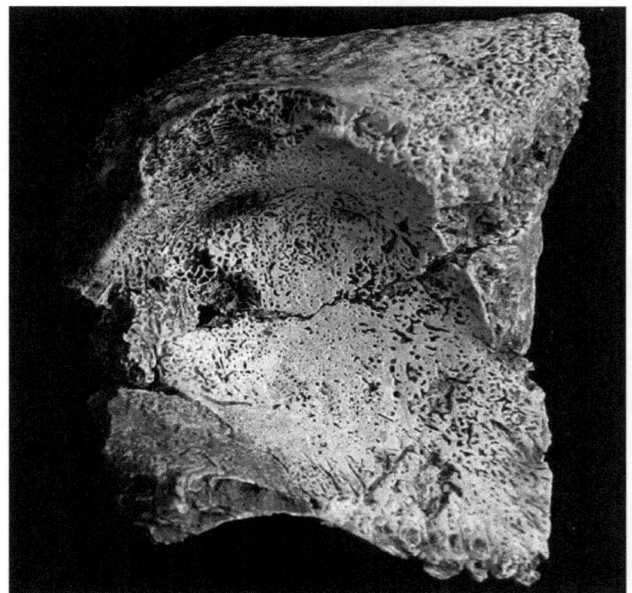

Figure 1. Bones present (shaded) and distribution of lesions (hatched) for Stanton Field 107.

Figure 4a. Reconstructed left orbit with inflammatory pitting and severe hypertrophy.

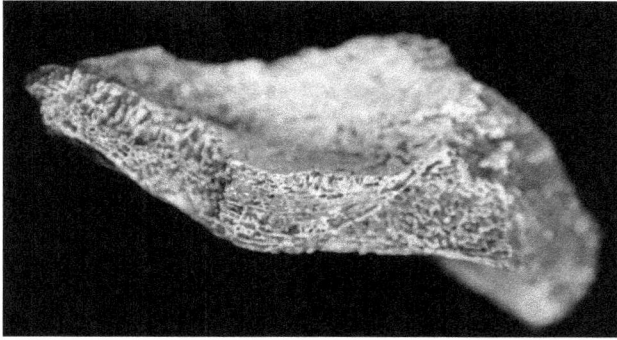

Figure 4b. Cross section of the left orbit showing successive layers of new bone formation indicative of a recurring condition.

Figure 5: Lateral view of the frontal bone showing hypertrophy and a large crest along the line of the metopic suture on the endocranial surface.

Burial 107: microscopic examination

Microscopic slides of the lesions were prepared to assist diagnosis. Small (approx 2cm diameter) fragments of cranial vault bone were infiltrated and embedded under low pressure in Araldite MY753/HY956 epoxy resin (Vantico Ltd, Duxford, UK). The resin-embedded specimens were then sectioned using a Leitz 1600 annular saw microtome (Leica Microsystems, Nussloch, Germany) to produce transverse sections through the vault, with a thickness of between 30 and 50 microns. The sections were mounted on glass microscope slides using Euparal mountant (Asco Laboratories, Manchester, UK). Bone microstructure was viewed on a Kyowa transmitted light microscope with the images displayed on a computer screen using a Pupil Cam digital camera and Vision Explorer software (Ken-a-Vision, Kansas City, USA). In order to have 'controls' by which to measure the cranial lesions, slides of non-adults from around the same age as burial 107 were prepared. These comprised a cranial fragment from a child skeleton showing no abnormal lesions, and cranial fragments from two skeletons exhibiting porotic hyperostosis from the medieval cemetery of Blackgate, Newcastle.

In the 'healthy' control specimen, the inner and outer laminas (tables) of the cranium are intact and the inner diploë shows a normal, well-organised trabecular structure (Fig 6). The skull of skeleton 107 has a very different microstructure (Figs 7). When viewed under plane-polarised light it is apparent that skeleton 107 has undergone greater post-depositional decay than the Blackgate skeleton, as less collagen is visible. The dark irregular deposits around the lacunae are soil inclusions. However, pathological changes are still evident. Due to the extent of pathological enlargement, two separate slide photographs were necessary to show the inner and outer tables of the cranial cross-section. The internal lamina is intact, although it does show some irregularity at the margins, and the trabeculae are elongated, enlarged and densely packed. This cranial section does not have macroscopic endocranial lesions. There is destruction of the external lamina with the ectocranial surface appearing irregular and porotic, and these features are continuous with the original cortex (Fig 7). The microstructure of this sample does not show the gracile characteristics observed in rachitic crania, where the external surface tends to be comprised of squamous plates, referred to as the 'rachitic osteophyte' (Schultz 2003: 85). This allows us to rule out rickets as a diagnosis. Osteomyelitis may also lead to the inflammation of the cranium. However, microscopic analysis revealed that there was no focal destruction of the trabeculae or secondary new bone formation characteristic of this infection (Schultz 2003: 99).

In cases of porotic hyperostosis associated with anaemia, a thickening of the diploë occurs due to the radial growth of trabecular bone and concurrent thinning of the outer table (Ortner 2003: 369). These alterations in bone microstructure are illustrated in the control sample of Blackgate 281 (Figs 8 & 9). The slides show the enlarged and vertically oriented trabeculae, thinning of the outer table and intact inner table. Overall the trabeculae tend to be elongated and gracile. These vertically oriented trabeculae produce a characteristic 'hair on end' effect that can be observed particularly well radiographically.

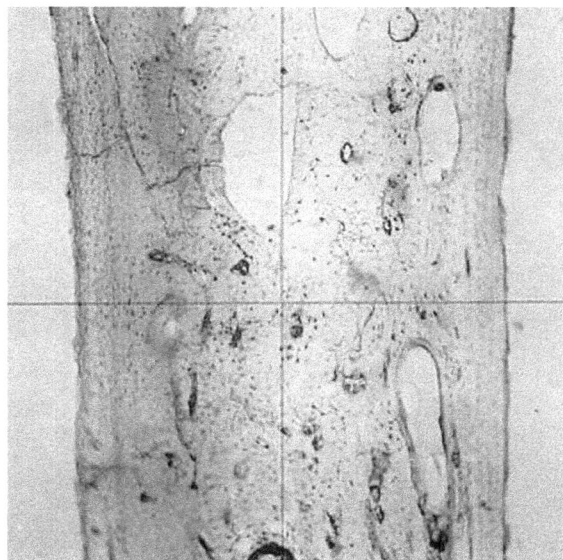

Figure 6. Microstructure of a cranial fragment cross-section from a 'healthy' child from Blackgate cemetery, Newcastle.

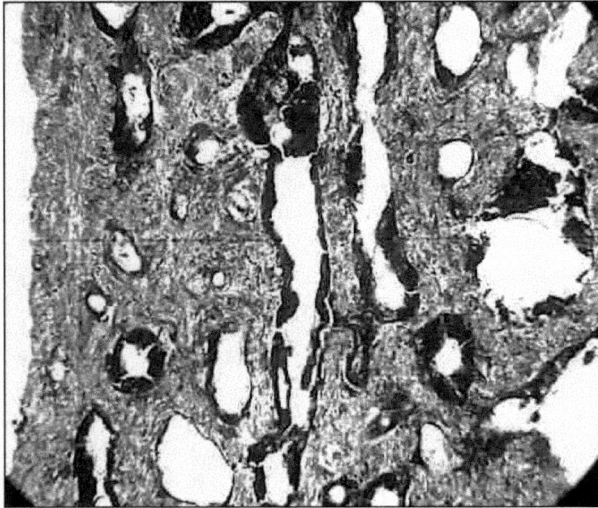

Figure 7. Cross-section of cranial sample from skeleton 107, showing the inner table (top of slide) and diploë. The irregular dark deposits around the trabeculae and Haversian canals are postmortem infiltrations.

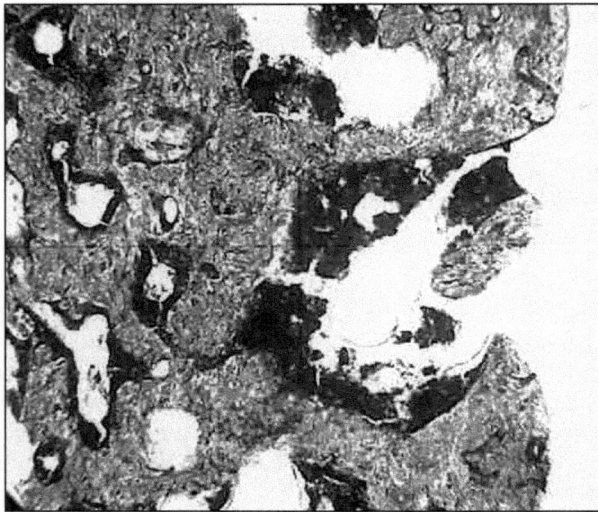

Figure 8: Microstructure of cranial cross-section of Blackgate 281 exhibiting vertically oriented trabeculae on the outer surface (left).

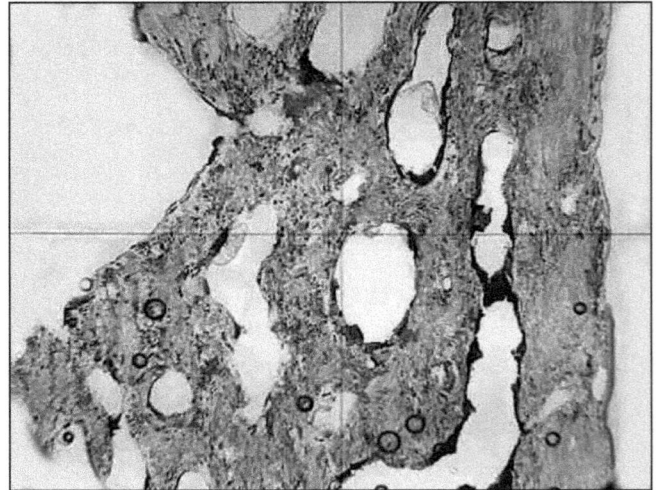

Figure 9: Microstructure of cranial cross-section of Blackgate 281 exhibiting elongated and gracile trabeculae and an intact inner table (right).

A final comparison was made with Blackgate 81 (Figs 10 & 11). This individual exhibited similar, but less severe, lesions to Stanton Field 107, including slight porosity of the sphenoid. An examination of the microstructure however, reveals a different condition. Blackgate 81 exhibits an intact inner table, and trabeculae are more enlarged and gracile than in skeleton 107 with the production of lamellar bone less pronounced. The pathological changes in skeleton 107, although similar in appearance to iron deficiency anaemia, differ from this condition, because the deposition of periosteal new bone also occurs on the surface of the original cortex of the cranial vault, rather than from an expansion within, and 'hair-on-end' trabeculae are not evident in Stanton Field 107. Furthermore, iron-deficiency anaemia rarely causes post-cranial changes. Although the changes to the frontal bones in particular have a stellate appearance reminiscent of caries sicca in congenital syphilis, the fact that skeleton 107 does not exhibit dental defects, the dental stigmata, or periosteal 'cloaking' of the long bones mitigates against this condition as a diagnosis. Due to the early date of the remains this is not surprising. In fact, the cranial lesions of Stanton Field 107 are far more severe and varied than any reported for congenital syphilis in the literature (e.g. see Ortner 2003).

Some of the lesions exhibited by burial 107, particularly on the sphenoid, mandible and long bones are very similar to those observed in scurvy. Indeed, sphenoid lesions have been argued to be pathognomonic of the disease (Ortner et al. 2001). The layers in the left orbit may be the result of repeated haemorrhaging and ossification. Melikian and Waldron (2003) illustrated a case of known scurvy from the Royal College of Surgeons, London with new bone formation on the frontal bone, overlying the metopic suture. However, such severe hypertrophy of the frontal and orbital bones has never been reported for scurvy. Microscopically, there is no evidence of bone apposition upon a normal outer lamina to suggest the thickening is the result of

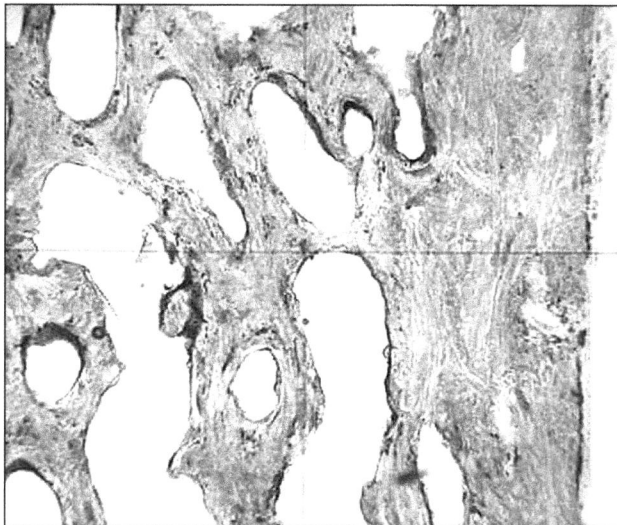

Figure 10: Microstructure of cranial cross-section of Blackgate 81 exhibiting enlarged, gracile and irregular trabeculae. Some of the outer table is still preserved (left).

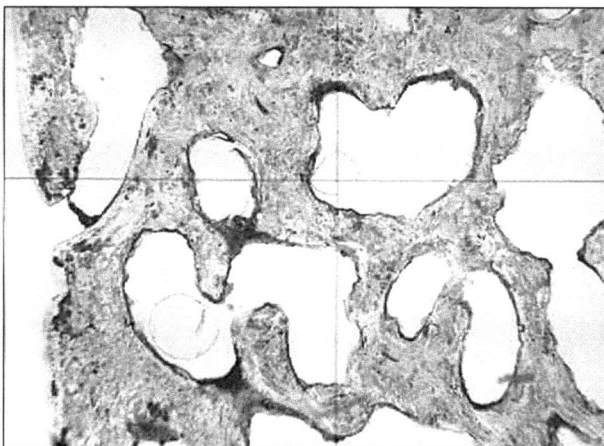

Figure 11: Microstructure of cranial cross-section of Blackgate 81 from Blackgate exhibiting enlarged, gracile and irregular trabeculae.

ossified haematomas (Schultz 2001). For these reasons, scurvy was not considered the most likely cause of the changes seen in the Stanton Field child. However, there is one chronic inflammatory condition that appears in infancy, causes 'lamellated' new bone under the periosteum, and affects the clavicle and mandible; infantile cortical hyperostosis. Lack of any tangible information on this condition prompted further research into its clinical features and a review of previously reported cases broadly contemporary with this burial, in order to assess the likelihood of the condition as a possible diagnosis for this child's disease.

Infantile cortical hyperostosis

Infantile cortical hyperostosis (ICH) or Caffey's disease is an uncommon condition. The reported incidence today is 3 per 1000 and the disease has been reported to be on

the decline since the 1950s, perhaps due to improved methods of diagnosis. It maintains a predilection for twins, and today, is managed with corticosteroids and anti-inflammatory drugs such as indomethacin (Couper et al. 2001). ICH denotes a triad of lesions comprising soft tissue swelling, and cortical thickening. The child becomes irritable, presents with a fever and may also suffer from painful pseudoparalysis, pleurisy and anaemia (Resnick and Niwayama 1988; Restrepo et al. 2004). The condition has both a familial and a sporadic aetiology, heals spontaneously, and has its onset and resolution in infancy. It is known throughout the world, affects all ancestral groups and has equal prevalence in boys and girls (Resnick and Niwayama 1988: 4118). Earlier reference to the condition was made in the German literature by Roske (1930) and it was alluded to by Caffey (1939) in a paper on infantile syphilis. But the condition was most famously described by Caffey and Silverman in 1945 and again by Smyth and colleagues (1946). Clinically, the condition persists over a period of several months, and manifests as a localised tender lump on a rib or the mandible, and with less frequency, on the long bone diaphyses (Aufderheide and Rodriguez-Martin 1998: 363). The average age of onset is nine weeks but the disease has been noted *in utero* (Barba and Freriks 1953; Lecollier et al. 1992). It is rarely reported after five months (Caffey 1978), although there have been active cases that have continued to recur into the fourth year of life and even in individuals up to 19 years of age (Keipert and Campbell 1970; Swerdloff et al. 1970; Thometz and DiRaimondo 1996).

In the early stages of the condition, the periosteum becomes thickened and cellular, with the loss of the outer fibrous layer, causing it to merge with the surrounding tissues. Osteoid is then deposited around the sheath and into the tissues. Profuse layers of new bone are formed causing the bone to appear thickened (Glorieux 2005). As the condition stabilises, the periosteum re-establishes its fibrous layer and the new layer of bone becomes incorporated into the original cortex. Remodelling begins from the endosteal surface, causing the medullary cavity to widen and the bones to become more fragile (Caffey 1978; Glorieux, 2005). The microscopic appearance of the affected bone is rarely described in the literature, but Langer and Kaufman (1986) identified densely packed, irregularly mineralised trabeculae, with an increased number of osteoblasts, in a cross-section of an affected ulna. This is reminiscent of the density of the trabeculae noted in the cranium cross-section from Stanton Field 107.

The skeletal distribution of the condition varies in the clinical literature (Table 1), with early studies noting lesions on the long bones (Barba and Freriks 1953), clavicle, scapula (Caffey and Silverman 1945; Neuhauser 1970), ribs (Barba and Freriks 1953; Caffey and Silverman 1945), hands and feet (Caffey and Silverman 1945), while later papers cite bone changes on the mandible as the most common (Blank 1975; Finsterbush and Husseini 1979; Swerdloff et al. 1970), suggesting it to be involved in almost 80% of cases (Fauré et al. 1977).

Table 1. Distribution of lesions

	Cranium	Mandible	Clavicle	Scapula	Long bones	Hands & Feet	Ribs
Roske (1930)					+		
Caffey & Silverman (1945)			+	+		+	+
Barba (1953)					+		+
Swedloff et al. (1970)		+					
Neuhauser (1970)	+	+	+	+			
Blank (1975)		+					
Finterbush & Husseini (1979)		+		+	+		
Lachaux et al. (1992)	+				+		+
Couper et al. (2001)		+	+		+		

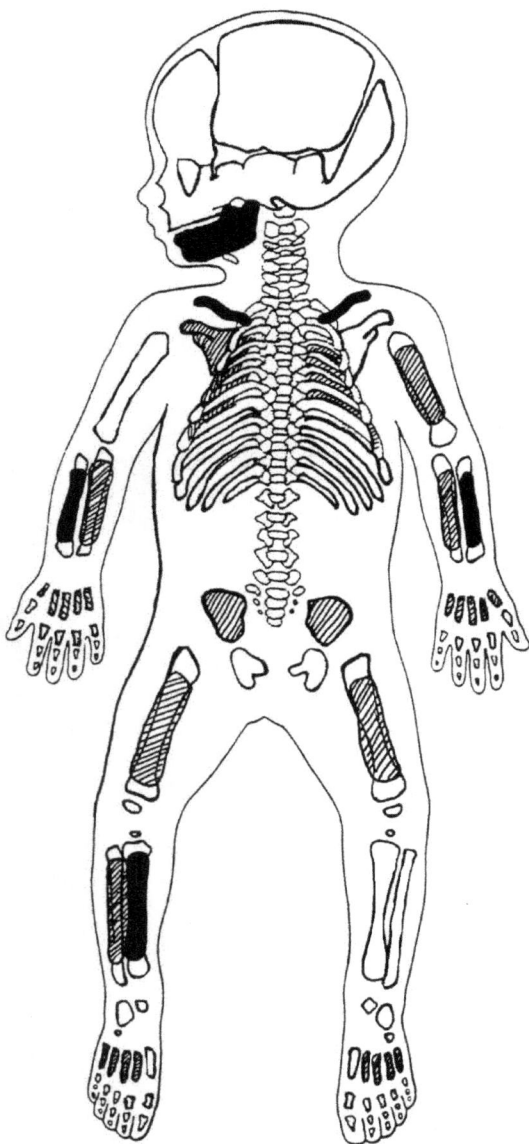

Figure 12: Distribution of lesions in infantile cortical hyperostosis (Lewis 2007: 145). Black areas indicate those most commonly affected, hatched areas indicate bones that are less frequently affected.

In around 20% cases, however, ICH can occur without mandibular involvement (Wilson 1969). A number of clinical cases also report thickening and sclerosis of the orbits and upper facial bones (Boyd et al. 1972; Fauré et al. 1977; Lachaux et al. 1992; Neuhauser 1970), although these bones are involved only infrequently. ICH does not involve the tarsals, carpals, phalanges and vertebrae, but the scapulae, ilia, and ribs may all be affected (Glorieux 2005; Ortner 2003: 417). The ulna is considered to be the long bone most likely to display obvious hypertrophic changes and bowing, next to an unaffected radius. All of these lesions may be asymmetric and, unlike rickets and scurvy, the metaphyses and epiphyses are spared (Caffey and Silverman 1945).

Scapula lesions are generally believed to be unilateral and are only noted during the first six months of life, mandibular lesions have not been reported in older infants, and clavicular lesions are found at all ages, appearing both unilaterally and bilaterally (Stein et al. 1955: 405) (Fig 12). More recent studies consider ICH as a diagnosis when lesions appear on the mandible, clavicle, and long bones (Couper et al. 2001). No dental lesions have been reported in the clinical literature.

The condition can completely resolve within three months without medical intervention, but recurring forms of the disease may persist for many years sometimes occurring at new sites (Glorieux 2005). Continued episodes of the disease may eventually lead to interosseous bridging of the radius and ulna, and between the ribs, dislocation of the radial head, mandibular asymmetry, bowing of the tibiae and other severe deformities (Barba and Freriks 1953; Blank 1975; Caffey 1978; Resnick and Niwayama 1988).

Clues to the aetiology of ICH lie in its clinical manifestation. As an infectious agent, the presence of high fever, occasional plural exudates and clustered cases are consistent, as is the inflammatory change of the periosteum. A viral infection is suggested by the similarity of lesions to a condition found in hamsters, and the lack of response to antibiotic therapy. Mossberger (1950) noted the death of an infant previously admitted with suspected ICH who tested positive for typhoid.

However, no bacterial or viral agents have ever been isolated in the disease (Resnick and Niwayama 1988). Familial, rather than sporadic, cases appear to have a slightly different distribution, with changes to the mandible, ribs and scapulae being less common, possibly suggesting a genetic aetiology in these instances (Borokowitz et al. 1991). An allergic aetiology has also been cited in the clinical literature, with an association in some instances related to milk allergies, or high numbers of asthma sufferers within a family (Ventura et al. 1983). Elevated levels of prostaglandin E have been noted in Caffey's patients (Ueda 1980). However, it is not known if these elevations are the cause of the consequence of the disease (Glorieux 2005). More recently, Gensure and colleagues (2005) reported that a mutation on the collagen gene (COL1A1), linked to the development of osteogenesis imperfecta, has been identified in ICH patients. But the significance of these results is still a matter of debate (Glorieux 2005). Its familial persistence may suggest that a previous environmental or viral aetiology of the sporadic forms of the disease has been overtaken by genetic underlying factors as the environmental conditions have been removed.

The dazzling array and variability of lesions thought to represent ICH may be the result of many misdiagnosed early cases, when clinicians were still wrestling with its aetiology. For example, the reported elevated levels of alkaline phosphatase reported by Resnick and Niwayama in 1988, is now considered pathognomonic of the rare hyperphosphatasia with osteoectasia rather than ICH (Couper et al. 2001). What seems clear is that the condition is characterised by lesions of the mandible and clavicles, with unilateral lesions on the scapulae. Long bones can be affected bilaterally or unilaterally with various degrees of frequency and that the calvarium and phalanges are normally unaffected.

Today, the disease is uncommon and many early signs of it could be easily missed both clinically and archaeologically. Child abuse has long been a differential diagnosis for Caffey's disease, however, the lack of metaphyseal and rib fractures in such children would rule out physical trauma as a cause. Hypervitaminosis A, vitamin deficiencies, viral infections and tumours also result in cortical thickening, but involvement of the mandible in these cases is unusual (Resnick and Niwayama 1988).

Archaeological evidence

Reported archaeological cases of infantile cortical hyperostosis are rare. Rogers and Waldron (1988) reported two cases; one in a 10-18 month Romano-British infant and the other in a one-year old from Anglo-Saxon England. The latter had evidence of profuse new bone on the ectocranial surface and the mandible, and periostitis on the shafts of the long bones. Bagousse and Blondiaux (2001) identified ICH from profuse appositional new bone formation on the cranium and long bones of a child from Roman Lisieux, France. Farwell and Molleson (1993) diagnosed the condition in a staggering 57 infants

from Poundbury Camp, Dorset. These cases are of particular interest to the study of burial 107 from Stanton Field because they are broadly contemporary. The affected children at this site range from birth to three years of age. The authors of the report cited recovery from smallpox (osteomyelitis variolosa) as the primary aetiology. However, the diagnosis of these individuals was not fully described, and there was no mention of how many of these children had mandibular involvement. A re-assessment of the Poundbury Camp ICH sample by the present authors suggests that, of the 57 cases; 27 had postmortem damage or normal growth that mimicked periosteal new bone formation and/or cranial lesions; 19 exhibited porotic hyperostosis indicative of iron-deficiency anaemia; six children had rickets, and there were four cases of scurvy. An improvement in our diagnostic techniques for rickets and scurvy in non-adult remains since the Poundbury Camp report was published now enables us to distinguish more of these diseases. In one case however, profuse lesions of the tibial shafts, and in particular, woven new bone formation along the crista frontalis suggested a similar condition to that of Stanton Field 107, and possibly ICH.

Given the above review, the most likely condition to cause 'lamellated' new bone under the periosteum, hypertrophy of the skull and affect the clavicle and mandible, is infantile cortical hyperostosis. Microscopically, the affected bone has densely packed, irregularly mineralised trabeculae that is not consistent with more commonly reported diseases such as rickets, scurvy, anaemia or syphilis. While the child is older than most clinically documented individuals that suffer from ICH, the cranial lesions suggest healing and re-occurrence of inflammation noted in the condition. It was the cranium that was the most severely affected in burial 107 and while ICH is less commonly observed in the skull in clinical cases, some have documented its involvement. It is possible that skeleton 107 also suffered from scurvy, and this would explain some of the new bone observed (e.g. on the sphenoid) that is at odds with the clinical literature on ICH.

Discussion and conclusions

The confusion surrounding the aetiology and manifestation of ICH in the medical literature seems to be reflected in palaeopathology, with ICH used as a 'catch-all' to describe widespread lesions on infant remains. The non-fatal nature of the disease means that those children who may have developed the condition could recover completely leaving no traces of the disease behind, and this may explain the paucity of such conditions reported in the archaeological samples. Future research into the skeletal manifestations of the disease is needed. Until then it is perhaps prudent to consider infantile cortical hyperostosis as descriptive of a series of lesions, rather than as a particular disease entity, in the same way that we now regard cribra orbitalia and porotic hyperostosis (Ortner 2003). Diagnosis of the disease suffered by burial 107 is hindered by the poor condition of the remains and lack of crucial elements, such as the bones of the forearm, particularly the ulnae which are commonly affected in ICH. Although many of the changes on the surviving skeletal elements are indicative of scurvy, neither the histology, nor the severity of the cranial changes are typical of this disease, and infantile cortical hyperostosis, whatever its aetiology, cannot be ruled out.

Regardless of the cause of the condition, the skeletal changes of burial 107 indicate that the child would have been visible ill to their family and community. The skin would have appeared bruised, inflamed and tender to the touch. The gums would have been swollen and bleeding, and the cranial changes may have led to skin lesions and bleeding into the hair follicles, disrupting hair growth (Aufderheide and Rodriguez-Martin 1998: 311). In addition, the extreme orbital changes are likely to have pushed the eyes forward (exophthalmos). The chronic changes in the skull indicate a long-term recurring condition and the child is likely to have experienced episodes of illness followed by short periods of comparative recovery. Whichever disease caused the gross pathological changes observed in skeleton 107, it is likely that the child had suffered with it for most, if not all, of its short life. The possibility of scurvy indicates that their specific diet may have been deficient in fruit and vegetables. However, this does not mean that the child was not well looked after, as there were different perceptions of what constituted a 'good' diet for infants in the past. Their survival with the condition over a long period of time indicates that the child was fed and nurtured, despite their illness.

Finally, inhumation was not the prevailing burial rite during the late Iron Age/ early Roman period in this region. The fact that of the five burials accorded this anomalous rite, two exhibited severe pathological changes to their skeletons is intriguing, as is the proximity of these burials to a natural spring. It is tempting to surmise that this area held a special ritual significance or symbolism associated with illness or healing. It seems that the pathological status of these individuals impacted on their identity within the community, not necessarily in any negative way, but to the extent that normative burial practices were not deemed appropriate.

Acknowledgements

We are grateful to Andrew Chamberlain (University of Sheffield) for preparing the histological slides and Joël Blondiaux (Centre d'Etudes Paleopathologiques du Nord) for his assistance with their interpretation. Jenny Moore and Substrata for providing the archaeological background to the Stanton Field case and Louise Humphrey and Robert Kruszynski (Natural History Museum, London) for access to the Poundbury Camp collection.

Literature cited

Aufderheide AC, and Rodriguez-Martin C. 1998. *The Cambridge Encyclopedia of Human Paleopathology.* Cambridge: Cambridge University Press.

Bagousse A-L, and Blondiaux J. 2001. Hyperostoses corticales foetal et infantile à Lisieux (IVe s.): retour à Costebelle. *Centre Archaéologique du Var Revue* 20: 60-64.

Barba WP, and Freriks DJ. 1953. The familial occurrence of infantile cortical hyperostosis *in utero. Journal of Pediatrics* 42:141-150.

Blank E. 1975. Recurrent Caffey's cortical hyperostosis and persistent deformity. *Pediatrics* 55:856-860.

Boyd R, Shaw D, and Thomas B. 1972. Infantile cortical hyperostosis with lytic lesions in the skull. *Archives of Diseases in Childhood* 47:471-472.

Burbank P, Lovestedt S, and Kennedy R. 1958. The dental aspects of Infantile Cortical Hyperostosis. *Oral Surgery, Oral Medicine and Oral Pathology* 10:1126-1137.

Caffey J. 1939. Syphilis of the skeleton in early infancy. *The American Journal of Roentgenology and Radium Therapy* 42:637-655.

Caffey J. 1978. *Pediatric X-Ray Diagnosis.* Chicago: Tear Book Medical Publishers, Inc.

Caffey J, and Silverman WA. 1945. Infantile cortical hyperostosis. Preliminary report on a new syndrome. *The American Journal of Roentgenology and Radium Therapy* 4:1-16.

Couper R, McPhee A, and Morris L. 2001. Imomethacin treatment of infantile cortical periostosis in twins. *Journal of Paediatrics and Child Health* 37:305-308.

Farwell DE, and Molleson TI. 1993. *Excavations at Poundbury 1966-80 Volume II: The Cemeteries.* Dorset: Dorset Natural History and Archaeological Society.

Fauré C, Beyssac J, and Montagne J. 1977. Predominant or exclusive orbital and facial involvement in Infantile Cortical Hyperostosis (de Toni-Caffey's Disease). *Pediatric Radiology* 6:103-106.

Finsterbush A, and Husseini N. 1979. Infantile cortical hyperostosis with unusual clinical manifestations. *Clinical Orthopaedics and Related Research* 144:276-279.

Gensure R, Makitie O, Barclay C, Chan C, DePalma S, et al. 2005. A novel COL1A1 mutation in infantile cortical hyperostosis (Caffey disease) expands the spectrum of collagen-related disorders. *The Journal of Clinical Investigation* 115:1250-1257.

Glorieux F. 2005. Caffey disease: an unlikely collagenopathy. *The Journal of Clinical Investigation* 115:1142-1144.

Gowland R, Chamberlain AC, and Lewis ME. 2003. *The Further Analysis of Skeletons 132 and 107 from Stanton Field Excavations.* Unpublished report for Bath Archaeological Trust.

Keipert JA ,and Campbell PE. 1970. Recurrent hyperostosis of the clavicles: an undiagnosed syndrome. *Australian Paediatric Journal* 6:97-104.

Lachaux A, Le Gall C, Loras C, Duclaux I, and Hermier M. 1992. Familial Infantile Cortical Hyperostosis (Caffey's Disease) with osteolytic lesions of the skull. *Archives of France Pediatrics* 49:525-528.

Langer R, and Kaufmann H. 1986. Case Report 363. *Skeletal Radiology* 15:377-382.

Leucolier B, Bercau G, Gonzales M, Afriat R, Rambaud D, and Mulliez N. 1992. Radiography, haematological, and biochemical findings in a fetus with Caffey disease. *Prenatal Diagnosis* 12: 637-41.

Lewis M. 2007. *The Bioarchaeology of Children. Perspectives from Biological and Forensic Anthropology.* Cambridge: Cambridge University Press.

Melikian M, and Waldron T. 2003. An examination of skulls from two British sites for possible evidence of scurvy. *International Journal of Osteoarchaeology* 13:207-212.

Moore J. 1993. *Stanton Field, Newton Loe, Bath. Additional Report 2: Osteological and Radiocarbon Analysis.* Unpublished report for Bath Archaeological Trust.

Mays S, and Michael Taylor G. 2003. A first prehistoric case of tuberculosis from Britain. *International Journal of Osteoarchaeology* 13: 189-196.

Moorrees CFA, Fanning EA, and Hunt EE. 1963. Formation and resorption of three deciduous teeth in children. *American Journal of Physical Anthropology* 21:205-213.

Mossberger JI. 1950. Infantile Cortical Hyperostosis: report of a case with observations at autopsy. *American Journal of Diseases in Children* 80:610-620.

Neuhauser E. 1970. Infantile Cortical Hyperostosis and skull defects. *Postgraduate Medicine* 48:57-59.

Ortner DJ ed. 2003. *Identification of Pathological Conditions in Human Skeletal Remains.* New York: Academic Press.

Ortner DJ, Butler W, Cafarella J, and Milligan L. 2001. Evidence of probable scurvy in subadults from archaeological sites in North America. *American Journal of Physical Anthropology* 114:343-351.

Resnick D, and Niwayama D eds. 1988. *Diagnosis of Bone and Joint Disorders.* Philadelphia: WB Saunders Company.

Rogers J, and Waldron T. 1988. Two possible cases of Infantile Cortical Hyperostosis. *Paleopathology Newsletter* 63:9-12.

Roske G (1930) Eine eigenartige knochenerkrankung im säuglingsalter. *Monatsschr f Kindeh* 47:385.

Scheuer L, and Black S. 2004. *The Juvenile Skeleton.* London: Elsevier.

Schultz M. 2001. Palaeohistopathology of bone: a new approach to the study of ancient diseases. *Yearbook of Physical Anthropology* 44:106-147.

Schultz M. 2003. Light microscopic analysis in skeletal palaeopathology. In DJ Ortner (ed.) *Identification of Pathological Lesions in Human Skeletal Remains.* London: Academic Press, pp 73-107.

Smyth F, Potter A, and Silverman W. 1946. Periosteal reaction, fever and irritability in young infants: a new syndrome? *American Journal of Diseases of Children* 71:333.

Stein I, Stein RO, and Beller ML. 1955. *Living Bone in Health and Disease.* London: Pitman Medical.

Swerdloff BA, Ozonoff MB, and Gyepes MT. 1970. Late recurrence of Infantile Cortical Hyperostosis (Caffey's disease). *American Journal of Roentgenology* 108:461-467.

Thometz J, and DiRaimondo C. 1996. A case of recurrent Caffey's disease treated with naproxen. *Clinical Orthopaedics and Related Research* 323:304-309.

Ueda K, Saito A, Nakano H, Aoshima M, Yokota M, Muraoka R, and Iwaya T. 1980. Cortical hyperostosis following long term administration of prostaglandin E1 in infants with cyanotic congenital heart disease. *Journal of Pediatrics* 97:843-846.

Venture A, Casini P, and Ferrante L. 1983. Different clinical picture in early and late onset cortical hyperostosis. *Pediatria Medica e Chirurgica* 5: 359-363

Wilson A. 1969. Infantile Cortical Hyperostosis. Review of the literature and report of a case without mandibular involvement. *Clinical Orthopaedics and Related Research* 62:209-217.

Tuberculosis of the Hip in Victorian Britain

Benjamin Clarke, and Piers D Mitchell

Faculty of Medicine, Imperial College London, 7E Charing Cross Hopsital, Fulham Palace Road, London W6 8RP.
p.mitchell@clara.co.uk

Abstract

Tuberculosis (TB) of the hip is less common than the infection of the lungs, but leads to lasting disability in those individuals who survive the illness. The aim of this research is firstly to describe the pathological changes noted in skeletal examples of TB of the hip dating from the 1800s that are preserved in the pathology museum of Imperial College London. These range from loss of subchondral bone on the articular surfaces, to destruction of the entire femoral head and neck as well as the acetabular floor. Secondly, we aim to investigate the medical treatment of patients with TB hip in Victorian records from the Alexandra Hospital for Children with Hip Disease and scientific articles in medical journals. The medical journals in the late 1880s recommended splinting of the involved hips to allow them to become stiff or fuse in a position compatible with their later use during walking. Other treatments included needle aspiration of fluid from the infected hip joint, cautery around the hip joint, and surgical excision of involved soft tissues around the joint. Case records from the Alexandra Hospital describe how all of these approaches were employed. While the Victorians had no effective method to cure tuberculosis, it seems that their approach to splinting the infected hip was a reasonable one that may well have improved the mobility of those who survived the disease.

Keywords: Tuberculosis, hip, treatment, Victorian, Britain

Introduction

Western healthcare is currently looking afresh at tuberculosis, and overcoming the relative complacency surrounding its treatment following the introduction of streptomycin in 1943 (WHO 2004). However, before the advent of anti-tubercular drugs, tuberculosis was a daunting prospect for healthcare professionals. Whilst a great deal of literature has focused on past efforts to provide healthcare for pulmonary tuberculosis (Myers 1977, Bryer 1988, Smith 1998), so far very little has looked at the plight of the skeletal TB sufferer. The extra-pulmonary manifestations of tuberculosis presented entirely different challenges to the doctors of the time. This was almost exclusively due to haematogenous spread, with bones containing significant areas of active marrow such as the spine, pelvis and long bones being mainly affected. The exudative and granuloumatous reactions of the host's immune system to the *Mycobacterium tuberculosis* tended to cause destruction of the articular surfaces in joints, with resorptive grooving, which could lead to a secondary arthritis (Ortner 2003: 227-230).

The principal aim of this paper is to present pathological evidence for TB infection of the hip as a problem encountered in Victorian times. Secondly, we will investigate the treatment of TB hip around this time, and its relation to the observable pathology.

Sources of evidence

To study the methods used to treat TB, one must first understand the manifestations of the disease. The Imperial College pathology museum houses two examples of TB hip that are both undated, but their description cards were of a type that was discontinued in 1900. In consequence we can conclude that they were definitely indexed before 1900. Since the cards may date as early as 1840, the specimens are likely to have come from the Victorian period. The lesions evident in these examples help to explain the nature and extent of the problems caused by the infection.

While this skeletal evidence demonstrates the damage such an infection would cause, relating this to the treatment requires a comparison with historical sources. There are a number of Victorian sources on the subject, including books, journals and surgical and nursing manuals which may be used to determine how and when treatment evolved. Of these, the surgical texts give us the greatest amount of detail about ideas and treatment at the time. Historical journals and history books provide the historical context, including information about the formation of hospitals and sanatoria. However, in these the main focus is on pulmonary tuberculosis, so they are of limited value in providing information about treatment of the hip.

Having examined the literary evidence, it is also important to verify that such ideas were actually being put into practice, for which more direct historical evidence may be used. The Alexandra Hospital records, together with case histories form the same hospital, give important clues as to what was being practised. The records are incomplete in places, so can only be relied on for a general picture of treatment practices in the hospital.

Materials and methods

Specimens held in the pathology museum (Catalogue numbers W0712 and W0715) were studied for lesions. In each case the hemipelvis and proximal femur of the involved hip was preserved, but the rest of the skeleton was not. Medical texts from the 1800s were consulted at the Wellcome Library and the British Library, which between them hold the most extensive collection of medical history literature in the UK. Texts from a range of professions (including pathologists, surgeons and nurses) were selected to try to give a varied perspective, and minimise the bias that might be encountered by purely intra-professional publications. For example, the fierce competition between surgeons at the time could have possibly led to exaggeration of the merit or practice of preferred operations. For hospital and sanatorium records, the Access to Archives database was accessed online, giving access to the listings of the National Archives.

Results: pathological specimens

The first pathological example (museum catalogue number W7012) was a specimen of right hemipelvis and proximal femur (Fig 1). Museum records revealed that it was from a 21-year-old woman, who presented with knee pain, weight loss, weakness and a fever and died after 10 weeks in hospital. On post-mortem examination, she was found to have pathology consistent with TB infection in her right hip: her pelvic viscera were knotted, with collections of pus around each broad ligament. The periosteum was detached from the internal surface of the ilium and the upper third of the femur, and the soft tissues of the hip joint were completely disorganised.

Upon inspection, of the preserved skeletal specimen, there were bony changes that would support the diagnosis of tuberculosis. The most obvious abnormality was visible in the medial aspect, where there was near complete destruction of the acetabular floor (Fig 2), with a perforation through the ischium into the pelvis, measuring 4x5 cm. Also, there was erosion of the surface of the femoral head, where the loss of cortical bone rendered the surface porous. On the posterior view, this extended right up to the femoral neck.

This intra-articular distribution combined with some sparing of the subchondral bone, and absence of new bone formation, gives us a classic appearance of TB infection (Roberts and Manchester 1995).

The second specimen (museum catalogue number W7015) was also a right hemipelvis with upper femur, with pelvic morphology suggestive of female sex (Fig 3). In this specimen, there was greater destruction, and indeed on the lateral view, it was seen that the head of the femur -which should lie medial to the greater trochanter- was completely destroyed (Fig 4). This would have caused the joint to lose its point of fulcrum. In consequence, the hip abductor muscles would have

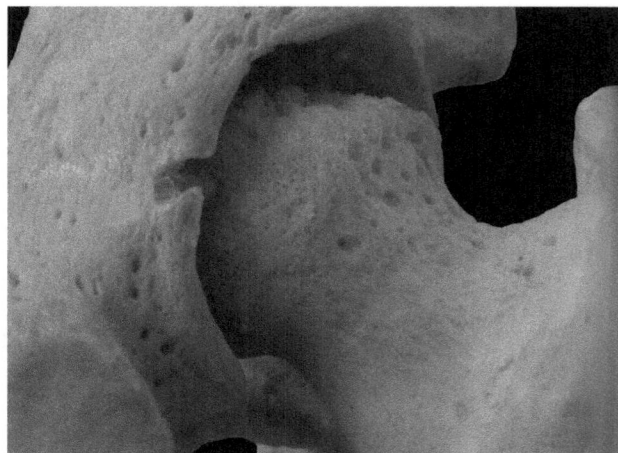

Figure 1. Specimen 1 (Catalogue number W0712), posterior view of lytic lesion extending up to femoral neck

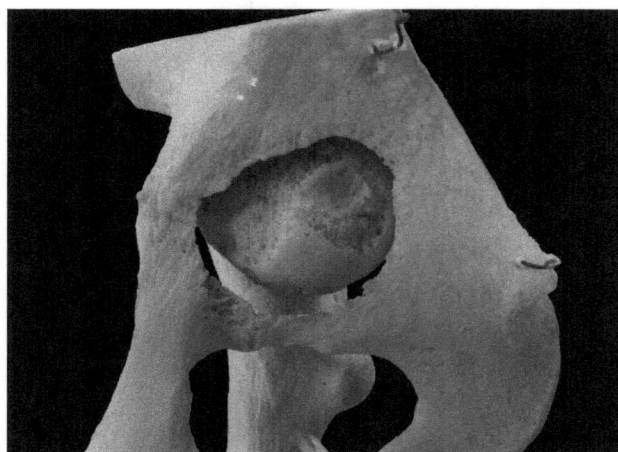

Figure 2. Specimen 1 (Catalogue number W0712), medial view. Extensive destruction of acetabular floor. Deep lytic lesion on femoral head, but some sparing of articular surfaces.

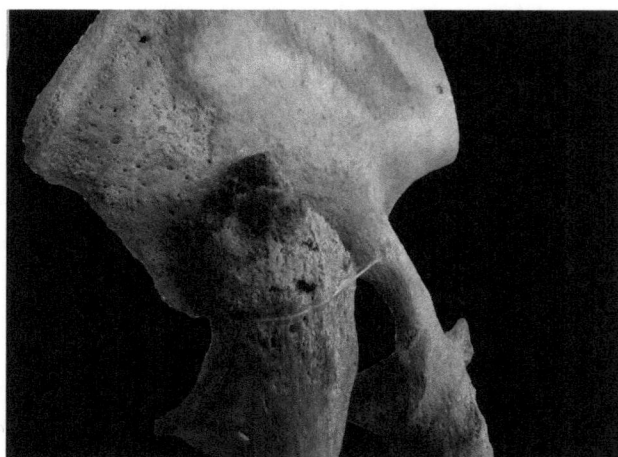

Figure 3. Specimen 2 (Catalogue number W0715), lateral view. Femoral head destroyed, with 2.5cm proximal displacement of femur relative to ilium.

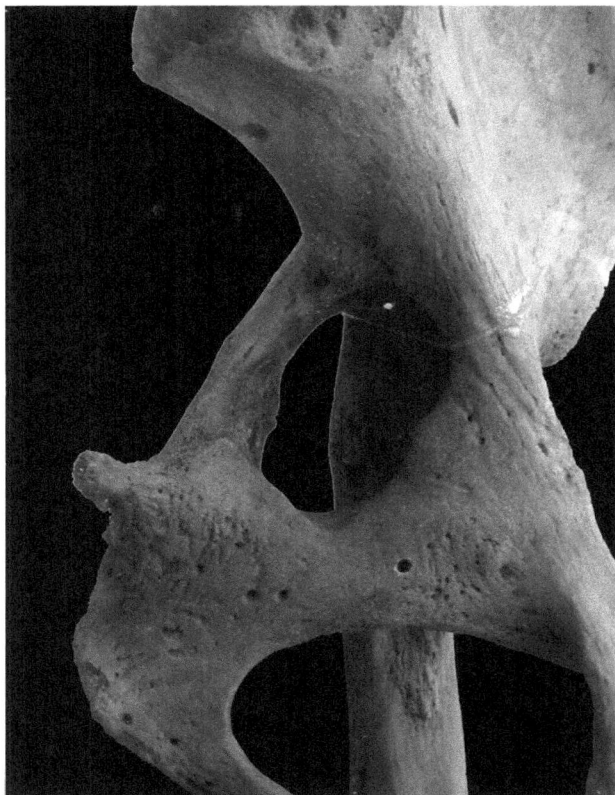

Figure 4. Specimen 2 (Catalogue number W0715), medial view. Extensive destruction of acetabular floor. Smoothed edges indicate bony remodelling.

the effect of displacing the femur proximally. On the medial aspect, it was noted that that the acetabulum was again completely eroded, but this time there were smoothed edges, which would indicate bony remodeling. Thus, it is likely that this person would have lived with the infection for a number of years. The narrow diameter of the femoral shaft is also consistent with disuse atrophy from long term hip disease.

Treatment: literary sources

Black, C (1859) - The Pathology of Tuberculous Bone
By 1859, Cornelius Black had published a thorough examination of the pathology of skeletal TB using microscopic observation. Taken in the context of being written twenty-nine years before Koch's discovery of the TB bacillus, it demonstrates a detailed knowledge of the disease without knowing the aetiology. Black wrote in depth of the micro-architecture of bone, and the structural and exudative changes that occur in TB infection. In the first stage of the disease he recognised 'active congestion' of the bone lacunae, so recommended 'local depletion' by absolute rest of the affected area, achieved by bed rest or splinting and crutches where necessary (Black 1859: 16). In the second stage, Black addressed the need for local growth of blood vessels to deal with the exudation. For this he recommended accelerating the circulation through exercise to increase the free supply of oxygen, though

maintained that the affected joint must be kept still through splinting.

Thomas, HO (1875) - Diseases of the Hip, Knee and Ankle Joints and Their Treatment by a New and Efficient Method. T. Dobb & Co, Liverpool
Hugh Thomas wrote one of the seminal orthopaedic texts of the Victorian era, and his techniques influenced much of the literature of the following fifty years. He was a great advocate of prompt immobilisation of tuberculous hips through splinting, commenting that "friction is a greater evil than pressure" (Thomas 1875: 2-25). In light of this, he scrutinised many of the splint variations available in Europe and the US at the time (Fig 5).

He dismissed the favourites from both France and the US for using the 'perineal extension' method (which relied on a stabilising frame in contact with the patient's perineum), which he criticised for providing inadequate mechanical support, and even commented that Sayre's splint necessitated excision of the joint more than would be expected with other splints. Of the 'ischiatic support' splints, he conceded that they did well in taking the weight off the affected hip, but failed to control joint movement, so were relatively useless by his judgement.

The splint he recommended, he termed the 'old fashioned long splint' which subsequently came to be referred to as a 'Thomas splint' (Fig 6). It was simpler than the other variations, and ran from the level of the axilla right the way down to the ankle, so providing a generous amount of support. Constructed from a single piece of iron, it was bent to match the contours of the back and leg, and to it were riveted curved crosspieces to provide support to the trunk and leg, and the whole device was attached with strapping and bandages.

Thomas also described a protocol for treatment. He broke the course of treatment into four stages, beginning with immediate immobilisation by use of the aforementioned splint, and in stage one being confined to bed until night pains had ceased. Stage two allowed the patient to be mobile by use of crutches with a metal patten on the good leg, to raise the splinted leg out of harm's way. Stage three commenced when the affected limb was "well atrophied around the greater trochanter" (Thomas 1875: 27) and allowed the removal of the frame at night time in bed. Stage four, which usually started after three to four months, allowed complete removal of the frame, and for the patient to use crutches and patten only, until satisfactory healing was demonstrated.

Cheyne, W (1888) - Harveian Society, The Lancet vol. 131, 3376: 925; and 1895- Tuberculous Disease of Bones and Joints: Its Pathology, Symptoms, and Treatment.
Watson Cheyne's text (1895) dealt in depth with tuberculous hips. He described the pathology of tubercles on a microscopic level, mentioning central parts containing epithelial and giant cells, and outer parts comprising of fibrous walls. Treatment, he divided into general-, local- and directly-acting. General treatment

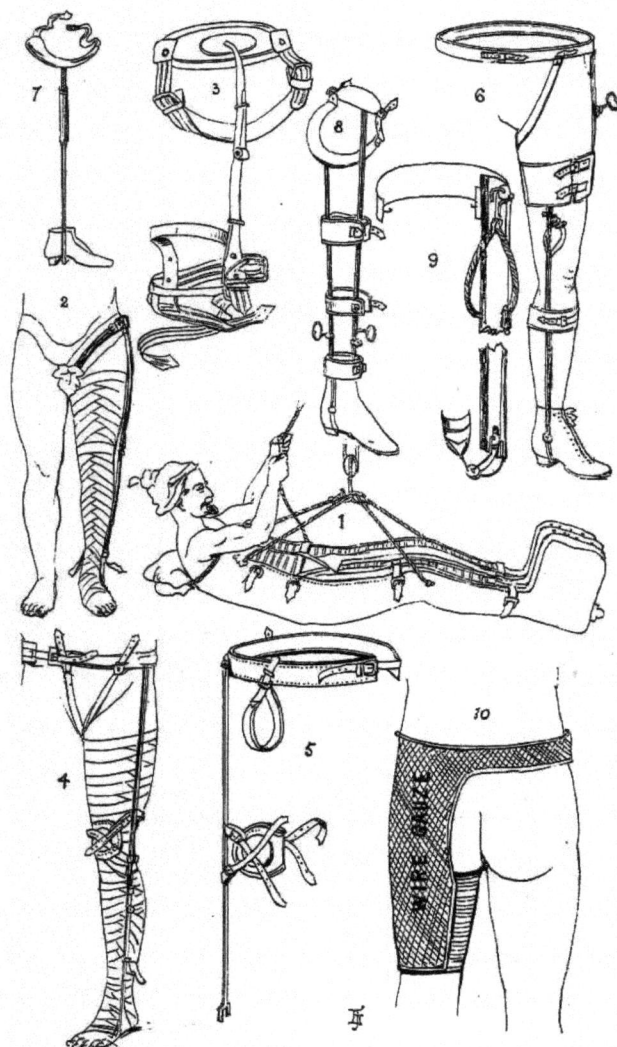

Figure 5. Apparatus as reviewed by Thomas, 1875.

Figure 6. Thomas' Hip Splint (Thomas, 1875)

included measures such as: good air and ventilation, a recumbent position combined with massage and exercise, and a diet as digestible and nutritious as possible. However, he was confident that his local treatments were more efficacious than the general measures, which should be reserved for the early stages of disease, or after operations; this is a continuing concept in later texts. For immobilisation and extension, he recommended a Thomas hip splint, or for more severe cases a 'Bennet's wire cuirass' or 'Phelps box' (both methods for immobilisation through a frame). He stressed that the role of extension should be to tire out the flexor and abductor muscles of the hip, rather than achieve joint surface separation, which he viewed as more damaging than beneficial. He prescribed extension until the pull of the muscles was reduced, and so the chances of deformity minimised. Local treatment was also comprised of counter-irritation in the form of blisters and cautery. Cheyne recommended cautery to the front of, and behind the trochanter, with the resulting sores being kept open for six weeks. Directly-acting

treatment encompassed administration of tuberculin or tissue loading (both of which Cheyne was very cautious of), but was mainly the realm of surgery.

According to Cheyne, the choice of operation was threefold. Arthrectomy was the surgical removal of solely the diseased tissue, whilst preserving joint tissues and ligaments as much as possible to give best functional result. More radical was total joint excision, where all joint tissues were removed, ensuring all infection was removed and optimising chances of cure. More radical still was the amputation of the affected limb; although completely removing function, its advantages lay in safety, as shock was less likely than in the other types of operation, as was recurrence of disease. Cheyne was of the opinion that in skilled hands, a thorough arthrectomy gave the most satisfactory result, but should be done early and before the appearance of abscesses, which could complicate the case. Cheyne (1888) promoted the drainage and antisepsis of abscesses and sinuses.

Evidence from the Alexandra Hospital for children with hip disease

The Alexandra Hospital opened in 1867, and as its name suggests, catered specifically for children with orthopaedic hip problems, which at the time was primarily TB infection. Over the period of 1888 to 1897, the case note cards and admission statistics (Alexandra Records AMR-2, -4 and -16) reveal record of 568 admissions; an average of 63 cases per year. Considering the lengthy duration of treatment, this is a high turnover in comparison to the hospital's capacity of around 68 inpatients, and an outpatient list of two to three times this size. Given that the times of these records roughly correspond with Hugh Thomas' 1895 text, one would expect the treatment to be similar to the way he described it. The case history (described below) pre-dates the text by 10 years, but does continue over a period of 5 years, and thus, is presumably fairly close to the period in which the text was being conceived.

In our example which comes from the record card of a Mr Bowlby, of a patient admitted 15th January, 1900 (Alexandra Hospital patient record card SBHA/MR/15/18):

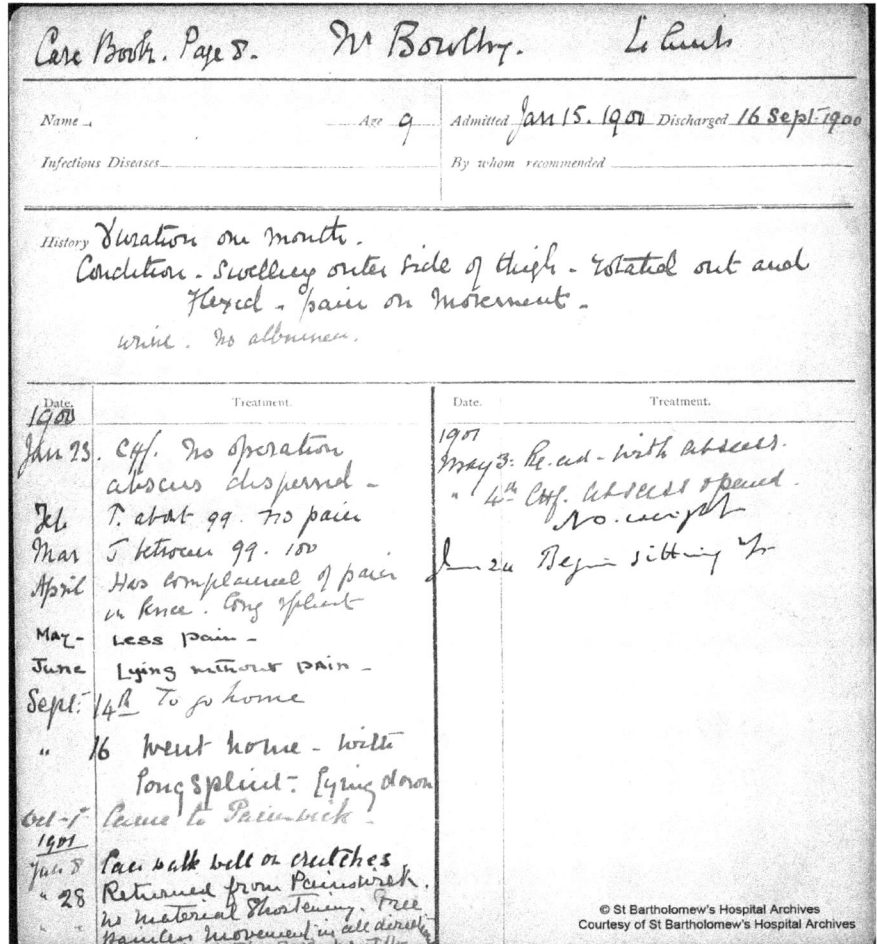

Figure 7. Alexandra Hospital patient record card (SBHA/MR/15/18), 1900, showing reference to Painswick Convalescent home. © St Bartholomew's Hospital Archives. Courtesy of St Bartholomew's Hospital Archives.

Following two years of outpatient care and some unsuccessful splinting, on May 1st 1867, the child's leg was manipulated under chloroform to "an obtuse angle." This done, the child was placed in a "back splint" with an extension weight of 4 lbs placed on the limb. Three days following removal, a "long splint" was applied [presumably a Thomas's hip splint] and weight-extension continued. From July to November of that year, the child was alternated between a back splint and a long splint, changing when the fit was unsatisfactory. On Christmas Eve, cautery was applied to the joint, with less pain reported afterwards. May 7th 1868 brought lancing of the joint capsule with a grooved needle, and removal of "thick synovial fluid." The joint was lanced once more, and continued to be splinted until October 1890, when the child was removed by his parents. The medical officer noted "discharging sinuses on either side of the knee" (which was by this time infected also) when the child left, so the case was not considered successful.

The 1888-97 records show the hospital's large dependence on convalescent homes. The discharge of 97 of the 568 admitted patients was to convalescent homes, and indeed many case histories do record stays in the

hospital's convalescent home in Painswick, Gloucestershire. A patient from 1900 was discharged home wearing a long splint, and still lying down after eight months in the hospital. A month later she came to Painswick where she stayed for four months, then returned to the Alexandra Hospital for further treatment (Fig 7).

Discussion

Evidence for TB of the hip in Victorian times

Given the distribution of the lytic changes in the first pathology specimen (W0712), one would assume that the disease was intra-articular during life. This is characteristic of tuberculous infection, and in view of the absence of other features that would detract from the museum's diagnosis of tuberculosis, it is sensible to support this view. The extent of destruction of the acetabular floor suggests severe infection, and the perforation would imply a route of infection into the pelvis, explaining the soft tissue findings. In the second pathology specimen (W7015), the changes are also consistent with tuberculous infection. The gross destruction of the femoral head would have caused apparent shortening of the limb during life. This would have been caused either by bearing weight on the limb, or simply through unopposed contraction of the hip muscles. Without the fulcrum effect of the femoral head to initiate flexion or abduction, these muscles would have pulled the femur proximally. This shortening would have changed the sufferer's gait, and combined the loss of stability in the joint, would have been very debilitating.

Treatment Methods

Modern treatment of TB hip is based upon pharmacology (Watts and Lifeso 1996). Such is the efficacy of anti-tuberculous agents that surgery is reserved for decompression of the spinal cord, or washing out infected joints. Accordingly, before the advent of such potent drugs, what did the Victorian doctors and nurses have to offer our two hip cases?

In Black's (1859) pre-Koch perspective gives us valuable insight into how ideas and practices of treatment were developing before knowledge of the bacteria. Black's explanation for the pathology he observed revolved around the exudations, so his suggestions for treatment consequently addressed this as the cause of symptoms. His disease-management ideas concentrated on the inflammatory response as though it was the causative agent. His inferences show logic given his observations. One can suppose the rest and splinting he advised would have offered the best chance of natural recovery, whilst the exercise would have acted to boost the general health of the patient. We can infer from Black that in 1859, medicine was gaining confidence in its knowledge of the infection, and although not yet offering widely agreed ideas on its cause, had structured ideas regarding treatment.

However, even with evolving ideas about the cause of disease, we see the persistence of older practice in the advocation of cautery by Cheyne (1895). This practice evidently survived several years after the discovery of the cause of TB, but it seems that the ideas around it changed. Rather than being based upon ideas of exudate, his use of the term 'counter-irritation', and the context in which it is described suggest the idea of activating the immune system, and drawing resources to the area.

Thomas shows that by 1875, immobilisation was the mainstay of treatment, and his four stages of immobilisation form an entire treatment regime. His rationale behind such treatment seems to be simply gaining functional results for the patients, as opposed to fighting an unknown cause. This may be due to the text being of a surgical rather than pathological nature, but in any case serves to maintain the relevance of the text even after Koch's discovery seven years later.

It is this change in the rationale for treatment that marks the most significant step for treatment of TB hip in Victorian times. With treatment focused on improving joint function rather than pain or symptoms, the patient finally had a hope for a life after treatment, and indeed

this theme continues throughout the later texts, representing a major change in attitude towards the meaning of benefit for the patient.

Cheyne (1895) stresses how the function of limb extension should be to tire out the flexor and abductor muscles of the hip so as to prevent deformity, as observed in our second pathological specimen. This would allow the patient better limb function and quality of life should they recover from their illness. He also talks of the operation of choice being a partial arthrectomy, as opposed to a total joint excision, so preserving the joint tissues, to a similar functional effect. Cheyne also mentioned the benefit of open-air living conditions for patients. These ideas for TB treatment seemed to have been taken on quickly in Britain by the orthopaedic institutions due to the pre-existing beliefs of the benefit of sunlight and fresh air for other bone and joint afflictions. The Royal National Orthopaedic Hospital started its Brockley Hill convalescent home in 1882, and from 1892 onwards was reserving the outdoor verandas of its Great Portland street hospital for children with tuberculous joints (Hunt 1907).

Did clinical practice follow the literature?

We can see from the Alexandra Hospital records that there is definite evidence that the medical texts of the time did reflect the hospital practice. For example, there is record of Thomas hip splints being used for immobilisation and extension weight applied. However, not all of the treatments or concepts correspond: the constant changing of the splint would seem to negate the concept of prompt immobilisation. This could well be the result of a struggling child, with nursing staff battling to achieve proper immobilisation (the records do not reveal this). Cautery was not advocated by Thomas, but would correspond with Cheyne's practice in the 1880s and 90s. The major difference that one would question is the treatment of children as outpatients, the child in the example record card having been seen as an outpatient for two years before he was admitted. Although none of the surgical texts specifically mention that patients should be treated only as inpatients, the nature of the immobilisation and the equipment and nursing required leads to the conclusion that treatment solely took place in hospitals. This assumption could be completely ill-founded: records of home nursing will not exist, and it is more than likely that many people could not afford to pay the hospital fees at the time. Therefore, it is quite likely that hospitals only served to primarily diagnose and initiate treatment, with patients enduring the convalescent stage at home or elsewhere.

Conclusion

We have seen the extent of damage caused by TB in the skeletal evidence, and so can begin to imagine the kind of disability it caused. The literary and historical sources allow us to see the evolution of treatment in the Victorian era, and vital to the understanding of this are the recurring themes of splinting to reduce friction and weaken the muscles, and surgery to remove disease but preserve as much of the joint as possible. These ideas were emerging to try to prevent what we noted in the second pathology specimen: joint deterioration, shortening and disability.

The evidence demonstrates a remarkable change during the 1800s. The fact that splinting and surgery evolved from vague measures addressing symptoms into the more precise art of maximising functionality over the course of the Victorian era shows how fast this area was developing. The fact that the hospital records confirm the literary evidence reinforces the importance of this progression for the treatment of skeletal TB. Perhaps the artificial pneumothorax was a comparable treatment for pulmonary consumptives, but this did not appear in Britain until 1910, by which time orthopaedic surgeons such as Cheyne had already been perfecting the best function-preserving arthrectomies for over 15 years. The fact that TB hip cases were being sent by the Alexandra Hospital to convalescent homes for recovery from its inauguration in 1867 almost pre-empted the sanatoria system of the next century, with the role of convalescent home being shifted to sanatoria in later years.

So it seems that those who drove this progression were ahead of their time in healthcare's assault on TB, and although their struggle was of smaller scale and fame than the pulmonary equivalent, it was of no less importance, and perhaps deserves more recognition than it has achieved so far.

Literature cited

Access to Archives UK National Archives online resource: www.a2a.org.uk. Accessed April 2006.

Alexandra Hospital for Children with Hip Disease 1867-1958, St Bartholomew's Hospital Archives and Museum:

AMR2: Medical Reports with Statistics of admissions, discharges and deaths 1884-99, prepared for meetings of the committee of management and signed by the senior medical officer.

AMR4: Case notes for inpatients 1867-70 and outpatients 1860-70, giving name, age and case history. Volumes I (1866-8) and II (1868-70)

MMR15: Record cards of patients (mainly Mr. Antony Bowlby's cases) 1884-1905, giving name, age, and date of admission, history of illness and infectious diseases and record of treatment.

AMR16; Case notes of patients 1903-6, apparently selected for long-term follow-up, giving patient's name, age, condition, treatment, and remarks on condition 1912-13

Black C. 1859. *The Pathology of Tuberculous Bone*, Sutherland and Knox, Edinburgh.

Bryer L. 1988. *Below the Magic Mountain: A Social History of Tuberculosis in Twentieth Century Britain.* Clarendon Press, London.

Cheyne WW. 1888. Harveian Society. *The Lancet,* vol. 131 (3376): 925.

Cheyne WW. 1895. *Tuberculous Disease of Bones and Joints: Its Pathology, Symptoms, and Treatment*, Young J. Pentland, London

Hunt AG. 1907. Baschurch and after II- fourteen years on. *The Cripple's Journal* 1(2):193

Myers J. A. 1977. *Captain of All These Men of Death: Tuberculosis Historical Highlights.* W H. Green, London.

Ortner DJ. 2003. *Identification of Pathological Disorders in Human Skeletal Remains*, Academic Press, New York.

Pennington TH. 1995. Listerism, its Decline and its Persistence: the Introduction of Aseptic Surgical Techniques in Three British Teaching Hospitals, 1890-99. *Medical History* 39: 35-60

Roberts CA and Manchester K. 1995. *The Archaeology of Disease*. A Sutton, Stroud.

Smith FB. 1998. *The Retreat of Tuberculosis 1850-1950*, Croom Helm, London.

Thomas HO. 1875. *Diseases of the Hip, Knee and Ankle Joints and Their Treatment by a New and Efficient Method,* T. Dobb & Co, Liverpool.

Watts HG. and Lifeso RM. 1996. Current concepts review - tuberculosis of bones and joints. *Journal of Bone and Joint Surgery America*, 78(2): 288

W.H.O. 2004. *Anti-Tuberculosis drug resistance in the world. The WHO/IUATLD Global Project on anti-tuberculosis drug resistance surveillance.* Report number 3 Geneva.

The Re-Analysis of Iron Age Human Skeletal Material from Winnall Down

Justine Tracey

Archaeology Department, University of Reading, Whiteknights, PO Box 217, Reading, Berkshire, RG6 6AH
j.t.tracey@reading.ac.uk

Abstract

The period from the end of the Bronze Age through to the Late Iron Age in Britain witnessed a 'break' in evidence for formal burial practices. Individual burials, either inhumations or cremations, under a round barrow with grave goods, were common rites in the Early Bronze Age (c. 2300-1400) BC. By the Middle Bronze Age (c.1400-1000 BC), communal cremation cemeteries were flourishing. However, during the Late Bronze Age (c.1000-700 BC) this rite disappeared from the archaeological record. By the Later Iron Age (c.90 BC) there is once again a rise of cremation cemeteries, such as Westhampnett, West Sussex. For some, between these periods there appears to be very little evidence for formal burial rites and a radical change of attitude suggesting a different treatment of the corpse.

This research re-examine the human remains from a prehistoric settlement, Winnall Down, Winchester, in Hampshire that was originally excavated thirty years ago. These remains are being reviewed in the light of more recent research and studies from the multi-disciplinary viewpoints of forensic taphonomy and anthropology. The aim is to discriminate between the various taphonomic processes in order to reconstruct and expand on mortuary and burial practices for the Early and Middle Iron Ages (c.700 BC). Therefore, differentiate cultural behaviour from natural processes using Winnall Down's human remains as a case study to see if further information can be retrieved from the skeletal record. The results correlate with the 'break' in burial traditions and provide evidence for a cultural choice of change in burial location and context type. The results also show a change in funerary behaviour from fragmentation of the corpse in the Early Iron Age to keeping the individual complete in the Middle Iron Age.

Keywords: Forensic taphonomy, prehistory, anthropology, cultural behaviour, natural processes.

Introduction

Early literary accounts first raised the issue of the apparent lack of archaeological evidence for formal mortuary and burial rite/s in the Early and Middle Iron Ages. From the late 1800s, the comparatively few complete inhumations found in pits gradually became accepted as the normal mortuary and burial rite, in contrast to the numerous fragmented skeletal assemblages (Pitt-Rivers 1887, 1888). Later, Cunnington (1932: 31) wrote that: '...in comparison to the evidence available concerning the lives of the British Celts in the Iron Age, there was very little evidence of their death'. This led Hodson (1964) to refer to this lack of evidence as a 'negative' fossil trait. Whilst Harding (1974) suggested that these remains represented the minority, perhaps criminal or social outcasts who were denied the customary funeral ceremony.

Ethnographic and anthropological studies hav been utilised to bring meaning to the British burial evidence. Analogies were made with societies that practiced secondary funerary rituals, a two-stage process of the dead, e.g. a tree burial. The deceased was laid in a canoe suspended high in the tree and exposed to the elements. After a period of time the second stage took place; cultural skeletal selectivity, where only the skull was removed for burial (Metcalf and Huntington 1991).

Following this approach, Cunliffe (1984) considered the wide-ranging skeletal assemblages found in numerous storage pits at Danebury to be akin to this ideology or even an expression ancestral lineage continuity and agricultural production (Bradley 1981). British burial evidence was likened to the burial system practiced by the West African 'Asante'. This is where the 'unclean' received distinctive mortuary rituals and deposition in a village midden (Ucko 1969:270; McLeod 1981). Cunliffe (1984) also referred to ancient texts (e.g. Polybius Histories III, 67, and Diodorus 29) as a means to identify common themes and disposal patterns of human remains, and developed skeletal categories (e.g. D comprising of skulls or parts of skulls and E comprising of pelvic girdles). He suggested that this type of discrimination followed the pattern of Iron Age mortuary traditions outlined by Celtic ideology (Cunliffe 1984). However, these classical authors were not British pre-Roman Iron Age people, and may well have been writing with biases.

The presence of the 'other', less complete skeletons and wide-ranging skeletal assemblages have given rise to a variety of hypotheses over the years. Liddell (1935:25) suggested a general disregard in the treatment of the dead as bodies were deposited in 'an indiscriminate manner' and he likened this phenomenon to being part of the sites' general rubbish. Similarly, Richardson (1951:131) suggested that the remains were, 'not a burial in the proper sense' and that 'bodies were thrown into a convenient rubbish pit'. However, others have considered these types of human remains reflective of head cults and trophy collection (Walker 1984), products of excarnation by exposure and secondary burial rites (Clarke 1962; Ellison and Drewett 1971; Harding 1974; Whimster 1981; Wilson 1981; Walker 1984; Carr and Knüsel 1997), and pre-Roman Iron Age cannibalism (Dunning 1976). Hill (1995) surmised that these and other similar accounts had embedded the mortuary rite of excarnation by exposure for the majority of the population.

These earlier approaches did not include an in-depth analysis of preservation issues and did not consider the complexity of both intrinsic and extrinsic taphonomic factors. Carr and Knüsel (1997:167) reviewed this 'archaeologically invisible' mortuary rite and found 'bodies and body parts', either isolated assemblages or disarticulated joints, in a variety of locations: pits, ditches, hillfort ramparts and enclosure boundaries. They noted that no formal assessment of any archaeological indicators or signatures to substantiate the practice of excarnation had taken place. As a result, their method included ethnographic examples of secondary burial rites, mortuary theory and taphonomic bone studies that could identify archaeological indicators for excarnation by exposure.

Materials

The Early and Middle Iron Age human remains from Winnall Down, a prehistoric settlement at Winchester, Hampshire, were re-examined as part of the current research. This prehistoric settlement spanned the time before and after the so-called 'archaeologically invisible' periods, and was excavated by Peter Fasham in 1976-7. In the original report, the human remains were divided into two main categories; complete or near complete inhumations comprising 31 individuals (6 adults and 25 non-adults) and 78 'odd' skeletal assemblages (separate instances or accounts of scattered bone). The complete, or near complete inhumations received most discussion within the report, with the identification of sex, age and any pathology (Fasham 1985). The 'odd' skeletal assemblages were just noted with their location.

Methods

The chronology of the site, contexts and their contents was based on the original reports that used ceramic ware and radiocarbon dating of charcoal, human and animal bone. Only contexts and their contents, where such dating evidence was provided, were included in the study sample (n=39).

Adult age estimations were based on methods outlined by Buikstra and Ubelaker (1994); cranial suture closure (Meindl and Lovejoy 1985); pubic symphysis degeneration (Brooks and Suchey 1990); auricular surface morphology (Lovejoy et al. 1985); sternal rib ends (İşcan and Loth 1986) and dental attrition (Ubelaker 1989; Hillson 1996; Miles 2001). Where possible, sex was evaluated using cranial and greater sciatic notch characteristics (Buikstra and Ubelaker 1994) and the pubic portion of the os coxae (Phenice 1969).

The recording of non-adult assemblages was guided by several works (Fazekas and Kosa 1978; Buikstra and Ubelaker 1994; Scheuer and Black 2000; Lewis 2007). Skeletal age was established from long bone measurements and fusion of bone epiphyses. Dental age as established using methods from several studies (Moorrees et al. 1963; Ubelaker 1989; Smith 1991).

All assemblages were scrutinised with a hand-held 10x magnifying lens and in some instances, underwent further microscopic analysis to determine their nature. To identify any form of skeletal patterning, each of Fasham's categories of 'odd' skeletal assemblages were re-analysed to include the identification of skeletal elements, number of skeletal elements present; age of the individual/s and the zonation value (Knüsel and Outram 2004). Context type, location, and type of any other assemblage/s found within the same context or layer were also recorded in order to identify any pattern of commingling (Brickley and McKinley 2004).

Taphonomy studies were used to identify post-mortem modifications, including scavenging (Haglund 1997; Haglund et al. 1988), weathering (Behrensmeyer 1978; Lyman and Fox 1997), density and survival rates (Galloway et al. 1997), and peri- and post-mortem surface modifications (Loe and Cox 2005; Blumenschine and Selvaggio 1988; Shipman and Rose 1983; Shipman 1981).

During the re-examination of Winnall Down it was noted that some complete inhumations were now missing skeletal elements. For example, when the bones of one particular skeleton were compared to original excavation photograph, the skull, ribs and all the right arm bones were missing. As a result, the state of preservation derived from indices such as the Anatomical Preservation Index (API; Bello 2001), Bone Representation Index (BRI; Dodson and Wexlar 1979) or Qualitative Bone Index (QBI: Bello 2001) were deemed impractical. However, this research developed a new category system to record Early and Middle Iron Age human remains based on repetitive skeletal patterning.

Results

The original evaluation of Winnall Down's complete or near complete individuals for Late Bronze Age (LBA), Early and Middle Iron Ages (EIA and MIA) and the Later Iron Age/Early Roman (LIA/ER) period are presented in Table 1 (Fasham 1985: 120).

Table 1. Winnall Down's complete or near complete human remains (original results).

Age and sex	LBA	EIA	MIA	LIA/ER	Total
Neonate	0	0	1	0	1
<1 year	0	1	9	0	10
1-12 years	0	0	2	0	2
<15 years	0	0	1	0	1
Female	0	0	2 + ?2*	0	2 +?2
Male	0	0	1	0	1
Total	**0**	**1**	**18**	**0**	**19**

*refers to 2 definite female and 2 probable females

Table 2 provides the revised count of human remains. The sex evaluation of the adults remained the same as the original report. The decrease in infant inhumations from the original report is due to the omission of four 'complete infant inhumations' three of which, on re-examination, proved to be infant animal bones, The fourth could not be located.

There are no human remains dating to LBA and LIA/ER periods on this settlement (Tables 1 and 2). These data correlate with burial evidence for these periods; i.e. Bronze Age barrow cemeteries and Later Iron cremation cemeteries.

Table 2. Winnall Down's complete or near complete human remains (revised results).

Age	LBA	EIA	MIA	LIA/ER	Total
Infant	0	1	2	1	4
Birth-sized (neonatal)	0	1	6	0	7
Over birth-sized (< 3 months)	0	0	2	0	2
Adolescent	0	0	1	0	1
Adult	0	21	14	0	35
Total	**0**	**23**	**25**	**1**	**49**

Table 3. 'Odd bones' at Winnall Down (original results).

Age (years)	LBA	EIA	MIA	LIA/LR	Total
<1	0	2	7	0	9
1-14.6	0	0	1	0	1
14.6 -17	0	0	1	0	1
17-25	0	0	0	0	0
26-35	0	0	5	0	5
46+	0	0	0	0	0
Total	**0**	**2**	**14**	**0**	**16**

Therefore, EIA and MIA burials within the domestic setting can be seen as a clear break from burial tradition of the periods before and after, which segregated the living from the dead. The number of complete infant and adult inhumations has dramatically increased in the MIA.

Table 3 provides the data for Fasham's (1985) 'odd bones' category and Table 4 provides the revised estimates. 'Odd bones' are instances or counts of human bone that are wide ranging in bone assemblage type and typical of EIA and MIA sites. At Winnall Down, this catergory ranged from just a single complete skeletal element, to an assemblage that contains numerous skeletal elements, but which did not contain sufficient material to be considered a complete inhumation.

Table 4. 'Odd bones' from Winnall Down (revised results).

Age (years)	LBA	EIA	MIA	LIA/ER	Total
<1 year	0	0	10	0	10
1-14.6	0	0	0	0	0
14.6-17	0	0	0	0	0
17-25	0	0	0	0	0
26-35	0	18	15	0	33
46+	0	0	0	0	0
Total	**0**	**18**	**25**	**0**	**43**

On re-assessment of these 'odd bones' repetitive skeletal patterning emerged, and the following new categories were developed:

- *A single complete inhumation*: a complete skeletal assemblage of one individual with no other human skeletal material present.
- *A single skeletal element*: any type of skeletal element found in the entire depositional context.
- *Small bone assemblages*: comprising less than six human skeletal elements of any sort.
- *Medium bone assemblages*: comprising more than six human skeletal elements of any type, but insufficient skeletal material to indicate a single inhumation.
- *Commingled assemblages*: comprising more than one of the skeletal assemblages listed above in any one context. For example, a pit may consist of one complete inhumation and a medium bone assemblage.
- *Mixed assemblages*: comprising both animal and human bone assemblages.

An overview of the re-categorised types of deposition of human remains found on this settlement is presented in Figure 1. There was no patterning based on age or sex, where they could be determined. Infant inhumations were found singly, or with other infants and adults. Commingling was also practiced. In the EIA, 79% of the assemblages were commingled, compared to 54% in the MIA.

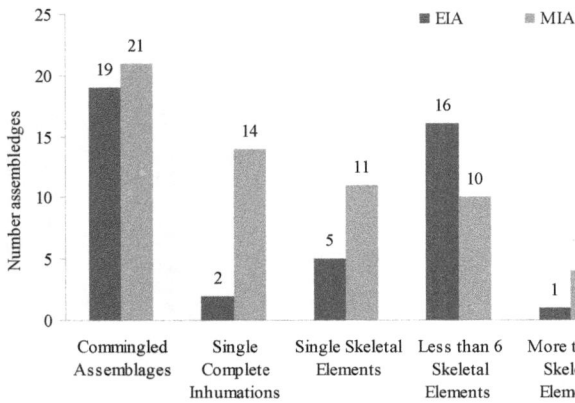

Figure 1. Types of deposition of human remains (revised results).

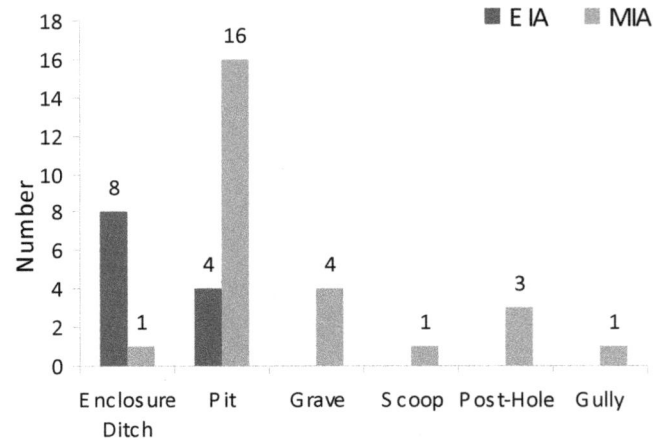

Figure 2. Type of depositional contexts

In the EIA, the commingling of small skeletal assemblages is the dominant depositioning type. This pattern changes during the MIA, when commingling is in decline at the same time as single complete inhumations increase. Thus, the evidence shows the change from fragmentation in EIA, to keeping the corpse complete in the MIA.

Discussion

Extrinsic factors
Both intrinsic and extrinsic factors were considered as agents that could affect the formation of skeletal assemblages. The burial environment is a complex interactive site, with wide ranging variables in which human remains will individually respond (Henderson 1987). In the last 15 years, research has proven that extrinsic factors related to the burial environment itself, (e.g. water table, temperature, humidity, soil pH, depth of burial, floral and faunal activity), will affect the physical or chemical nature, and hence the preservation, of human remains (Haglund and Sorg 2002; Lyman 1994). Bone loss could be the result of one, or a combination of a number of these factors, rather than caused by cultural behavior. Therefore, repetitive depositional contexts were considered as a means of identifying any mortuary manipulation or selectivity of human remains. Figure 2 shows that during the EIA, the enclosure ditch was a favoured depositional context (mainly adult small assemblages). Whereas during the MIA, pits were the dominant depositional context type (adult and infants assemblages).

The burial contexts, with their respective burial environments, were considered as factors that could affect the formation and preservation of skeletal assemblages. Thus, creating the wide-ranging types of skeletal assemblages observed on this settlement and other Iron Age sites. Consequently, three different MIA depositional contexts; grave, scoop and pit that contained the same human remains category (complete inhumation) were compared for skeletal element content to determine

Table 5: skeletal elements present by grave type.

Element	Grave	Scoop	Pit
Skull	X	X	X
Maxilla			X
Mandible			X
Teeth	X	X	X
Vertebrae	X	X	X
Sternum			X
Scapulae		X	X
Clavicles		X	X
Ribs	X	X	X
Sacrum			X
Pelvis		X	X
Femora	X	X	X
Fibulae		X	X
Tibiae	X	X	X
Patellae			
Foot bones			X
Humerii	X	X	X
Ulnae		X	X
Radii		X	X
Hand bones			X

whether there was any skeletal element variation (Table 5). The grave and scoop contained the remains of infants (under 1 year), while a pit contained the remains of a 15-17 year-old.

The infant inhumation in the grave had fewer skeletal elements surviving than either of the individuals buried in the scoop or pit. Interestingly, the scoop and the grave were in close proximity to each other. Skeletal representation could be expected to be similar, as the overall burial environment was the same. But this was not the case. The scoop contained more skeletal elements than the grave. The pit clearly had more skeletal elements surviving, or present, than either of the inhumations buried in the grave or scoop, although the absence of the patella was notable. The grave, considered the 'formal' depositional context, contained the least skeletal elements, whilst the pit, the so-called 'rubbish' or 'casual' burial context, contained the most.

The depth of the burial could be a factor that affected skeletal content of assemblages. Infant burials are considered to have been shallower than those of adults, leaving the infant more susceptible to displacement and damage due to ploughing, or machined stripping during excavations (Lewis 2007). Research has shown that cadavers buried at a depth of 0.3m (1 ft) or less below the soil surface attracted mammalian carnivores and carrion insects (Rodriguez and Bass 1985). However in this case, the burials were within a domestic setting that could possibly deter such activity.

Intrinsic factors

Intrinsic factors, related to the nature of the bone itself, can also influence the preservation of skeletal remains (e.g. bone chemistry, shape, size, density and age (see Henderson 1987:44). It has been suggested that bone density varies with age (Galloway et al. 1997) and thus, the actual size of the bone could be a significant factor in bone diagenesis. With this in mind, some authors have considered that the very young might have a higher rate of skeletal decay, increased vulnerability to faunal activity, disturbance and loss through human activity (Henderson 1987).

A comparison of age and skeletal representation in one context type, the pit burial, was carried out. Three MIA complete inhumations were compared for skeletal content and variation; a 1 year old infant, a 15-17 year old non-adult, and a 17-25 year old young adult (Table 6).

Table 6. Representation of elements in pits by age

Element	1 yr	15-17 yrs	17-25 yrs
Skull	X	X	X
Maxilla	X	X	X
Mandible	X	X	X
Teeth	X	X	X
Vertebrae	X	X	X
Sternum		X	X
Scapulae	X	X	X
Clavicles	X	X	X
Ribs	X	X	X
Sacrum		X	X
Pelvis	X	X	X
Femora	X	X	X
Fibulae	X	X	X
Tibiae	X	X	X
Patellae		X	X
Foot bones		X	X
Humerii	X	X	X
Ulnae	X	X	X
Radii	X	X	X
Hand bones	X	X	X

Table 6 illustrates that it is possible to have an equivalent skeletal representation from one burial context type, in this case, the pit. So, in this instance, factors such as bone size and density associated with the age of the individual did not affect the survival of skeletal elements. In fact, it is significant that the age of the individual and size of the bone had no bearing on the skeletal content. The infant assemblage lacked only a few elements, which could be attributed to osteological familiarity or recovery and retrieval methods which did not include sieving.

Commingled assemblages

Commingled human assemblages are commonly found on many Early and Middle Iron Age sites (Knüsel and Outram 2004: 85). This is where one or more individuals, or parts of individuals, are found in the same depositional context. In some cases, both human and animal bone assemblages are found together. Winnall Down was no different. For example, Pit 2418 was reported to contain one complete or near complete infant, and the bones of at least two, but possibly as many as six, other infants (Fasham 1985:26). In the original report, each skeletal assemblage was given its own reference number, and recorded either as 'complete or near complete' or as 'odd' child bones. In total, there was one count of both left and right iliae, scapulae and clavicles, four femora, tibiae and fibulae, two ulnae and radii, two separate accounts of mandible fragments, rib fragments and five separate accounts of skull fragments.

A conjoining exercise was carried out, and long bone fragments from two different assemblages from adjacent stratigraphic layers were conjoined. Hence, these originated from the same individual. One of these long bone fragments was also found in the same stratigraphic layer as the 'near' complete infant inhumation and so, these three assemblages could be part of the same individual. Therefore, the original human remains number of 'odd bones' assemblages have reduced. Further work will be carried out on other commingled 'odd bones' assemblages.

Mixed assemblages

During the research it became evident that faunal remains (e.g. sheep, goat, dog and horse) were often deposited in the same context as human remains, something not noted in the original report. This study's preliminary results show the number of contexts with mixed assemblages to be: EIA n=11 (81%) and MIA n=10 (38.5%). This evidence suggests that mixed assemblages were more commonly practiced in the EIA and reduced popularity during the MIA.

Interestingly, two EIA mixed assemblages both found in the enclosure ditch, may demonstrate structured and interchangeable skeletal elements. One assemblage contained a human skull and animal long bones, whilst the other had the skeletal elements reverse, a sheep/goat skull with human long bones. This evidence would support Hill's (1995) theory that structural skeletal patterning, with 'rules' for the placement of human and faunal remains, was in practice during the Iron Age.

Surface modifications

For both periods, there was very low incidence of canid tooth marks (Haglund et al. 1988; Haglund 1992). Few human skeletal assemblages exhibited faunal damage; MIA n=4 (1%) and was most likely incidental. However, the presence of teeth marks is not necessarily conclusive, and may be an under-representation, as some research has shown that not all bone retains such marks (Kent 1981).

Conversely, evidence for root etching (irregular channelling or grooved impressions on the outer cortex) was much more prolific in both the EIA and MIA assemblages, which may indicate similar burial depths. Invading roots can eventually degrade skeletal remains so much that it could explain some wide-ranging bone loss from shallow graves (Rodriguez and Bass 1985).

It has been put forward that if excarnation was a rite practiced in the EIA and MIA, bones should exhibit some degree of weathering (Morse et al. 1983; Behrensmeyer 1978). However at Winnall Down, there was little evidence of surface modification to support any long term weathering and thus, excarnation.

Zonation

Skeletal elements were assessed using zonation method described by Knüsel and Outram (2004), in order to determine whether any skeletal zone patterning could be addressed by bone density and survival rate patterns. Although the sample size is small, the femoral and humeral shafts were more likely to be present, with damage observed on the greater and lesser trochanters. Apart from long bones, skull fragments were frequently recorded, for adult skull fragments there seemed to have been no particular zone trend.

Conclusions

Early work on EIA and MIA human remains compared the skeletal assemblages to ethnographic and anthropological funerary studies. These early interpretations have shaped our current understanding and expectations of burial and mortuary traditions for these periods.

This paper has reviewed EIA and MIA human remains, originally excavated some thirty years ago, from a settlement that spanned the LBA through into the ER period. The settlement's burial evidence supports early literary accounts that suggest a break in burial and mortuary tradition. That is, there were no human remains dating to the LBA or LIA/ER periods on this settlement which correlate with BA barrow cemeteries and LIA/Early Roman cremation cemeteries. Winnall Down's EIA and MIA populations broke away from previous funerary traditions and buried their dead within the domestic setting.

Changes were also observed between the EIA and MIA in the choice of depositional contexts; from the enclosure ditch being the main depositional context of the EIA, to mainly pits, a few graves, and a 'scoop' during the MIA. During the EIA the dead were not leaving the settlement and entering a designated burial area, but were placed on the boundary between the living and the dead. During the MIA, some of the dead even penetrate the living space. However, the onset of LIA sees the location of the dead taken away from the settlement back to cremation cemeteries. At Winnall Down there was also a major change in the human remains assemblage type from fragmentation of the EIA, to keeping the individual whole or complete in the MIA.

Both intrinsic and extrinsic factors were considered to be involved with the formation of the Winnall Down's skeletal assemblages. In one context type, the age of the individual did not create any significant skeletal element variation, but there was between context types. The grave has been considered the formal burial but contained the least skeletal elements in comparison to a scoop or pit assemblage. Whilst the individual, or parts of an individual, found in pits has been considered to be a 'casual' burial or be part of the 'rubbish' of IA settlements.

This research has identified repetitive skeletal patterning as one means to provide evidence of cultural behaviour that demonstrated changes in funerary activity, skeletal manipulation and skeletal selectivity. Finally, this research has demonstrated the importance of conjoining commingled assemblages as this could alter original human reports and the need to explore mixed assemblages as they may provide a different funerary picture.

Acknowledgements

I thank Dave Allen, Kay Ainsworth and Alan Jacobs from Hampshire Museum Services, Winchester, and Professor Richard Bradley and Mary Lewis from the University of Reading.

Literature cited

Behrensmeyer AK. 1978. Taphonomic and ecologic information from bone weathering. *Paleobiology* 4: 150-162.

Bello S. 2001. *Taphonmie des restes osseux humans. Effet des processus de conservation du squelette sur les paramètres anthropologiques. Marseilles: Università degli Studi di Firenze, Florence, Italy and Université de la Méditerranée.* Unpublished PhD.

Bello S. 2005. The reciprocal effects of taphonomy, funerary practices and anatomical features on the state of preservation of human remains. In: Zakrzewski SR and Clegg M (eds.) *Proceedings of the Fifth Annual Conference of the British Association for Biological Anthropology and Osteoarchaeology.* BAR International Series 1383. BAR Publishing: Oxford, pp 1-10.

Bello S and Andrews P. 2006. The intrinsic pattern of preservation of human skeletons and its influence on the interpretation of funerary behaviours. In: Gowland R and Knüsel C (eds.) *Social Archaeology of Funerary Remains*. Oxford: Oxbow, pp 1-13.

Blumenschine RJ and Selvaggio MM. 1988. Percussion marks on bone surfaces as a new diagnostic of hominid behaviour. *Nature* 333:763-765.

Bradley R. 1981. Economic growth and social change: two examples from prehistoric Europe. In: Sheridan, A and Bailey, G. (eds.) *Economic Archaeology* British Archaeological Reports (International Series 96). Oxford: BAR Publishing, pp 231-8.

Brickley M and McKinley J. 2004. *Guidelines to the Standards for Recording Human Remains*. London: IFA and BABAO.

Brooks S and Suchey JM. 1990. Skeletal age determination based on the os pubis: A comparison of the Acsádi-Nemeskéri and Suchey-Brooks methods. *Human Evolution* 5:227-238.

Buikstra J and Ubelaker D. 1994. *Standards for Data Collection from Human Skeletal Remains*. Arkansas Archaeological Survey Research Series 44. Arkansas: Fayetteville

Carr, G and Knüsel, C 1997. The ritual framework of excarnation by exposure as the mortuary practice of the Early and middle Iron Ages of central southern Britain. In: Gwilt A and Haselgrove C (eds.) *Reconstructing Iron Age Societies. New Approaches to the British Iron Age*. Oxford: Oxbow Monograph 71, pp 167-173.

Clark JGD. 1962. *Prehistoric England*. London: BT Batsford Ltd.

Cunliffe, B 1984. *Danebury: An Iron Age Hillfort in Hampshire. Volume 2. The Excavations 1969-1978: The finds*. London: CBA Research Report 52.

Cunnington M. 1932. Was there a second Belgic invasion represented by bead-rim pottery? *Antiquaries Journal* 12: 48-58.

Dodson P and Wexlar D 1979. Taphonomic investigations of owl pellets. *Paleobiology* 5: 279-284.

Dunning G. 1976. Salmonsbury, Burton-on-the-Water, Gloucestershire. In: Harding D (ed.) *Later Prehistoric Earthworks in Britain and Ireland*. London: Routledge, pp75-118.

Ellison A and Drewett P. 1971. Pits and post-holes in the British early Iron Age. *Proceedings of the Prehistoric Society* 31: 183-194.
Fazekas Gy and Kosa F. 1978. *Forensic Fetal Osteology*. Budapest: Akadémiai Diaodó.

Fasham PJ. 1985. *The Prehistoric Settlement at Winnall Down, Winchester. Winchester. Hampshire Field Club and Archaeological Society*. Monograph No.2: M3 Archaeological Rescue Committee Report No. 8. Gloucester: Alan Sutton Publishing.

Galloway A, Willey P, and Snyder L. 1997. Human bone mineral densities and survival of bone elements: a contemporary sample. In: Haglund WD and Sorg MH (eds.) *Forensic Taphonomy: The Postmortem Fate of Human Remains* London: CRC Press, pp 295-315.

Haglund WD. 1992. Contribution of rodents to postmortem artefacts of bone and soft tissue. *Journal of Forensic Sciences* 37: 1459-1465.

Haglund WD. 1997. Dogs and coyotes: postmortem involvement with human remains. In: Haglund WD and Sorg MH (eds.) *Forensic Taphonomy: The Postmortem Fate of Human Remains* London: CRC Press, pp 367-379.

Haglund WD, Reay DT, and Swindler DR. 1988. Canid scavenging/disarticulation sequence of human remains in the Pacific Northwest. *Journal of Forensic Sciences* 34: 587-606.

Haglund WD and Sorg MH. 1997. *Forensic Taphonomy: The Postmortem Fate of Human Remains*. London: CRC Press.

Harding D. 1974. *The Iron Age in Lowland Britain*. London: Routledge.

Hill JD. 1995. *Ritual and Rubbish in the Iron Age of Wessex. A study on the formation of a specific archaeological record*. BAR British Series 242. Oxford: BAR Publishing.

Hillson S. 1996. *Dental Anthropology*. Cambridge: Cambridge University Press.

Henderson J. 1987. Factors determining the state of preservation of human remains. In: Boddington A, Garland AN, and Janaway RC (eds.) *Death, Decay and Reconstruction. Approaches to Archaeology and Forensic Science*: Manchester: Manchester University Press, pp 43-54.

Hodson F. 1964. Cultural grouping within the British pre-Roman Iron Age. *Proceedings of the Prehistoric Socitey* 30: 99-110.

İşcan MY and Loth SR. 1986. Estimation of age and determination of sex from the sternal rib. In: Reichs KJ (ed.) *Forensic Osteology: Advances in the Identification of Human Remains*. Springfield, Illinois: CC Thomas, pp 68-69.

Kent S. 1981. The dog: an archaeologist's best friend or worst enemy – the spatial distribution of faunal remains. *Journal of Field Archaeology* 8: 367-372.

Knüsel CJ and Outram AK. 2004. Fragmentation: the zonation method applied to fragmented human remains from archaeological and forensic contexts *Environmental Archaeology* 9: 85-97.

Lewis ME. 2007. *The Bioarchaeology of Children. Perspectives from Biological and Forensic Anthropology.* Cambridge: Cambridge University Press.

Liddell DM. 1935. Report on the Hampshire Field Club's excavations at Meon Hill. *Proceedings of the Hampshire Field Club* 13: 7-54.

Loe L and Cox M. 2005. Peri- and post mortem surface features on archaeological human bone: why they should not be ignored and a protocol for their identification and interpretation: Peri- and post-mortem surface features. In: Zakrzewski SR and Clegg M (eds.) *Proceedings of the Fifth Annual Conference of the British Association for Biological Anthropology and Osteoarchaeology.* BAR International Series 1383. Oxford: BAR Publishing, pp 11-21.

Lovejoy CO, Meindl RS, Pryzbeck TR and Mensforth RP. 1985. Chronological metamorphosis of the auricular surface of the ilium: A new method for the determination of adult skeletal ages at death. *American Journal of Physical Anthropology* 68: 15-28.

Lyman RL. 1994. *Vertebrate Taphonomy. Cambridge Manuals in Archaeology.* Cambridge: Cambridge University Press.

Lyman RL and Fox GL. 1997. A critical evaluation of bone weathering as an indication of bone assemblage formation. In: Haglund WD and Sorg MH (eds.) *Forensic Taphonomy: The Postmortem Fate of Human Remains.* London: CRC Press, pp 223-243.

McLeod, MD. 1981. *The Asante.* London: British Museum.

Meindl RS and Lovejoy CO. 1985. Ectocranial suture closure: a revised method for the determination of skeletal ages a death based on the lateral-anterior sutures. *American Journal of Physical Anthropology* 68: 57-66.

Metcalf P and Huntington R. 1991. *Celebrations of Death. The Anthropology of Mortuary Ritual.* Second Edition. Cambridge: Cambridge University Press.

Miles AEW. 2001. The Miles method of assessing age from tooth ear revisited. *Journal of Archaeological Science* 28: 973-982.

Moorress CFA, Fanning EA and Hunt EE. 1963. Formation and resorption of three deciduous teeth in children. *American of Physical Anthropology* 21: 205-213.

Morse D, Duncan J and Stoutamire J. 1983. *Handbook of Forensic Archaeology and Anthropology.* Tallahasee, Florida: Rose Printing.

Phenice TW. 1969. A newly developed visual method of sexing in the os pubis. *American Journal of Physical Anthropology* 30: 297- 301.

Pitt-Rivers A. 1887. *Excavations in Cranbourne Chase, Vol. I.* Privately Published.

Pitt-Rivers, A. 1888. *Excavations in Cranbourne Chase, Vol. II.* Privately Published.

Richardson KM. 1951. The excavation of Iron Age villages on Boscombe Down West. *Wiltshire Archaeological Magazine* 54: 123-168.

Rodriguez WC and Bass WM. 1985. Decomposition of buried bodies and methods that may aid in their location. *Journal of Forensic Sciences* 30(3): 836-852.

Scheuer L and Black S. 2000. *Developmental Juvenile Osteology.* London: Academic Press.

Shipman P. 1981. Applications of scanning electron microscopy to taphonomic problems. In: Cantwell AE, Griffin JB and Rothschild NA (eds.) *The Research Potential of Anthropological Museum Collections.* New York: Annals of the New York Academy of Science, pp 357-385.

Shipman P and Rose J. 1983. Early hominid hunting butchering and carcass process behaviours: approaches to the fossil record. *Journal of Anthropological Archaeology* 2: 57-98.

Smith BH. 1991. Standards of human tooth formation and dental age assessment. In: Kelley MA and Larson CD (eds.) *Advances in Dental Anthropology.* New York: Wiley-Liss, pp 143-168.

Walker L. 1984. Population and behaviour. In: Cunliffe B (ed.) *Danebury: An Iron Age Hillfort in Hampshire. Volume 2, the excavations 1969-1978: The finds.* London: CBA Research Report 52, pp 442-463.

Whimster R. 1981. *Burial Practices in Iron Age Britain.* Oxford: British Archaeological Reports 90.

Wilson C. 1981. Burials within settlements in southern Britain during the pre-Roman Iron Age. *Bulletin of the Institute of Archaeology of the University of London* 18: 127-169.

Ubelake, DH. 1997. Taphonomic applications in forensic anthropology. In: Haglund WD and Sorg MH (eds.) *Forensic Taphonomy: The Postmortem Fate of Human Remains.* New York: CRC Press, pp 77-87.

Ubelaker DH. 1989. *Human Skeletal Remains: excavation, analysis, Interpretations*. Washington DC: Taraxacum.

Ucko PJ. 1969. Ethnography and archaeological interpretation of funerary remains. *World Archaeology* 1(2): 262-280.

Can we estimate post-mortem interval from an individual body part? A field study using *Sus scrofa*

Branka Franicevic[1] and Robert Pastor[2]

[1] Department of Forensic and Investigative Science, University of Central Lancashire, Preston, PR1 2HE
[2] Department of Anthropology, University of Oregon, Eugene, Oregon 97403, US
BFranicevic@uclan.ac.uk

Abstract

Taphonomical studies contribute to our understanding of how the ecology of various terrains impacts on the decomposition of human remains. In nature, where bodies are often found scattered by scavengers, naturally disarticulated or dismembered, a single bone such as a femur can often aid positive identification. This study explores the possibility of also estimating Post-Mortem Interval (PMI) from an individual body part, using the Accumulated Degree Day (ADD) method and the observation of decomposition stages in a terrestrial terrain. The decomposition patterns of two dismembered pigs (*Sus scrofa*) were compared to two whole pig carcasses. Over a 31 day period, a total of five stages of decomposition were observed in the whole pigs: Fresh, Putrefaction, Deterioration, Disintegration and Decay, with only the first three stages observed in the individual body parts. The ADD results did not work in accordance with decomposition patterns, yielding an ADD mean of 62.3 for dismembered upper and lower limbs, and a mean of ADD 74.1 for heads, indicating more rapid decomposition in comparison to a mean ADD of 21657 for whole carcasses. These results demonstrate that firstly, individual body parts cannot accurately represent the PMI of a whole body, and secondly that ADD analysis is not a reliable method of PMI estimation for individual body parts in this terrain. Therefore, further taphonomic research on individual body parts is necessary, since PMI techniques have previously only been studied on whole corpses. The possibility that overlooking the different decomposition processes of individual body parts might affect the accuracy of PMI estimation has a direct bearing on forensic investigations, and the PMI determination of well-preserved archaeological human remains in advanced stages of decomposition.

Keywords: Individual body parts, postmortem inverval, taphonomy, Croatia

Introduction

The length of time between death and the discovery of the remains, or the Post-Mortem Interval (PMI), can be vital in determining the post-mortem history of the subject, as well as in eliminating possible suspects in a medico-legal enquiry. Lacunae in our knowledge of the decomposition patterns of dismembered and naturally disarticulated human body parts are particularly significant, since the field of PMI research historically has been designed for, and from, whole corpses and carcasses. The apparent lack of decay models for individual body parts poses the potential danger of miscalculation of PMI for forensic cases involving dismemberments and scattered human limbs. Consequently, this shortcoming may affect the accuracy of medico-legal investigations in reconstructing post-mortem events. Decomposed remains (partially to completely skeletonised) also make up part of the archaeological record. Therefore, contemporary taphonomic fieldwork might reveal how the manner of death influences the taphonomic history of ancient remains. Studies of disarticulated material can further help in investigating whether skeletonised remains represent an active or a passive accumulation, or in clarifying factors associated with the manner of death, such as skeletal analyses of human decapitations.

Evidence from taphonomic studies would suggest a different decomposition pattern of individual body parts is likely. Alteration of intrinsic factors through dismemberment may cause more dependency on external factors in decomposition, consequently affecting its speed. Intrinsically, decomposition is initially triggered by the internal chemical breakdown of tissue from liberated enzymes (autolysis). This process progresses more rapidly with higher water content tissues such as the brain, and higher enzyme content tissues, such as the liver (Vass 2001), resulting in an uneven decomposition, even in whole bodies. Putrefaction follows autolysis and is mostly a bacterially driven process (Mayer et al. 1997). It progresses through two stages, hydrolysis and acidification, by continuing the destruction of the soft tissues to their dissolution into salts, liquids and gases. Microscopic decomposers – bacteria, actinomycetes, fungi and protozoa – are introduced from both the intestine and the external environment. In the case of single-limb decay, only the external environment influences the rate of decomposition.

The speed of post-mortem change to hard tissues at the microscopic level is also not conclusive. Bell et al. (1996) found evidence of microbial attack in bone three months post-mortem. Although Syssovena (1958, cited in Bell et al. 1996) found no change to the microstructure of teeth buried for 70 years. As the abdominal area is the main source for bacterial putrefaction, dismemberment around the time of death may prevent bacteria invading bone tissue, leading to greater density and better preservation of bone (Bell et al. 1996). The preservation of sharp-force trauma in dismembered bone is another speculative issue. A few studies have focused on post-mortem skeletal butchery marks in fossil animal bone (Hill 1979; Hill and Behrensmeyer 1985). Others, such as Symes et al. (2002) investigated the taphonomic context of cut marks in closed forensic cases. To date, no experimental findings on the taphonomic factors, either in creating pseudo-cut marks or altering their signature in bone, have been published.

This project investigates the way in which intrinsic and extrinsic factors affect the preservation of individual body parts, and the subsequent estimation of post-mortem intervals using these remains. The aim is to establish the decomposition pattern of individual body parts in comparison to whole carcasses in a terrestrial habitat. The first goal was to establish the intrinsic factors affecting decomposition for any differences between body parts and whole corpses, by means of analysing post-mortem gross changes and loss of body mass. Secondly, as biological systems under field conditions are rarely comparable with the precision attained in the laboratory, the second research aim was to evaluate the external influencing factors in a more realistic external setting. This was achieved by recording and correlating taphonomic factors known to affect decomposition, to include climate factors, entomological and microbial succession. Retrospective PMI estimation in forensic cases and archaeological contexts is often restricted in its accuracy due to many influencing factors responsible for the destructive process that are no longer traceable and/or measurable. Hence, the third research aim concerned quantifying PMI using the Accumulated Degree Days (ADD) method, based on temperature as the principal influencing and traceable variable, as opposed to qualitative gross observations of soft tissue decay. This method allows the retrospective calculation of PMI, as well as predictive stage of decomposition, by means of averaging daily temperatures (Magyesi et al. 2005; Vass et al. 1992). The goal was to establish the level of accuracy, standardisation and replication for the ADD method in other contexts.

Materials and methods

Experimental site
Fieldwork involved the decomposition analysis of individual body parts in a terrestrial habitat during the winter season. The study site was located 2km from the city of Opuzen, Croatia (43.02° N 17.57° E), with restricted public access. Samples were exposed to the sun and deposited on salt marsh soil in the Neretva River delta surrounding limestone terrain (Ramsar 2002). The warming influence of the sea meant the average winter temperature was 7.4˚C, with warmer autumn temperatures (16.5˚C) than in the spring (14.7˚C). The summer mean temperature was 24.2˚C. The relationship between decomposition rates and soil moisture conditions in a marshy soil was not investigated in this project. Air temperature and relative humidity (RH) data readings were obtained from the local Hydro-Meteorological Station, located 50 metres from the site.

Animal model
Sus scrofa is widely accepted as a reliable model for human decomposition, as it is assumed to decompose similarly to a human cadaver in terms of its fat distribution, digestive process, skin type, quantity of body hair and ability to attract insects (Catts and Goff 1992). Additionally, they are easily obtainable and selected for uniform mass and sizes. Four domestic pigs (*Sus scrofa*), two males and two females of the Bulgarian White breed, were used as animal analogues in this study, to mimic human decomposition processes. Two whole carcasses were compared to two dismembered pig remains in order to estimate the relationship between variables. The carcasses ranged in size from 21 to 23 kg. The animals were conventionally reared in raised decks and were in a good state of health. They were slaughtered in accordance with the relevant European animal welfare and environmental regulations. They were approximately one year of age at death, killed by a local farmer by means of an electric gunshot and dismembered peri-mortem within an hour from death. Dismemberments included decapitation and upper and lower joint disarticulation, leaving the trunk isolated.

Procedures
All post-mortem changes during decomposition were recorded from the day of death, with the Time Since Death (TSD) of approximately seven hours that allowed dispatch from the slaughter house to the field site. The experiment was conducted in November 2006 and lasted 31 days. Samples were initially chilled and kept in double sealed plastic bags during transportation prior to exposure at the site to avoid premature insect activity. Once on the site, the carcasses were weighed and kept in metal cages for the duration of the experiment, to protect them from large scavengers. The cage dimensions were 0.72m x 0.76m x 0.78m, spread around a 34m² plot, each cage fitted with an improvised supported steel hinged lid, allowing easy access for photography and weighing. They allowed entry to smaller vertebrates and for the natural rise and fall of the carcass during decomposition. To have opened up the experiment to allow large scavengers access to the remains would have limited its ability to facilitate specific findings as to how decomposition is affected by micro-environmental and geographical factors, although it is recognised that in forensic conditions, these animals would generally have a role to play in the decomposition process. Three of the four carcasses per habitat were sampled for invertebrates at daily intervals. The fourth carcass was used as a control to assess visually whether frequent sampling disrupted the natural decomposition process, as suggested by Adlam and Simmons (2007). The environmental data was recorded in the diary log for the purpose of determining their correlations with stages of decomposition. Temperature data was obtained from the hourly data logger recordings. Daily temperature mean figures were calculated per observation, and divided by the number of observations. This way, the mean as opposed to the median was assumed to be more applicable for the statistical analysis.

Table 1. Summary of decomposition subcategories used for the ADD method

Decomposition category	Point	Post-mortem changes
A. Fresh	1	Fresh, no discolouration
B. Putrefaction	2	Pink-white appearance of the skin
B. Putrefaction	3	Cream to light brown discolouration of the skin with slight skin slippage
C. Early Disintegration	4	'Fisherman skin' (soggy ash white skin with green and black stripes visible)
C. Early Disintegration	5	Further skin slippage
D. Advanced Disintegration	6	Skin colour pink to red, skin texture crispy
D. Advanced Disintegration	7	Skin colour light red with dark red patches
D. Advanced Disintegration	8	Skin sagging and flaking off in most parts
E. Early Decay	9	Skin structure leathery to stringy with evident fatty tissues.
E. Early Decay	10	Substantial greasy substance, decomposed tissues, cartilage and tendons exposed.
F. Advanced Decay	11	Formation of moisture thin white-grey substance on bone trauma ends
F. Advanced Decay	12	Bone exposure of most of the samples with greasy substances and decomposed tissue.

Its effect on the decomposition process may, however, be presumed to have been fairly constant throughout the experiment, given that relative humidity conditions did not fluctuate markedly during the period. Wind velocity information was gathered from the Croatian official weather condition web-sites for the area. The extraction of micro-organisms from the soil and sediment was processed following the '*Berlese funnel*' technique that proved useful in coastal settings (Davis and Goff 2000). Micro-organism extraction was conducted three times a week from the 'drip zone' (the immediate area of sediment from the samples). The process of decomposition recording derived from direct observation was conducted throughout week one, twice a day, and in weeks two to four, once a day. Observation entailed examination of the physical condition of the remains, and visible invertebrate and vertebrate activity. The possibility of direct extrinsic contamination of instars was minimised by collection of insects, netting adults first and preserving in 75% ethanol. Entomological cross-contamination of samples during the migration of instar stage three could not be entirely excluded, but the risk was minimised by labelling the jars with geographical location, date and hour of collection, case number, location of the body where collected, and name of the collector as per Byrd and Castner (2001). A combination of methods was utilised in order to increase accuracy of taxonomic identification as recommended by Borror et al. (1976). Data were analysed using a Kruskal-Wallis test.

Statistical analysis
Correlation analysis was performed to test whether temperature can be used as a variable to estimate PMI quantitatively in retrospect when dealing with individual single remains, as an alternative to the gross observation of post-mortem changes. Statistical procedures were conducted using SPSS 15.0 for Windows. Due to the characteristics of samples and the nature of the

experiment, data were not assumed to have normal distributions. Consequently, Spearman's coefficient was chosen to calculate the correlation between decomposition and the main environmental variable.

The relationship between temperature (as the primary variable) and the decomposition process was tested by the Accumulated Degree Day method (ADD) using the linear regression formula:

$$ADD=10^{(0.002*TBS*TBS+1.18)}\pm388.16$$

This technique is used for quantitative post-mortem estimations to examine the possibility of estimating the PMI by using a combination of Total Body Score (TBS) and ADD. The model was adopted from Megyesi et al. (2005), where it was tested on archived data from closed forensic cases. Decomposition was divided into five broad observed decomposition categories, and subdivided into a further eight subcategories that described the appearance of the remains (Table 1). Stages were modified into a sequential ranking so that the final decomposition scores reflected the total amount of accumulated decomposition (Megyesi et al. 2005). The scores of all anatomical regions were then added up to provide the TBS. This total of scored points reflects how much accumulated decomposition has occurred. Data were plugged into the mathematical equation above to estimate ADD. The correction factor 0.1667 was applied for the individual body parts weighting less than 20kg Vass et al. (1992). The post-mortem interval was then calculated by dividing ADD figures by the average daily temperatures.

Results

A maximum of five decomposition stages were recorded for whole carcasses, and three for individual body parts. Average values are demonstrated in Table 2.

Table 2. Summarised stages of decomposition

Category 1. Fresh 2. Putrefaction 3. Deterioration 4. Disintegration 5. Decay	Observation day 1-31	Decomposition stage duration (days)	Odour 1. No odour 2. Minimal 3. Some 4. Substantial
Whole carcasses			
1	1-3	3	1
2	4-20	17	2
3	21-26	6	3
4	27-29	3	4
5	30-31	2	3
Individual body parts			
1	1-6	6	1
2	7-12	6	3
3	13-31	19	3

Fresh
The experimental samples in this category retained a general fresh appearance without discolouration or odour. A sharp decrease in body temperature was observed with whole carcasses, reaching levels below ambient temperature within first three hours. The fresh stage was considered terminated with the first signs of lividity, exhibited as purple colouration of the skin as a result of gravitational movement of blood within the vessels.

Putrefaction
All remains still preserved a fresh appearance, but with a degree of lividity. The first signs of bloating typical of this stage were noticed on the whole carcasses. An indication of this early stage on the individual body parts was a pink-white skin discolouration, and an increase in odour level. Further signs of putrefaction were evident as green to black stripes visible under the skin. Body temperature increased during this stage for whole carcasses as a result of insect activity and the putrefaction process.

Deterioration
The strongest odour was recorded during this stage. As the stage progressed, the skin colour changed to cream-grey with evidence of some skin slippage around the joints. Scavenging activity was evident during this stage, mostly on the whole carcasses. The preferred body locations were the body orifices, but scavenging marks were also noticed on other parts of the body. The deterioration stage was the last observed decomposition stage for individual body parts (Table 2).

Disintegration
During the disintegration stage, the texture of the carcass skin was significantly thinner and crispy to the touch. As the stage progressed, the remains exhibited brownish to black discolouration, and abundant decomposed tissues from the skin slippage were evident causing some bone

exposure. A peak in body temperature in the whole carcasses was reached during this stage, which was evident with the body-mass loss.

Decay
This was the shortest observed stage, due to the controlled termination of the fieldwork. Scavenging succession increased and lasted until the end of the experiment for the whole carcasses. Rats were observed feeding on flesh regularly until the last day of the experiment. Skin disintegration progressed to soft tissue decay, and bone detachment began with carpals and tarsals.

Biomass removal showed similar rates of breakdown duration for whole carcasses (Figure 1). However, with the exception of the trunk, which in both samples showed a mean weight loss of 70%, the individual body parts lost little weight throughout the decomposition period, supporting a slow decay rate, with a mean body-weight loss for limbs of 7.6%, and for heads of 16.14%.

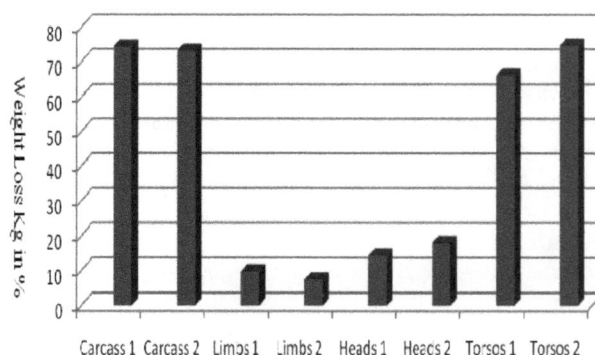

Figure 1. Rates of decomposition for whole carcasses and individual body parts

Table 3. Summarised list of taxa collected from the remains

Order	Family	Genus/Species	Decomposition stage	Development stage	Location on the body
Diptera	Calliphoridae	Calliphora vicina	1-2-3-4	E-Y-O-A	Orifices IBPs/C
		Lucilia illustris	2-3-4	A-P-O	Orifices IBPs/C
		Phaenicia eximia	3-4	Y-O-P	Orifices/trauma areas IBPs
	Sarcophagidae	Sarcophaga bullata	2-3-4	E-Y-O-P-A	Orifices C
	Muscidae	Fannia canicularis	3-4-5	A-P-O	Trauma areas IBPs
		Fannia scalaris	3-4-5	A-P-O	Orifices C
		Musca domestica	2-3-4-5	Y-O-P-A	Orifices/soft tissue C
	Scathophagidae	Scatophaga stericoraria	3-4	Y-O	Orifices/soft tissue C
		Poecilosomella angulata	3-4-5	Y-O	Orifices/soft tissue C

Key: 1-Fresh 2-Putrefaction 3-Deterioration 4-Disintegration 5-Decay; E-Eggs Y-Young larva O-Older larva P-Pupa A-Adult; IBPs-Individual Body Parts C-Whole carcasses.

Decomposition associated taxa

In total, 100 samples of larvae, pupae and adult individuals were collected. Only dominant taxa were collected from the 'drip zone' of the remains and recorded in the study. This area was designated as secondary site of activity due to the nutrient materials falling from the animal model (Shalaby et al. 2000). Therefore, complete taxonomical classification and the exact number of the insects are unknown. In this manner, the arthropod succession observed is a preliminary report typical for this geographical region, giving a very general baseline for further research. All taxa were of the order *Diptera*, belonging to three families and nine species. Within *Diptera*, two families were predominant; *Calliphoridae* (70% of all *Diptera*), evident within the first half hour on all remains, and *Muscidae* (20%). The other two families were found in lesser numbers but distinctively divided between whole carcasses and individual body parts. In contrast to *Calliphoridate* and *Muscidae* taxa that demonstrated no general preference between whole carcasses and individual body parts, *Scathophagidae* and *Sarcophagidae* were mostly collected from whole carcasses (Table 3). Disturbance did not prove to inversely affect either the carcass weight loss or the insect succession pattern.

Statistical analysis

Spearman rank correlation coefficients (r and r^2) were derived for the correlation analysis. Ambient temperature, the environmental variable assumed to affect the rates of decay the most, is correlated with percentages of body loss of both whole carcasses and individual body parts. The average standard error for the r-values of all samples was 0.035. The effect of ambient temperature on decomposition provided the most explanatory power on whole carcasses where the correlation as Spearman's rank coefficient was significant. The significant positive correlation was noted between temperature and weight loss for Whole Carcass 1 is +0.90, $r^2= 0.81$, and for Whole Carcass 2 is +0.91, $r^2= 0.82$ where correlation is significant at 0.05 level (2-tailed). The values of the correlations for individual body parts are probably

appropriate to be used to detect the relationships with rates of decay generally but no more accurate estimates could be yielded. With the exception of some body elements – Head 1, that correlated significantly with ambient temperature (r = + 0.92, $r^2= 0.84$ at the 0.05 level); Torso 2 (r = +0.90, $r^2 = 0.81$ at the 0.01), and Lower Limbs 1 that yielded perfect correlation (+1.00, $r^2=1.00$ at the significance level of 0.01) – no other body parts correlated significantly with ambient temperature. These data suggest that temperature, as a variable, would not be appropriate to be used quantitatively to detect the relationship with rates of decay of individual body parts.

Accumulated Degree Days

Since it is widely accepted that temperature, and not just time, is a significant variable in the decomposition process, it was hypothesised that the post-mortem interval could be calculated quantitatively from the ambient temperature averages in retrospect. The ADD method was applied to whole carcasses and to individual body parts to assess further the non-significant correlations observed. Total Body Score for the data ranged between three (Putrefaction) for Limbs 1 to 36 for Whole Carcass 1 (Advanced Decay). The ADD for all cases ranged from 66.0 to 25118 (Table 4).

Table 4. Quantitative estimation of decomposition categories

Body elements	TBS	ADD	Av. daily temp (F)	PMI (days)
Carcass 1	36	25118	53.6	31
Carcass 2	35	18197	53.6	31
Head 1	5	72.4	53.6	31
Head 2	6	75.8	53.6	31
Limbs 1	3	66.0	53.6	31
Limbs 2	4	69.1	53.6	31
Limbs 3	4	69.1	53.6	31
Limbs 4	4	69.1	53.6	31
Torso 1	8	85.1	53.6	31
Torso 2	7	79.4	53.6	31

The ADD calculations did not work in accordance with decomposition patterns of either whole carcasses or individual body parts, further disproving the hypothesis of temperature being the main variable in the decomposition process of individual body parts. The maximum decomposition time for individual body parts, regardless of differences in body weight for both whole carcasses and individual body parts, is 17.8 days. The actual Advanced Decay stage in the experiment was reached for whole carcasses by the end of day 31, while some individual body parts were still in the Putrefaction stage. Further, applying the ADD estimation formula, the appearance of whole carcasses would be consistent with death occurring between 274 and 379 days, meaning that if undisturbed, whole carcasses would decompose within approximately one year in this region, whilst individual body parts would be skeletonised within a week.

Discussion

Intrinsic factors affecting decomposition
The post-mortem physiological changes followed a recognised sequence of decomposition stages with individual body parts. A bloating stage was, however, not observed in any individual body parts, probably due to the absence of necessary intestinal gases. Autolysis and putrefaction to a lesser extent established the sequences through which the soft tissues decomposed. Generally, tissues whose cells conduct the highest rates of ATP synthesis, biosynthesis and membrane transport decomposed first, such as intestines and organs of digestion (Ubelaker 1997). They were followed by tissues that contain substantial amounts of macrophages whose lysosomes release hydrolytic enzymes, activated at lowered cytoplasmic pH. These are, for instance, air passages and lungs, followed by the brain and nervous tissues that contain neurons, the most metabolically active and among the first to autolyse. Upper and lower limbs that decomposed the slowest include skeletal muscles, connective tissues and integuments that contain the protein collagen that is difficult to hydrolyse (Ubelaker 1997). Thus, it is possible in this environment, a leg detached from the body would decompose at a slower than the rest of the corpse.

Extrinsic factors affecting decomposition
Some studies suggest that larger remains (e.g. whole carcasses) do not necessarily attract more insects (Kuusela and Hanski 1982), implying that individual body parts would not be subject to different levels of insect succession. However, Haskell and colleagues (1989) demonstrated that the rate of decomposition is related to the amount of carrion present. Our findings confirm this result by demonstrating larger and more varied taxa associated with the decomposition process on whole carcasses than on individual body parts, which supports greater weight loss and consequently, a faster decomposition process. Body weight could be associated with more frequent scavenger succession on whole carcasses as well. Rats were regularly observed feeding on the remains throughout decomposition, but were only occasionally spotted around individual body parts.

Not all body parts release the necessary amount of gases needed for the insect succession, further contributing to slower decomposition. The lack of succession of insects that are normally at their highest during the Putrefaction stage could be attributed to the water factors and limitations for larvae development, and also because following death, biochemical fermentation processes release compounds from the intestine. For instance, nitrogen (N_2), ammonia (NH_3), hydrogen sulphide (H_2S) and carbon dioxide (CO_2), to which necrophagous insects respond in effect to accelerate the putrefaction process (Anderson 2001; Smith 1986). The release of these gases was assumed minimal in this study. The lack of a bloating stage for all individual body parts in the absence of the necessary intestinal gases could have also contributed towards slower decomposition in regards to attracting both flies and scavengers. This could be supported with the fact that more insect and scavenger succession was noticed towards the end of the experiment, as the decomposition progressed, than in its early days. These successional differences are forensically significant since they demonstrate different data for estimates based on similar conditions, so more confidence could be placed in the inference made for time of death.

Determining PMI for individual body parts
Temperature is by far the most important environmental factor affecting the decomposition process. Insect succession is temperature dependent, as is the rate of internal bacteria breaking down protein into fatty acid. Therefore, since chemical elements are found in different concentrations in various parts resulting in non-symmetrical decomposition with whole carcasses, once body parts are detached, the harmonious process of decomposition will be affected. The findings of this pilot study confirmed this hypothesis, showing different decomposition processes based on observational and quantitative strategy. It is not possible to estimate PMI from an individual body part to account for a whole body. This study showed that the body element to decompose at a rate most closely approximating that of the whole carcass is the torso. Recommendations based on the findings include an explicit entomological analysis that may be beneficial for a more comprehensive understanding of the impact of two major factors in decomposition, insect and temperature variables, on individual body parts.

Conclusion

A model of the decomposition pattern of isolated single remains in the terrestrial setting was presented, with reference to the rates of decay specific to south-eastern Europe in winter time. The project demonstrated the complexity of taphonomical issues associated with the decomposition of individual body parts pertaining to the disappearance of soft tissue in a different manner from on whole carcasses, even in the same vicinity. A general baseline of the decomposition model outlined creates a basis for further research that could be beneficial in both forensic and archaeological contexts, and may prove useful for PMI estimation for regions of similar climates. An outstanding issue surrounding PMI estimation for dismembered body parts is distinguishing peri-mortem from post-mortem dismemberment and natural disarticulation of remains found in advanced stages of decomposition.

Literature cited

Adlam, RE. and Simmons, T. 2007. The effect of repeated physical disturbance on soft tissue decomposition. Are taphonomic studies an accurate reflection of decomposition? *Journal of Forensic Sciences* 52(5):1007-1015.

Anderson, GS. 2001. Insect succession on carrion and its relationship to determining time of death. In: Byrd, JH. and Castner, JL. eds. *Forensic Entomology: The Utility of Arthropods in Legal Investigations.* Boca Raton, Florida: CRC Press, pp 143-176.

Bell, LS, Skinner, MF, and Jones, SH. 1996. The speed of post mortem change to the human skeleton and its taphonomic significance. *Forensic Science International* 82(2) 30: 129-140.

Borror, DJ, Delong, DW. and Triplehorn, CA. 1976. *An Introduction to the Study of Insects.* New York: Holt, Rinehart & Winston.

Byrd, JH. and Castner, J. eds. 2001. *Forensic Entomology: The Utility of Arthropods in Legal Investigations.* Boca Raton, Florida: CRC Press.

Catts, EP. and Goff, ML. 1992. Forensic entomology in criminal investigations. *Annual Review of Entomology* 37:253-272.

Davis, JB, and Goff, ML. 2000. Decomposition patterns in terrestrial and inter-tidal habitats on Oahu Island and Coconut Island, Hawaii. *Journal of Forensic Sciences* 45(4): 836-842.

Haskell, NH; McShaffrey, DG, Hawley, DA; Williams, RE, and Pless, JE. 1989. Use of aquatic insects in determining submersion interval. *Journal of Forensic Sciences* 34(3): 622-632.

Hill, A. 1979. Butchery and natural disarticulation: an investigatory technique. *American Antiquity* 44(4): 739-733.

Hill, A. and Behrensmeyer, AK. 1985. Natural disarticulation and bison butchery. *Antiquity* 50(1): 141-145.

Kuusela, S. and Hanski, I. 1982. The structure of carrion fly communities: the size and the type of carrion. *Holarctic Ecology* 5: 337-348.

Magyesi, MS, Nawrocki, SP. and Haskell, NH. 2005. Using accumulated degree-days to estimate the post-mortem interval from decomposed human remains. *Journal of Forensic Sciences* 50(3): 618-626.

Mayer, BX, Reiter, C, and Bereuter, TL. 1997. Investigation of the triacylglycerol composition of iceman's mummified tissue by high temperature gas chromatography. *Journal of Chromatography* 692: 1-6.

Ramsar convention on wetlands. 2002. *Lower Neretva valley transboundary wetland.* From: http://www.ramsar.org/wn/w.n.neretva_workshop2.htm [Viewed 05/01/2006].

Shalaby, OA, de Carvalho, LM, and Goff, ML. 2000. Comparison of patterns of decomposition in hanging carcass and a carcass in contact with soil in a xerophytic habitat on the island of Oahu, Hawaii. *Journal of Forensic Sciences* 45(6): 1267-73.

Smith, K. 1986. *A Manual of Forensic Entomology.* London: Trustees of the British Museum (Natural History).

Symes, SA. Williams, JA., Murray, EA, Hoffman, JM, Holland, TD, Saul, MJ, Saul, FP, and Pope, A. 2002. Taphonomic context of sharp force trauma in suspected cases of human mutilation and dismemberments. In: Haglund, W. and Sorg, MH. eds. *Advances in Forensic Taphonomy: Method, Theory, and Archaeological Perspectives.* CRC Press, Inc., pp403-434.

Syssovena, PR. 1958. Post mortem changes to human teeth with time. *Sudebnd-Medisthinskaya Ekspertiza I Kriminalistika na sluzhbe Sletsshviya* 2: 213–218.

Ubelaker, DH. 1997. Taphonomic applications in forensic anthropology. In: Haglund, WD. and Sorg, MH. *Forensic Taphonomy: The Post-Mortem Fate of Human Remains.* Boca Raton, Florida: CRC Press, pp77-99.

Vass, AA; Bass, WM, Wolt, JD, Foss, JE, and Ammons, JT. 1992. Time Since Death determinations of human cadavers using soil solution. *Journal of Forensic Sciences* 37(5):1236-1253.

Vass, AA. 2001. Beyond the grave-understanding human decomposition. *Microbiology Today* 11:190-192.

The expression of asymmetry in hand bones from the medieval cemetery at Écija, Spain

Lisa A. Cashmore and Sonia R. Zakrzewski

Centre for the Archaeology of Human Origins (CAHO) Archaeology, University of Southampton, Avenue Campus, Southampton, SO17 1BJ
lac1@soton.ac.uk

Abstract

The unique nature of 'handedness' in modern humans poses questions about the development of this trait in both extinct hominid species and archaeological populations. An examination of the expression of hand preference in skeletal material is required to answer such questions. The main focus of previous research on asymmetry and hand preference has been on the bones of the upper limb, rather than those of the hand. This study addresses this issue by exploring the expression of asymmetry in the metacarpals and phalanges in 65 adult skeletons from the Medieval Muslim cemetery in Écija, Spain. From comparisons of metric properties of the bones and muscle marker development, varying patterns of asymmetry distribution were found. Sex was found to have a highly significant effect on metric properties, but not on asymmetry scores or muscle development. Age was not found to be significant in any of the analyses. These results suggest that the expression of hand preference varies throughout the hand, and is influenced by the method with which it is assessed. The bones of the hand have an important contribution to make to handedness research, as long as care is paid to associated methodological issues.

Keywords: bilateral asymmetry, handedness, musculoskeletal stress markers

Introduction

Anatomical and functional differences between the left and right hands have long been of interest to researchers. This interest stems, in part, from the observation that in living modern human populations, up to 90% of individuals exhibit a strong preference for performing tasks with the right hand (Heçaen and de Ajuriaguerra 1964; McManus 1999). This strong, population-level hand preference is in contrast to that of non-human primate species. For example in chimpanzees, conflicting findings regarding the pattern of handedness distribution are found. An extensive meta-analysis of hand use in free-ranging chimpanzees (McGrew and Marchant 1997) found little evidence for lateralised behaviour, and concluded that population-level 'handedness', as displayed in modern humans, is not present in the great apes. Studies of captive chimpanzees, however, have identified a much stronger degree of lateralised hand use (Hopkins et al. 2002, 2005; Hopkins and Cantalupo 2005). In light of these conflicting results, it is not currently possible to draw any firm conclusions about hand preference in non-human primates.

The question now remains as to when 'handedness' in modern humans emerged and developed. Examination of skeletal material is potentially the most informative way of answering this question (Lazenby 2002). Traditionally, the approach to identifying hand preference in skeletal material has been through the assessment of upper limb bilateral asymmetry, particularly in the humerus (Stirland 1993, Steele 2000, Steele and Mays 1995, Blackburn and Knüsel 2006). The bones of the hand have been largely absent from studies of hand preference. One reason for this is the difficulty of studying hand bones, either in terms of the paucity of accurately sided material available

for study (particularly for extinct hominid species), or the minute differences in asymmetry due to the small size of the bones (Robb 1998). Some studies have attempted to look at the relationship between asymmetry and hand preference in the second metacarpal of humans (Garn et al. 1976; Plato et al. 1980; Roy et al. 1994; Mays 2002) and chimpanzees (Sarringhaus et al. 2005). They found that hand bones could be informative regarding the nature of the skeletal expression of handedness. However, more work is required to gain a complete understanding of the relationship between function and structure across the whole hand.

The aim of this study is to investigate the potential for the bones of the hand to provide a more complete picture of bilateral asymmetry in the upper limb. It also aims to shed light on the relationship between the expression of handedness in archaeological populations and living samples. To this end, the current study examines a range of data on the metacarpals and phalanges from an archaeological sample of modern humans. Both metric and musculoskeletal stress marker (MSM) analyses were performed. This allowed a comparison of two popular techniques, rarely used in tandem, to assess upper limb asymmetry. It will also explore the utility of MSM to provide information on the expression of asymmetry in the hand, an approach which has previously been avoided.

Materials

The Medieval Islamic site at Écija is situated approximately 80km east of Seville in southern Spain. It was a key town in the Muslim caliphate of al-Andalus during the Medieval period in the Iberian peninsula and the site of a significant battle in AD 711 (Jiménez nd;

Table 1. Measurements taken on metacarpals and phalanges (adapted from Bräuer 1988).

Code	Metacarpal and phalanx measurements	Description of measurement
mc*L	Length	Distance from the middle point of the surface of the base to the topmost point of the head
mc*RU	Radio-ulnar midshaft diameter	Maximum distance from the radial to the ulnar side at the midshaft, perpendicular to the long axis of the bone
mc*DP	Dorso-palmar midshaft diameter	Maximum distance from the radial to the ulnar side at the midshaft, parallel to the long axis of the bone
mc*PB	Maximum proximal breadth	Maximum breadth of the proximal end of the bone, measured perpendicular to the long axis of the bone
mc*DB	Maximum distal breadth	Maximum breadth of the distal end of the bone, measured perpendicular to the long axis of the bone
pp*L	Length of proximal phalanx	Distance from the middle point of the surface of the base to the topmost point of the head
ip*L	Length of intermediate phalanx	Distance from the middle point of the surface of the base to the topmost point of the head
dp*L	Length of distal phalanx	Distance from the middle point of the surface of the base to the topmost point of the head

*denotes metacarpal or phalanx number, e.g. mc1L, pp2L

Ortega nd; Román nd). Excavation of the town's Plaza de España between 1997 and 2002, uncovered the extensive Muslim cemetery, which appears to have been in constant use from the first post-Visigothic settlement in the early 8th century, until the region began to return to Christian rule in the 11th century. In osteological terms, Écija is of interest due to the size of the collection, the preservation of the material and the clear cultural identity of the sample. Rules regarding burial in Islamic society state that all individuals are equal in death. Bodies of the deceased must be wrapped or dressed in simple cloth and placed in graves without coffins, on their right side, facing Mecca. The depositing of grave goods is not permitted (Insoll 1999). Despite some variation in the adherence to these rules, these practices leave a clear archaeological signature, confirming the Muslim status of the Écija cemetery.

A total of over 4500 skeletons were excavated from the Écija site. Although the general preservation of individuals across the site was very good, several skeletons exhibited crushing due to the number of grave layers deposited on the site. Therefore, not all individuals were suitable for study. A total of 65 adults were included in the study. These were selected primarily on the basis of good preservation of the hand bones, and if possible, the humerus. Skeletons exhibiting pathologies likely to impair the proper functioning of the upper limb were excluded from analysis. Age and sex was determined by the methods outlined by Brothwell (1981), Lovejoy et al. (1985), Buikstra and Ubelaker (1994), Schwartz (1995) and O'Connell (2004). Within each of the sex categories, individuals were defined as either 'young adult' (17-30 years), 'middle adult' (30-45 years) or 'old adult' (45+ years). Only five individuals were classed as 'old adult', with majority scored as either

'young adult' (n=35), or 'middle adult' (n=25). Of the 65 skeletons, 35 (53.8%) were male and 30 (46.2%) female.

Methods

For each individual, a series of measurements were taken on the metacarpals and phalanges, on both the left and right sides. For the most part, hand bones were bagged according to side immediately after excavation. However, for a number of individuals, all hand bones were bagged together. On these occasions, metacarpals were siding using the methods described in Matshes et al. (2005). Although the siding of phalanges is known to be problematic, siding of mixed phalanges was attempted using the method proposed in Case and Heilman (2006). While the exact accuracy of this method on the Écija sample can not be known, it was considered accurate enough to warrant inclusion of this data in the current study, and potential siding issues were considered during the interpretation of the results of the phalanx data analysis.

The measurements encompassed both the metric properties of the bones, as well as analysis of MSM development. For the metacarpals and phalanges the measurements, taken from Bräuer (1988), are outlined in Table 1.

Radiographic and computer tomographic (CT) scanning facilities were not available for this study, so metric data was favoured over geometric data. Studies by Stock and Shaw (2007) and Pearson et al. (2007) have found a clear correlation between externally-derived and cross-sectional diaphyseal properties, suggesting that standard metric measurements still have relevance to analyses of diaphyseal robusticity. Due to time constraints, it was not

Table 2. Measurement error (mm) in the Great Chesterford metacarpal sample.

	Side	N	Average error	% error
mc1L	L	19	0.5	1.13
	R	17	0.3	0.77
mc2L	L	20	0.3	0.48
	R	21	0.5	0.69
mc3L	L	18	0.4	0.58
	R	23	0.3	0.41
mc4L	L	16	0.2	0.41
	R	20	0.5	0.86
mc5L	L	14	0.3	0.49
	R	19	0.3	0.53
mc1RU	L	18	0.3	2.64
	R	18	0.2	1.92
mc2RU	L	22	0.4	4.25
	R	21	0.3	4.12
mc3RU	L	20	0.1	1.58
	R	24	0.2	2.17
mc4RU	L	21	0.2	3.37
	R	21	0.2	3.45
mc5RU	L	17	0.5	6.25
	R	20	0.4	5.52
mc1DP	L	18	0.2	2.44
	R	18	0.2	2.22
mc2DP	L	22	0.2	2.76
	R	21	0.3	3.45
mc3DP	L	19	0.2	2.31
	R	24	0.2	2.28
mc4DP	L	21	0.3	4.27
	R	21	0.2	3.09
mc5DP	L	17	0.4	6.26
	R	20	0.5	6.86
mc1PB	L	19	0.4	2.70
	R	17	0.3	1.90
mc2PB	L	20	0.5	3.16
	R	21	0.7	4.22
mc3PB	L	17	0.6	4.26
	R	23	0.5	3.79
mc4PB	L	18	0.4	3.63
	R	20	0.3	2.71
mc5PB	L	12	1.0	8.33
	R	21	1.0	7.93
mc1DB	L	18	0.4	3.04
	R	18	0.5	3.18
mc2DB	L	19	0.7	4.97
	R	19	0.3	2.19
mc3DB	L	17	0.3	2.46
	R	22	0.5	3.29
mc4DB	L	19	0.3	2.35
	R	19	0.3	2.75
mc5DB	L	15	0.2	1.95
	R	18	0.2	1.31

cemetery site of Great Chesterford, Essex (Evison 1994), curated at the University of Southampton. Measurement error was quantified as the absolute difference between two corresponding measurements, following Sarringhaus et al. (2005). Table 2 provides the results of this analysis for the Great Chesterford metacarpal material, represented as the average difference between corresponding measurements and this average difference as a percentage of the average measurement value. Table 3 provides the results of this analysis for the Great Chesterford phalanx material.

From Table 2, it can be seen that average measurement error for the metacarpals is low, with no variable showing an error greater than 1mm. These errors appear larger when considered as a percentage of the average measurement value. This is most likely due to the small size of the metacarpal measurements. This is evident when metacarpal length percentages, which represent the largest measurements, are compared with other metacarpal dimensions. While the majority of percentage errors are below 5%, six out of 50 (12%) are over 5%. These measurements are all for the fifth metacarpal, suggesting particular issues in taking measurements on this bone.

Again, this may be a reflection of the gracile nature of this bone relative to the other metacarpals. Observer experience may also contribute to the level of error, as this was limited in pilot study. Table 3 shows a low level of measurement error in the phalanx sample. With the majority of measurements having an average difference of less than 1mm. Twenty-six (93%) out of 28 measurements show a percentage error of less than 2%, and within acceptable limits (Auerbach and Ruff 2006). Small sample size is likely to be the cause of the greater than 2% measurement error found for left and right dp4L. Taken together, these results suggest that care must be exercised when taking hand bone measurements to ensure low measurement error.

Asymmetry in the Écija metacarpals and phalanges was assessed by calculating the percentage difference between corresponding left side and right side measurements using the equation by Trinkaus et al. (1994):

$$(\text{min value} - \text{max value})/\text{min value} \times 100$$

This equation has been used in a number of studies (e.g. Churchill and Formicola 1997; Rhodes and Knüsel 2005; Sarringhaus et al. 2005; Lieverse et al. 2008), and benefits from maximising the perceived asymmetry between the sides, particularly in cases where the variation is small and stochastic in nature. This analysis was performed on a combined-sex, combined-age sample. To assess whether side dominances identified were statistically significant, Wilcoxon tests were performed on each pair of left and right measurements, and on the combined-age and combined-sex sample. To assess the effects of sex and age, an univariate General Linear Model (GLM) ANOVA was performed. A Mann-

possible to collect the duplicate data required to calculate measurement error for the Écija sample. However, measurement error was calculated for the metacarpal and phalanx material used in an earlier pilot study to assess the suitability of the methods. This pilot study was carried out on 26 skeletons from the Anglo-Saxon

Table 3. Measurement error (mm) in the Great
Chesterford phalanx sample

	Side	N	Average error	%error
pp1L	L	19	0.4	1.52
	R	19	0.4	1.32
pp2L	L	16	0.5	1.38
	R	18	0.3	0.79
pp3L	L	16	0.4	1.00
	R	20	0.4	0.83
pp4L	L	17	0.6	1.41
	R	20	0.5	1.19
pp5L	L	16	0.4	1.34
	R	17	0.2	0.60
ip2L	L	11	0.4	1.79
	R	10	0.2	0.96
ip3L	L	13	0.3	0.92
	R	14	0.5	1.79
ip4L	L	10	0.3	1.21
	R	12	0.4	1.31
ip5L	L	10	0.2	0.92
	R	15	0.1	0.64
dp1L	L	9	0.3	1.40
	R	9	0.3	1.14
dp2L	L	5	0.3	1.55
	R	2	0.1	0.58
dp3L	L	6	0.3	1.34
		9	0.3	1.63
dp4L	L	2	1.2	6.67
	R	4	0.4	2.12
dp5L	L	5	0.3	1.85
	R	6	0.2	1.03

Whitney U test was carried out to assess the effects of sex on asymmetry scores.

Asymmetry was also assessed through the analysis of MSM development. Traditionally, the development of muscle attachments has been scored on an ordinal scale (i.e. Hawkey and Merbs 1995). In this system, features such as robusticity, stress lesions and ossification exostoses are graded on a scale of 0-4, with each number representing an increase in the expression of that feature. This system has a certain subjective element, as each researcher must establish the scale for each skeletal collection studied. While this method can be suitable for the long bones of the body (where the size of the muscle and therefore, the resulting muscle attachment site is relatively large), it is not suitable for the hand, where the muscle attachment sites are smaller and show less variation (Robb 1998). Instead, the current study uses an alternative method for assessing MSM proposed by al-Oumaoui et al. (2004). Rather than using a scalar method, MSMs are rated on a simple presence/absence basis. While an individual scoring system has to be set up for each sample, this method allows for muscle attachments of a smaller size to be studied and standardises MSM analysis for cross-study comparisons. Figure 1 illustrates the criteria used to determined presence and absence of MSM for the *opponens digiti minimi*.

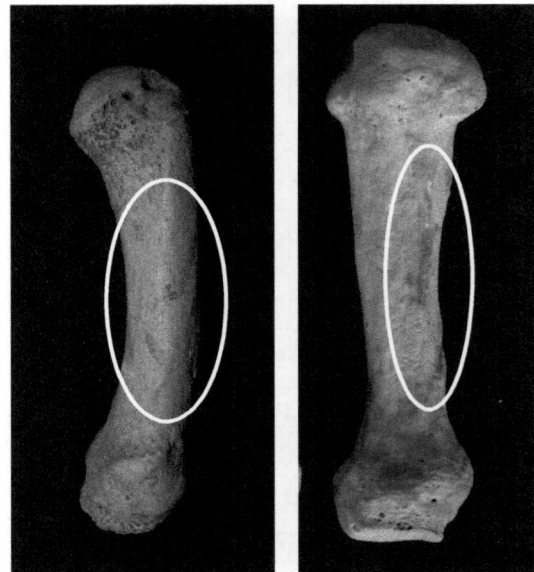

Figure 1. Criteria used to assess the (a) absence (left), and (b) presence (right) of the *opponens digiti minimi* muscle attachment on the medial side of the fifth metacarpal. The areas of absence and presence are within the area of the circle marked on each picture.

A pilot study was conducted to test the applicability of the presence/absence methodology to the muscles of the hand. It was not possible to reliably identify and score a number of the muscle attachment sites on the metacarpals (where the majority of the muscles originate/attach). For this reason, muscles could not be selected based on their functional properties alone, (see Marzke et al. 1998). Instead, muscles were selected based on the ease at which they could be identified on dry bone. Table 4 outlines the muscles chosen for the current study. A McNemar test of association was performed to identify statistically significant differences between left and right MSM pairs. A chi-squared test (χ^2) was used to identify associations between sex, age and MSM score.

Results

Metric analysis

Figure 2 and Table 5 summarise the results of the asymmetry calculation for the metacarpals, plotted as percentage asymmetry values. These results indicate clear right-side dominance in the metacarpals, or that all of the measurements, are larger on the right side than the left. The magnitude of this right-side dominance, however, is variable, ranging from only 51% (mc3L) to 91.5% (mc5DP). In modern studies, the natural right to left side dominance has been estimated at around 90% (e.g. Heçaen and de Ajuriaguerra 1964; McManus 1999). In total, only 11 out of the 25 measurements exhibit an asymmetry value greater than 70%, suggesting that the expression of asymmetry across, and within, the metacarpals is more variable than might have been expected.

Table 4. Muscles of hand scored for development of musculoskeletal stress markers.

Code	Muscle	Location of measurement	Action of muscle
FPL	Flexor pollicis longus	Palmar surface of base of distal pollical phalanx	Flexion of thumb
APT	Adductor pollicis (transverse)	Palmar surface of third metacarpal	Adduction and flexion of thumb
ODM	Opponens digiti minimi	Medial edge of fifth metacarpal	Rotation of mc5 into opposition with thumb, draw mc5 forward, assists in flexion of 5th carpometacarpal joint
FDP	Flexor digitorum profundus 2,3,4 and 5	Palmar surface of base of distal phalanges 2,3,4 and 5	Flexion of distal interphalangeal joints of 2-5. Assists in adduction of 2nd, 4th and 5th digits and flexion at wrist
FDS	Flexor digitorum superficialis 2,3,4 and 5	Both sides of the palmar surface of intermediate phalanges 2,3,4 and 5	Flexion of intermediate phalanges of digits 2-5, and wrist
PI2	Palmar interosseous 2	Palmar surface of second metacarpal	Adduction of digits towards centre of 3rd digit, at metacarpophalangeal joints.
PI3	Palmar interosseous 3	Palmar surface of third metacarpal	Assist in flexion of digits at these joints
PI4	Palmar interosseous 4	Palmar surface of fourth metacarpal	Assist in flexion of digits at these joints
DI1	Dorsal interosseous 1	Medial edge of mc1 and lateral edge of mc2	Abduction of 2nd, 3rd and 4th digits from the midline of the hand
DI2	Dorsal interosseous 2	Medial edge of mc2 and lateral edge of mc3	Abduction of 2nd, 3rd and 4th digits from the midline of the hand
DI3	Dorsal interosseous 3	Medial edge of mc3 and lateral edge of mc4	Abduction of 2nd, 3rd and 4th digits from the midline of the hand
DI4	Dorsal interosseous 4	Medial edge of mc4 and lateral edge of mc5	Abduction of 2nd, 3rd and 4th digits from the midline of the hand

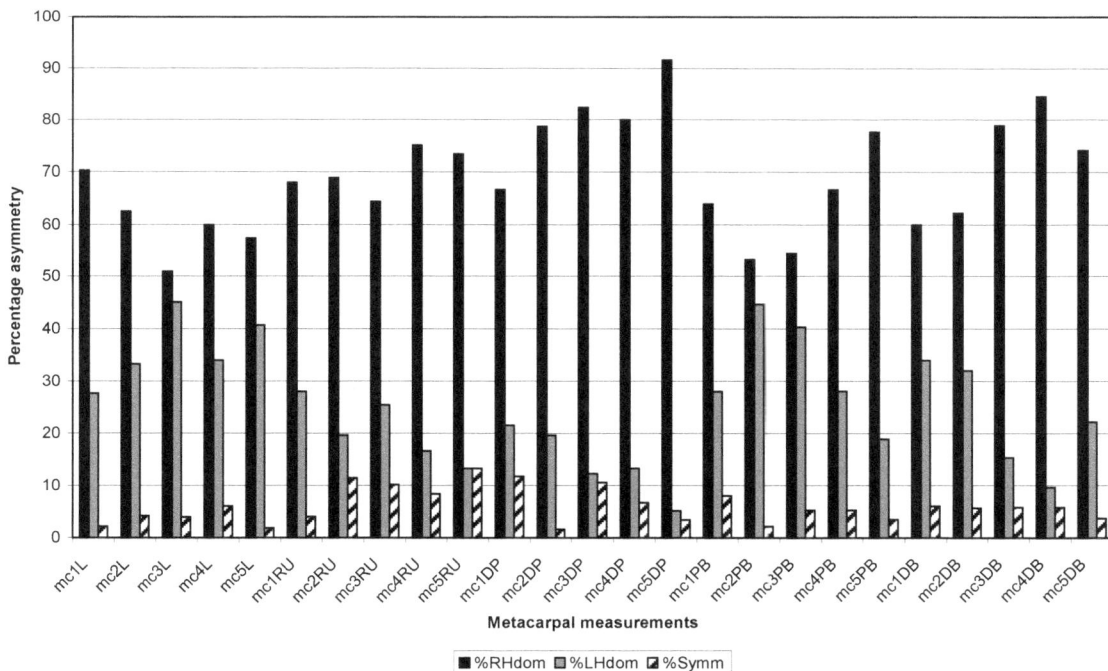

Figure 2. Percentage of right- and left-side dominant and symmetric individuals for all metacarpal measurements

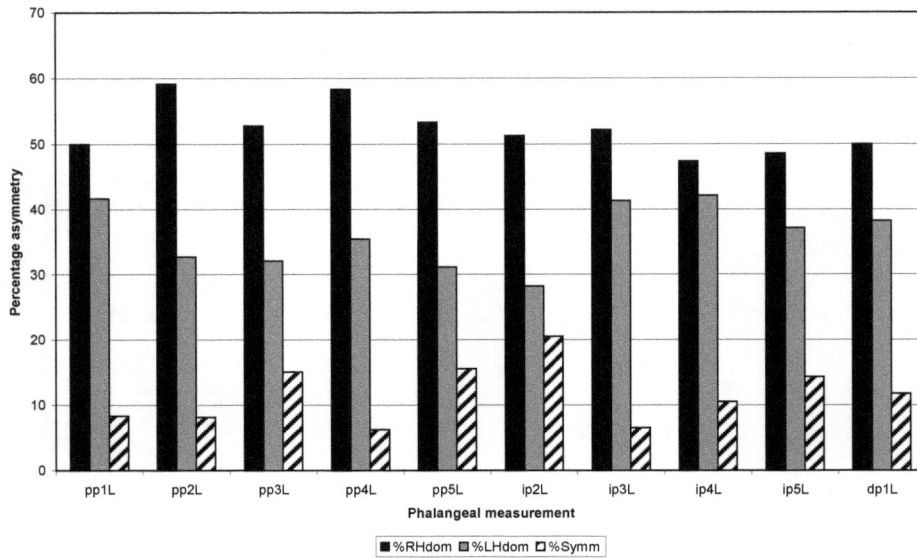

Figure 3. Percentage of right- and left-side dominant and symmetric individuals for all proximal and intermediate phalanx measurements. Due to small sample sizes, distal phalanges 2 to 5 were excluded from the analysis.

Looking at each of the metacarpal measurements in more detail identifies certain trends in the distribution of asymmetry. For metacarpal length, there is a decrease in asymmetry, moving medially across the metacarpal row (from mc1 to mc5), with a pronounced dip at mc3L, which is approaching symmetry. For the other metacarpal measurements, however, this pattern is reversed, with asymmetry increasing from mc1 to mc5.

While the level of asymmetry in the metacarpal measurements is generally low, there is variation between the measurements. The degree of asymmetry is greatest in the

dorso-palmar diameter measurements, with proximal breadth measurements showing the lowest levels of asymmetry. Generally, the metacarpal shaft, represented by mcRU and mcDP, appears to exhibit stronger right-side asymmetry than measurements of the head and base (mcDB and mcPB). This pattern supports the observation that, in the long bones, diaphyses tend to be more asymmetric than articular surfaces due to continued remodelling of the bone shaft after epiphyseal fusion (Ruff 2000).

When each metacarpal is studied individually, metacarpals 2 to 5 show a broadly similar pattern of asymmetry, with clear differences in asymmetry between the various measurements, but with the pattern remaining the same for each metacarpal. Metacarpal 1 is the exception, as asymmetry is almost constant across all measurements, with only a 10% difference between the largest and smallest right-side dominant values. Percentage asymmetry differences were also calculated for the phalanges, using the Trinkaus et al.'s (1994) equation (Table 6) Figure 3 plots these asymmetry values.

Table 5. Metacarpal asymmetry equation data.

	N	% left-side dominant	% right-side dominant	% symmetrical
mc1L	47	27.7	70.2	2.1
mc2L	48	33.3	62.5	4.2
mc3L	51	45.1	51.0	3.9
mc4L	50	34.0	60.0	6.0
mc5L	54	40.7	57.4	1.9
mc1RU	50	28.0	68.0	4.0
mc2RU	61	19.7	68.9	11.5
mc3RU	59	25.4	64.4	10.2
mc4RU	60	16.7	75.0	8.3
mc5RU	60	13.3	73.3	13.3
mc1DP	51	21.6	66.7	11.8
mc2DP	61	19.7	78.7	1.6
mc3DP	57	12.3	82.5	10.5
mc4DP	60	13.3	80.0	6.7
mc5DP	59	5.1	91.5	3.4
mc1PB	50	28.0	64.0	8.0
mc2PB	47	44.7	53.2	2.1
mc3PB	57	40.4	54.4	5.3
mc4PB	57	28.1	66.7	5.3
mc5PB	58	19.0	77.6	3.4
mc1DB	50	34.0	60.0	6.0
mc2DB	53	32.1	62.3	5.7
mc3DB	52	15.4	78.8	5.8
mc4DB	52	9.6	84.6	5.8
mc5DB	54	22.2	74.1	3.7

What is immediately clear from Figure 3 is that, while there is a right-side dominance of all of the phalanges, the level of asymmetry is greatly reduced compared to that of the metacarpals. Right-side dominance ranges from 47.4% (ip4L) to 59.2% (pp2L), compared to the metacarpals, where only four variables (mc3L, mc5L, mc2PB, mc3PB) out of 25 had a right-side asymmetry value of less than 60%. This shows a very uniform distribution in asymmetry in the finger bones, with no clear pattern emerging. This may be a reflection of functional differences in the utilisation of the fingers compared to the metacarpals.

Table 6. Data from phalanx asymmetry equation

	N	% left-side dominant	% right-side dominant	% symmetrical
pp1L	48	41.7	50.0	8.3
pp2L	49	32.7	59.2	8.2
pp3L	53	32.1	52.8	15.1
pp4L	48	35.4	58.3	6.3
pp5L	45	31.1	53.3	15.6
ip2L	39	28.2	51.3	20.5
ip3L	46	41.3	52.2	6.5
ip4L	38	42.1	47.4	10.5
ip5L	35	37.1	48.6	14.3
dp1L	34	38.2	50.0	11.8
dp2L	5	40.0	60.0	0.0
dp3L	14	42.9	42.9	14.3
dp4L	10	60.0	30.0	10.0
dp5L	6	33.3	50.0	16.7

Wilcoxon tests (Table 7) performed on each pair of left and right measurements found that, for the majority of metacarpal measurements, the difference between the left and right sides was highly significant (p<0.01). The exceptions were mc3L (p=0.49), mc5L (p=0.15), mc2PB (p=0.51) and mc3PB (p=0.36). This supports the findings of the previous analysis, where these four measurements were the only ones exhibiting right-side dominance less than 60%. In keeping with the analysis in Figure 3, the Wilcoxon significance test for the phalanges (Table 8) identified only three significant left/right differences, pp2L (p=0.05), pp3L (p=0.01), and ip2L (p=0.03). Again, this is in line with the trends identified in the asymmetry analysis.

The GLM ANOVA (Table 9) shows that, for the metacarpals, sex was highly significant, with the only exceptions being right mc2L (p=0.07), and left and right mc5PB (p=0.08 and p=0.82, respectively). For age, the opposite was true, with only left mc5DB (p=0.05) showing significance. This was repeated in the phalanges (Table 10), with sex being strongly significant, with age less so. Perhaps due to small sample sizes for the distal phalanges, the effect of sex was limited in the distal phalanges, but if these are excluded (as per the previous analysis), then it only left ip4L (p=0.06), right ip5L (p=0.15) and left and right dp1L (p=0.07 and p=0.21, respectively) that do not have significant *p*-values.

The Mann-Whitney U test for the metacarpals (Table 11) found that, in contrast to the ANOVA on the metric properties, the influence of sex on metacarpal asymmetry was very limited, with significance only being found for mc2RU (p = 0.03), mc3RU (p < 0.01), mc3DP (p = 0.05) and mc4PB (p = 0.02). For phalanx asymmetry (Table 12), the effect was limited further, with only dp4L showing a significant sex effect (p = 0.03).

MSM analysis
The MSM development at four muscle insertion sites and eight origin sites (Table 4)

Table 7. Wilcoxon test results for the Écija metacarpal sample.

	Side	N	Mean	SD	Sig. (2-tailed)
mc1L	L	55	42.97	3.18	**p < 0.01**
	R	56	43.77	3.08	
mc2L	L	54	64.95	4.02	**p = 0.01**
	R	53	65.22	3.99	
mc3L	L	57	62.60	4.16	p = 0.49
	R	59	62.66	4.17	
mc4L	L	52	55.77	3.78	**p = 0.03**
	R	62	55.84	3.61	
mc5L	L	58	51.74	4.02	p = 0.15
	R	61	51.96	3.44	
mc1RU	L	57	11.55	1.12	**p < 0.01**
	R	58	12.00	1.05	
mc2RU	L	62	8.09	0.77	**p < 0.01**
	R	64	8.28	0.82	
mc3RU	L	62	8.27	0.72	**p < 0.01**
	R	62	8.42	0.73	
mc4RU	L	60	6.65	0.62	**p < 0.01**
	R	65	6.98	0.71	
mc5RU	L	61	7.56	0.77	**p < 0.01**
	R	64	8.02	0.95	
mc1DP	L	57	8.40	1.16	**p < 0.01**
	R	58	8.53	0.96	
mc2DP	L	62	8.72	0.87	**p < 0.01**
	R	64	9.00	0.85	
mc3DP	L	62	8.84	0.91	**p < 0.01**
	R	62	9.28	0.80	
mc4DP	L	60	7.32	0.82	**p < 0.01**
	R	65	7.63	0.85	
mc5DP	L	61	6.80	0.86	**p < 0.01**
	R	63	7.28	0.89	
mc1PB	L	56	14.85	1.59	**p = 0.02**
	R	58	15.10	1.43	
mc2PB	L	55	16.53	1.54	p = 0.51
	R	56	16.37	1.63	
mc3PB	L	61	13.50	1.19	p = 0.36
	R	60	13.57	1.08	
mc4PB	L	58	11.81	0.99	**p < 0.01**
	R	63	12.04	0.99	
mc5PB	L	60	11.18	1.14	**p < 0.01**
	R	63	11.74	1.09	
mc1DB	L	57	13.71	1.34	**p < 0.01**
	R	58	14.01	1.21	
mc2DB	L	58	13.42	1.12	**p < 0.01**
	R	58	13.64	1.19	
mc3DB	L	58	13.26	1.09	**p < 0.01**
	R	59	13.60	1.07	
mc4DB	L	55	11.39	0.89	**p < 0.01**
	R	61	11.74	0.91	
mc5DB	L	58	11.06	0.73	**p < 0.01**
	R	61	11.25	0.84	

Significant p values highlighted in bold.

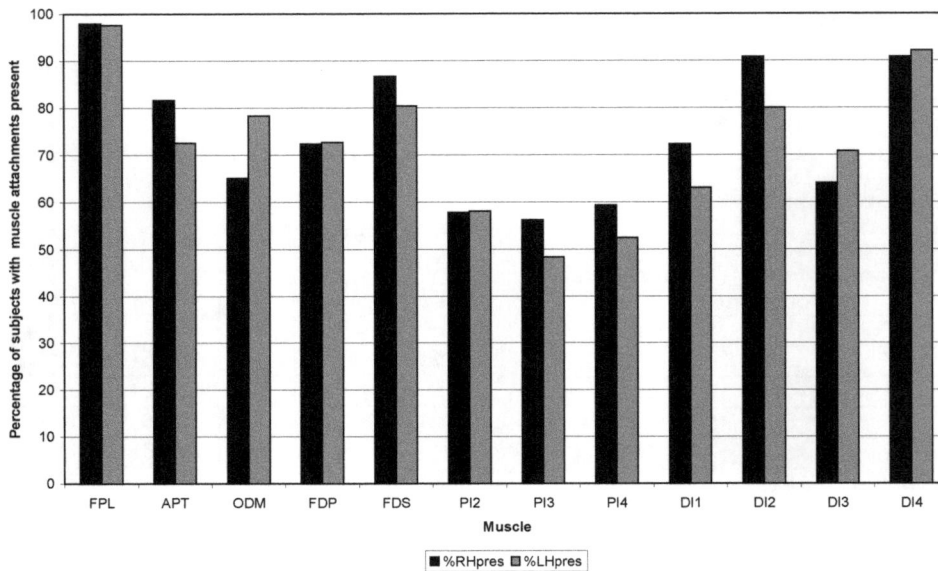

Figure 4. For all MSM, the percentage of individuals for which the muscle attachment was scored as 'present' for the right hand (black) and 'present' for the left hand (grey).

Table 8. Wilcoxon test results for the Écija phalanx sample.

	Side	N	Mean	SD	Sig. (2-tailed)
pp1L	L	53	28.53	2.30	p = 0.23
	R	53	28.64	2.31	
pp2L	L	53	38.48	2.55	**p = 0.05**
	R	54	38.38	2.56	
pp3L	L	57	42.52	2.94	**p = 0.01**
	R	59	42.81	2.77	
pp4L	L	52	40.25	2.63	*p = 0.07*
	R	58	40.10	2.84	
pp5L	L	52	31.51	2.09	*p = 0.08*
	R	52	31.89	1.96	
ip2L	L	45	22.77	1.83	**p = 0.03**
	R	49	23.00	1.76	
ip3L	L	50	27.59	2.67	p = 0.18
	R	53	27.80	2.58	
ip4L	L	41	26.27	1.93	p = 0.47
	R	48	26.19	1.80	
ip5L	L	41	18.54	1.64	p = 0.20
	R	51	18.38	1.60	
dp1L	L	42	21.52	1.76	p = 0.33
	R	46	21.84	1.82	
dp2L	L	11	17.01	1.19	p = 1.00
	R	14	16.49	1.15	
dp3L	L	18	18.09	1.30	p = 0.68
	R	26	18.22	1.34	
dp4L	L	17	17.63	1.52	p = 0.63
	R	16	17.61	1.17	
dp5L	L	10	16.42	1.90	p = 0.50
	R	17	16.14	1.60	

Significant p values highlighted in bold. P values approaching significance (i.e. between 0.055 and 0.1) highlighted in italics.

was scored as either 'present' or 'absent'. This scoring was repeated for MSM on both the left and the right hand. The percentage of individuals for which an attachment site was rated as 'present' was then plotted (Table 13, see appendix and Figure 4) in order to compare left and right hand MSM asymmetry.

Results shown in Figure 4 indicate that there is very little asymmetry in this sample in terms of MSM development.

Of the twelve MSM scored, seven showed a right-side dominance (i.e. scored as 'present' on the right side more frequently than on the left) and five showed a left-side dominance. The McNemar test of association (Table 14, see appendix) found that there were no statistically significant differences between left and right MSM pairs. The lack of asymmetry in the MSM is in contrast to the findings of the metric analysis, where all of the measurements showed clear right-side dominance.

Despite of the lack of asymmetry, a number of patterns can be identified in the right-side dominant muscles (FPL, APT, FDS, PI3, PI4, DI1, and DI2) compared to those that were left-side dominant (ODM, FDP, PI2, DI3 and DI4). While the flexors (FPL, FDP and FDS) and the mc5-centred muscles (ODM, PI4, dominance, muscles attached to the second metacarpal (DI1, DI2) and those attached to the third metacarpal (DI3, DI4) show the same pattern of dominance. While not conclusive, this suggests possible identifiable links between muscle function and the development of asymmetry.

It can be seen from Figure 4 that there are differences in the degree to which each muscle is rated as present. The *palmar interossei* (PI2, PI3, PI4) muscles in particular are recorded as 'present' less than 60% of the time. While this may be related to the function and expression of this muscle, it may also be a result of the difficulty with which these MSM sites were identified on dry bone. The FPL insertion site, by contrast, was identified as 'present' on approximately 98% DI4) do not show consistent patterns of side of occasions. While this muscle is readily identifiable on archaeological material, it is also a

functionally prominent muscle in the function of the human hand (Susman 1988; Marzke 2000).

The χ^2 test (Table 15) revealed that sex was only significantly associated with left-FDS (p=0.04), right-DI1

Table 9. GLM ANOVA results for the effects of sex and age on metacarpal properties.

	Side	N	Mean	Sex		Age	
				F	Sig.	F	Sig.
mc1L	L	55	42.97	37.10	**p < 0.01**	0.17	p = 0.85
	R	56	43.77	10.86	**p < 0.01**	0.92	p = 0.41
mc2L	L	54	64.95	10.94	**p < 0.01**	0.37	p = 0.69
	R	53	65.22	3.45	*p = 0.07*	1.28	p = 0.29
mc3L	L	57	62.60	22.68	**p < 0.01**	0.60	p = 0.56
	R	59	62.66	18.42	**p < 0.01**	1.51	p = 0.23
mc4L	L	52	55.77	22.42	**p < 0.01**	0.77	p = 0.47
	R	62	55.84	20.85	**p < 0.01**	0.39	p = 0.68
mc5L	L	58	51.74	26.02	**p < 0.01**	0.71	p = 0.50
	R	61	51.96	25.43	**p < 0.01**	0.14	p = 0.87
mc1RU	L	57	11.55	10.42	**p < 0.01**	0.47	p = 0.63
	R	58	12.00	12.42	**p < 0.01**	1.56	p = 0.22
mc2RU	L	62	8.09	21.80	**p < 0.01**	0.25	p = 0.78
	R	64	8.28	11.47	**p < 0.01**	0.82	p = 0.45
mc3RU	L	62	8.27	11.16	**p < 0.01**	0.39	p = 0.68
	R	62	8.42	9.29	**p < 0.01**	0.85	p = 0.44
mc4RU	L	60	6.65	9.95	**p < 0.01**	0.70	p = 0.50
	R	65	6.98	6.64	**p = 0.01**	0.56	p = 0.58
mc5RU	L	61	7.56	9.38	**p < 0.01**	0.20	p = 0.82
	R	64	8.02	8.57	**p < 0.01**	1.24	p = 0.30
mc1DP	L	57	8.40	14.57	**p < 0.01**	0.02	p = 0.98
	R	58	8.53	12.97	**p < 0.01**	0.05	p = 0.95
mc2DP	L	62	8.72	7.65	**p < 0.01**	0.63	p = 0.53
	R	64	9.00	8.50	**p < 0.01**	0.22	p = 0.81
mc3DP	L	62	8.84	8.34	**p < 0.01**	0.15	p = 0.86
	R	62	9.28	6.82	**p = 0.01**	0.53	p = 0.59
mc4DP	L	60	7.32	11.26	**p < 0.01**	0.65	p = 0.52
	R	65	7.63	9.70	**p < 0.01**	0.30	p = 0.74
mc5DP	L	61	6.80	7.18	**p = 0.01**	0.05	p = 0.95
	R	63	7.28	4.99	**p = 0.03**	0.08	p = 0.92
mc1PB	L	56	14.85	15.47	**p < 0.01**	1.72	p = 0.19
	R	58	15.10	14.19	**p < 0.01**	2.09	p = 0.13
mc2PB	L	55	16.53	8.27	**p < 0.01**	1.50	p = 0.23
	R	56	16.37	5.32	**p < 0.01**	0.05	p = 0.95
mc3PB	L	61	13.50	16.23	**p < 0.01**	0.14	p = 0.87
	R	60	13.57	1.59	**p < 0.01**	0.42	p = 0.66
mc4PB	L	58	11.81	13.81	**p < 0.01**	0.10	p = 0.90
	R	63	12.04	6.78	**p = 0.01**	0.50	p = 0.61
mc5PB	L	60	11.18	3.28	*p = 0.08*	0.87	p = 0.42
	R	63	11.74	0.05	p = 0.82	0.92	p = 0.41
mc1DB	L	57	13.71	33.17	**p < 0.01**	0.66	p = 0.52
	R	58	14.01	21.03	**p < 0.01**	2.56	*p = 0.09*
mc2DB	L	58	13.42	21.40	**p < 0.01**	0.68	p = 0.51
	R	58	13.64	13.14	**p < 0.01**	0.79	p = 0.46
mc3DB	L	58	13.26	21.63	**p < 0.01**	0.31	p = 0.73
	R	59	13.60	15.43	**p < 0.01**	0.07	p = 0.93
mc4DB	L	55	11.39	11.69	**p < 0.01**	0.26	p = 0.77
	R	61	11.74	13.46	**p < 0.01**	1.14	p = 0.33
mc5DB	L	58	11.06	10.47	**p < 0.01**	3.09	**p = 0.05**
	R	61	11.25	16.01	**p < 0.01**	0.95	p = 0.39

Significant p values highlighted in bold. P values approaching significance (i.e. between 0.055 and 0.1) highlighted in italics.

Table 10. GLM ANOVA results for the effects of sex and age on phalanx properties.

	Side	N	Mean	Sex		Age	
				F	Sig.	F	Sig.
pp1L	L	53	28.53	9.57	**p < 0.01**	0.58	p = 0.56
	R	53	28.64	16.76	**p < 0.01**	0.20	p = 0.82
pp2L	L	53	38.48	27.94	**p < 0.01**	0.43	p = 0.66
	R	54	38.38	24.48	**p < 0.01**	0.20	p = 0.82
pp3L	L	57	42.52	32.47	**p < 0.01**	0.03	p = 0.97
	R	59	42.81	28.95	**p < 0.01**	0.21	p = 0.81
pp4L	L	52	40.25	26.24	**p < 0.01**	0.06	p = 0.94
	R	58	40.10	14.44	**p < 0.01**	0.26	p = 0.77
pp5L	L	52	31.51	19.86	**p < 0.01**	0.20	p = 0.82
	R	52	31.89	9.48	**p < 0.01**	1.93	p = 0.16
ip2L	L	45	22.77	18.23	**p < 0.01**	0.38	p = 0.69
	R	49	23.00	9.36	**p < 0.01**	0.80	p = 0.45
ip3L	L	50	27.59	8.84	**p < 0.01**	0.22	p = 0.81
	R	53	27.80	7.03	**p = 0.01**	0.13	p = 0.88
ip4L	L	41	26.27	3.89	*p = 0.06*	0.76	p = 0.47
	R	48	26.19	4.24	**p = 0.05**	0.43	p = 0.65
ip5L	L	41	18.54	9.03	**p < 0.01**	0.04	p = 0.96
	R	51	18.38	2.11	p = 0.15	0.54	p = 0.58
dp1L	L	42	21.52	3.62	*p = 0.07*	1.21	p = 0.31
	R	46	21.84	1.61	p = 0.21	0.13	p = 0.88
dp2L	L	11	17.01	0.82	p = 0.40	0.23	p = 0.80
	R	14	16.49	0.53	p = 0.48	0.39	p = 0.69
dp3L	L	18	18.09	1.45	p = 0.25	0.98	p = 0.40
		26	18.22	9.51	**p < 0.01**	0.74	p = 0.49
dp4L	L	17	17.63	7.05	**p = 0.02**	0.33	p = 0.73
	R	16	17.61	8.43	**p = 0.01**	0.05	p = 0.95
dp5L	L	10	16.42	2.94	p = 0.13	0.52	p = 0.50
	R	17	16.14	0.99	p = 0.34	1.03	p = 0.39

Table 11. Mann-Whitney U test for the effect of sex on metacarpal asymmetry.

	N	mean	sd	U	Sig. (2-tailed)
mc1L	47	1.37	1.13	213.0	p = 0.22
mc2L	48	0.93	0.91	250.0	p = 0.54
mc3L	51	1.11	0.81	318.5	p = 0.95
mc4L	50	1.25	0.98	265.5	p = 0.45
mc5L	54	1.24	1.02	340.5	p = 0.79
mc1R	50	4.33	3.47	229.5	p = 0.14
mc2R	61	5.52	4.50	306.5	**p = 0.03**
mc3R	59	3.98	3.15	263.0	**p < 0.01**
mc4R	60	6.29	4.40	436.5	p = 0.90
mc5R	60	6.85	6.01	340.0	p = 0.12
mc1D	51	3.94	3.62	233.0	*p = 0.10*
mc2D	61	4.91	3.35	413.0	p = 0.55
mc3D	59	5.73	4.42	313.0	**p = 0.05**
mc4D	60	5.07	3.54	431.0	p = 0.83
mc5D	59	8.23	5.84	418.0	p = 0.84
mc1P	50	4.22	3.11	249.0	p = 0.28
mc2P	47	4.32	3.54	257.5	p = 0.94
mc3P	57	3.18	2.44	358.0	p = 0.45
mc4P	57	4.45	3.19	247.5	**p = 0.02**
mc5P	58	6.47	5.19	311.5	*p = 0.10*
mc1D	50	2.78	2.03	297.5	p = 0.84
mc2D	53	3.23	2.51	279.0	p = 0.24
mc3D	52	4.01	2.49	321.5	p = 0.83
mc4D	52	4.06	2.61	299.5	p = 0.54
mc5D	54	3.64	2.42	296.5	p = 0.27

Table 12. Mann-Whitney U test for the effect of sex on phalanx asymmetry.

	N	mean	sd	U	Sig. (2-tailed)
pp1L	48	1.47	1.34	195.5	*p = 0.08*
pp2L	49	1.13	0.78	248.5	p = 0.34
pp3L	53	1.16	0.98	263.0	p = 0.19
pp4L	48	1.55	3.64	284.0	p = 0.97
pp5L	45	1.38	1.13	239.5	p = 0.87
ip2L	39	1.39	1.31	180.0	p = 0.81
ip3L	46	2.19	4.73	223.5	p = 0.43
ip4L	38	1.51	1.15	138.0	p = 0.31
ip5L	35	1.88	1.31	128.0	p = 0.42
dp1L	34	2.43	2.93	133.0	p = 0.91
dp2L	5	3.94	3.03	2.0	p = 0.80
dp3L	14	2.41	1.85	22.5	p = 1.00
dp4L	10	2.42	2.65	2.0	**p = 0.03**
dp5L	6	1.63	1.31	2.0	p = 0.53

Significant p values highlighted in bold

Table 13. Data from MSM presence/absence analysis.

MSM	Side	N	% present	% absent
FPL	L	42	97.6	2.4
	R	48	97.9	2.1
APT	L	62	72.6	27.4
	R	60	81.7	18.3
ODM	L	60	78.3	21.7
	R	63	65.1	34.9
FDP	L	23	72.7	27.3
	R	31	72.4	27.6
FDS	L	56	80.4	19.6
	R	60	86.7	13.3
PI2	L	62	58.1	41.9
	R	64	57.8	42.2
PI3	L	60	48.3	51.7
	R	64	56.3	43.7
PI4	L	61	52.5	47.5
	R	64	59.4	40.6
DI1	L	65	63.1	36.9
	R	65	72.3	27.7
DI2	L	65	80.0	20.0
	R	65	90.8	9.2
DI3	L	65	70.8	29.2
	R	64	64.1	35.9
DI4	L	63	92.1	7.9
	R	65	90.8	9.2

Key: FPL = flexor pollicis longus, APT = adductor pollicis (transverse head), ODM = oppenens digiti minimi, FDP = flexor digitorum profundus (2-5), FDS = flexor digitorum superficialis (2-5), PI = palmar interosseous, DI = dorsal interosseous.

Table 14. McNemar test of association between left- and right-hand MSM.

MSM	N	Sig. (2-tailed)
FPL	35	p = 1.00
APT	57	p = 0.15
ODM	58	p = 0.18
FDP	19	p = 0.25
FDS	56	p = 0.29
PI2	61	p = 1.00
PI3	60	p = 0.15
PI4	60	p = 0.33
DI1	65	p = 0.24
DI2	65	*p = 0.07*
DI3	64	p = 0.45
DI4	63	p =1.00

N = number of comparisons performed. Due to the low number of instances where score changed between categories, binomial distribution was used instead of chi-squared statistic. See Table 4 for abbrievations used.

Table 15. Chi-squared (χ^2) test of association between sex, age and hand MSM.

MSM	Side	Sex		Age	
		χ^2	Sig. (2-tailed)	χ^2	Sig. (2-tailed)
FPL	L	1.51	p = 0.41*	0.67	p = 1.00*
	R	1.31	p = 0.44*	0.90	p = 1.00*
APT	L	0.03	p = 1.00	0.02	p = 1.00
	R	0.57	p = 0.52	1.34	p = 0.31*
ODM	L	0.05	p = 1.00	3.44	p = 0.11
	R	4.22	*p = 0.06*	4.68	**p = 0.05**
FDP	L	0.03	p = 1.00*	2.78	p = 0.16*
	R	0.07	p = 1.00*	0.07	p = 1.00*
FDS	L	4.99	**p = 0.04***	2.00	p = 0.19
	R	0.93	p = 0.45*	0.14	p = 1.00*
PI2	L	1.93	p = 0.20	0.25	p = 0.79
	R	0.39	p = 0.62	0.05	p = 1.00
PI3	L	1.13	p = 0.31	0.01	p = 1.00
	R	2.81	p = 0.13	1.89	p = 0.19
PI4	L	0.36	p = 0.61	0.001	p = 1.00
	R	0.01	p = 1.00	0.01	p = 1.00
DI1	L	4.09	*p = 0.07*	0.73	p = 0.43
	R	4.22	**p = 0.05**	1.47	p = 0.26
DI2	L	3.48	p = 0.12	0.81	p = 0.53
	R	1.12	p = 0.40*	0.19	p = 0.69*
DI3	L	1.49	p = 0.28	1.16	p = 0.40
	R	0.01	p = 1.00	0.06	p = 1.00
DI4	L	6.37	**p = 0.02***	1.19	p = 0.38*
	R	3.68	*p = 0.09*	1.05	p = 0.39*

Significant p-values highlighted in bold and values approaching significance (between 0.055 and 0.1) highlighted in italics. Values marked with an asterisk (*) indicate those comparisons where the Fisher's Exact Test p-value was used due to low cell counts (in most instances, this test provides the same results as the standard χ^2).

(p=0.05) and left-DI4 (p=0.02). This clearly contrasts with the results of the metric analysis, where sex had a strong effect on metacarpal and phalanx measurements (but not on asymmetry values) and suggests that, in this sample at least, sex is not associated with MSM as strongly as previously thought. In keeping with the metric analysis, however, the χ^2 test showed that age is not associated with MSM development. The only exception to this was right-ODM (p=0.04).

Discussion

A clear right-side dominant asymmetry was found in the hand bones of the Écija sample, which was more pronounced in the metric properties of the bones than for the MSM. While this implies a right-hand preference in this sample, the magnitude of the asymmetry is much reduced from what might be expected in modern humans (Heçaen and de Ajuriaguerra 1964). These results are in keeping with those of Blackburn and Knüsel (2006), who found a discrepancy between asymmetry in skeletal measurements (humeral epicondylar breadth) and self-reported handedness in a living sample. Together, these results suggest that care must be taken in assuming a direct relationship between 'real-world' hand use and its representation in skeletal material.

The metric analysis suggested some potential functional patterns in metacarpal asymmetry. The metacarpal shaft measurements appear more asymmetric than the other metacarpal measurements. This suggests that the actions of the *palmar interossei* and *dorsal interossei* muscles vary between the left and right hands. The difference in the pattern of asymmetry between metacarpal 1 and the rest of the metacarpal row again suggests that the functional uniqueness of this bone has led to a potentially identifiable asymmetry signature. In contrast to the metric analysis of the metacarpals, the analysis of the phalanges shows a reduced level of asymmetry. This may be due to the organisation of the musculature of the hand, resulting in left/right differentiation between the role of the fingers compared to the metacarpals. This could, however, be a result of the problems inherent in the siding of phalanges (Case and Heilman 2006; Ricklan (1988 np). The reliability of the method varies across the phalanges, with the accuracy of siding the distal phalanges particularly poor. In practice, the method can be difficult to apply, particularly for phalanges of a smaller size. Therefore, it is unclear whether all the phalanges will be correctly sided, and in turn, whether the asymmetry profile of the phalanges in this sample is accurate.

Sex and age had contrasting effects on the metric properties of the metacarpals and phalanges. While sex was found to be statistically significant for most measurements, age was found to have very little effect. This strong association of sex is in contrast to the weak association found by Pomeroy and Zakrzewski (in press) on humeral diaphyseal shape in a sample from Écija. This suggests that, in this population, there may be more gendered divisions of tasks that strongly recruit the bones of the hand. Interestingly, neither the current study, nor that of Pomeroy and Zakrzewski found a significant effect of sex on asymmetry values, which indicates that sex is more strongly associated with the ways in which the upper limb is employed than with the asymmetry between left and right sides. The lack of a strong age association is perhaps surprising, but may reflect recognised problems with the accurate assessment of age in skeletal material (Molleson and Cox 1993). It may also reflect the rather arbitrary nature of the separating the adults in this study into 'young', 'middle' and 'old' categories.

In comparison to the relatively strong right-side asymmetry found in the metric analysis, the MSM analysis found a much more even distribution of right- and left-side dominance. In addition, the relative magnitude of asymmetry was much reduced. This may reflect a difference in the response of metric properties of bone and muscle attachment sites to the activity of the hand. It could also be due to a lack of sensitivity in either or both, the method used to assess MSM development, or the muscle attachment sites to accurately represent lateralised hand use. The identification of possible

patterns in MSM asymmetry related to the second and third metacarpals suggest that there is potential for MSM of the hand to provide information regarding hand use and preference. Further investigation is required of the development of hand MSM to explore in more detail, the efficacy of the presence/absence approach for addressing questions of handedness, and also the choice of muscle attachment sites for study. Comparisons between the muscles of the hand and those of other regions of the upper limb (e.g. the humerus) would be informative.

Conclusions

This study has shown that the bones of the hand play an interesting and variable role in the expression of hand preference in skeletal material. The hand can, and arguably should, be included in discussions of handedness. Combining information from the hand with that from the rest of the upper limb will allow a more inclusive and revealing picture of bilateral asymmetry and its relationship to hand use in living populations. Comparisons of metric and MSM development in the hand has shown that the skeletal representation of hand use and preference is more fluid and more complex than had perhaps previously been thought and, therefore, care must be taken when assessing these traits. Selection of the appropriate methods of assessment and anatomical features for study is crucial. While methodological problems still surround analysis of the bones of the hand, further study will help to clarify these and ensure that the hand aids in a more comprehensive understanding of the unique functioning of the human upper limb.

Acknowledgements

Thank you to Antonio Fernández Ugalde and the staff of the Museo Histórico Municipal de Écija for providing access to the skeletal material and for their hospitality during our stay in Spain. This research was funded by a studentship from the British Academy Centenary Project – From Lucy to Language: The Archaeology of the Social Brain and a BABAO Small Research Project Grant. Thanks also to the two anonymous reviewers who provided many useful comments on an earlier draft of the manuscript.

Literature cited

al-Oumaoui, I, Jiménez-Brobeil, S and du Souich, P. 2004. Markers of activity patterns in some populations of the Iberian Peninsula. *International Journal of Osteoarchaeology* 14: 343-359.

Auerbach, BM and Ruff, CB. 2006. Limb bone bilateral asymmetry: variability and commonality among modern humans. *Journal of Human Evolution* 50: 203-218.

Blackburn, A and Knüsel, CJ. 2006. Hand dominance and bilateral asymmetry of the epicondylar breadth of the humerus. *Current Anthropology* 47: 377-382.

Bräuer, G. 1988. Osteometrie. In Knussman, R (ed.), *Anthropologie: Handbuch der Vergleichenden Biologie des Menchen.* Stuttgart: Gustav Fisher. 212-213.

Brothwell, DR. 1981. *Digging Up Bones.* (3rd ed). New York: Cornell UniversityPress.

Buikstra, JE and Ubelaker, DH. 1994. *Standards for Data Collection from Human Skeletal Remains.* Arkansas Archaeological Survey Research Series No. 44.

Case, DT and Heilman, J. 2006. New siding techniques for the manual phalanges: A blind test. *International Journal of Osteoarchaeology* 16: 338-346.

Churchill, SE and Formicola, V. 1997. A case of marked bilateral asymmetry in the upper limbs of an Upper Palaeolithic male from Barma Grande (Liguria), Italy. *International Journal of Osteoarchaeology* 7:18-38.

Evison, V (ed.). 1994. *An Anglo-Saxon Cemetery at Great Chesterford, Essex.* Council for British Archaeology Research Report 91.

Garn, SM, Major, GH and Shaw, HA. 1976. Paradoxical bilateral asymmetry in bone size and bone mass in the hand. *American Journal of Physical Anthropology* 45: 209–210.

Hawkey, DE and Merbs, CF. 1995. Activity-induced musculoskeletal stress markers (MSM) and subsistence strategy changes among ancient Hudson Bay Eskimos. *International Journal of Osteoarchaeology* 5: 324-338.

Heçaen, H and de Ajuriaguerra, J. 1964. *Left-handedness: manual superiority and cerebral dominance.* New York: Grune and Stratton.

Hopkins, WD, Cantalupo, C, Wesley, MJ, Hostetter, AB and Pilcher, DL. 2002. Grip morphology and hand use in chimpanzees (*Pan troglodytes*): Evidence of a left hemisphere specialization in motor skill. *Journal of Experimental Psychology-General* 131: 412-423.

Hopkins, WD, Cantalupo, C, Freeman, H, Russell, J, Kachin, M and Nelson, E. 2005. Chimpanzees are right-handed when recording bouts of hand use. *Laterality* 10: 121-130.

Hopkins, WD and Cantalupo, C. 2005. Individual and setting differences in the hand preferences of chimpanzees (*Pan troglodytes*): A critical analysis and some alternative explanations. *Laterality* 10: 65-80.

Insoll, T. 1999. *The Archaeology of Islam.* Oxford: Blackwell Publishers Limited.

Jiménez, A. n.d. El sector noroeste. In Romo, A (ed.) *Intervención Arqueológica en la Plaza de España, Ecija. Memoria Final. Volumen 1: Memoria 1.* 183-193 (Unpublished site report on excavations in the Plaza de España, Écija).

Lazenby, RA. 2002. Skeletal biology, functional asymmetry and the origins of "handedness". *Journal of Theoretical Biology* 218: 129-138.

Lieverse, AR, Metcalf, MA, Bazaliiskii, VI and Weber, AW. 2008. Pronounced bilateral asymmetry of the complete upper extremity: A case from the early Neolithic Baikal, Siberia. *International Journal of Osteoarchaeology* 18: 219-239.

Lovejoy, CO, Meindl, RS, Mensforth, RP and Barton, TJ. 1985. Multifactorial determination of skeletal age at death: a method and blind tests of its accuracy. *American Journal of Physical Anthropology* 68: 1-14.

Marzke, MW. 2000. Precision grips, hand morphology, and tools. *American Journal of Physical Anthropology* 102: 91-110.

Marzke, MW, Toth, N, Schick, KD, Reece, SP, Steinberg, B, Hunt, K, Linscheid, RL and An, K-N. 1998. EMG study of hand muscle recruitment during hard hammer percussion manufacture of Oldowan tools. *American Journal of Physical Anthropology* 105: 315-332.

Matshes, E, Burbridge, B, Sher, B, Mohamed, A and Juurlink, BH. 2005. *Human Osteology and Skeletal Radiology: An Atlas and Guide.* Boca Raton, Florida: CRC Press.

Mays, SA. 2002. Asymmetry in metacarpal cortical bone in a collection of British post mediaeval human skeletons. *Journal of Archaeological Science* 29: 435-441.

McGrew, WC and Marchant, LF. 1997. On the other hand: current issues in and meta-analysis of the behavioral laterality of hand function in nonhuman primates. *Yearbook of Physical Anthropology* 40: 201-232.

McManus, IC. 1999. Handedness, cerebral lateralization, and the evolution of language. In: Corballis, MC and Lea, SEG (eds.) *The Descent of Mind: Psychological Perspectives on Hominid Evolution.* Oxford: Oxford University Press, pp194-217.

Molleson, TI and Cox, MJ. 1993. Spitalfields: The Middling Sort. *The Spitalfields Project, Volume 2.* CBA Research Report 86, Council for British Archaeology.

O'Connell, L. 2004. Guidance on recording age at death in adults. In Brickley, M and McKinley, JI (eds.) *Guidelines to the Standards for Recording Human Remains.* Institute of Field Archaeologists Paper No. 7, pp 18-20

Ortega, M. n.d. El sector noreste. In Romo, A (ed.) *Intervención Arqueológica en laPlaza de España, Ecija. Memoria Final. Volumen 1; Memoria 1.* 117-182.

(Unpublished site report on excavations in the Plaza de España, Écija).

Pearson, OM, Petersen, TR and Grine, FE. 2007. Prediction of long bone geometrical properties from external dimensions. *American Journal of Physical Anthropology* 132 (Supplement S44): 185.

Plato, CC, Wood, JL and Norris, AH. 1980. Bilateral asymmetry in bone measurements of the hand and lateral dominance. *American Journal of Physical Anthropology* 52: 27–31.

Pomeroy, EP and Zarzewski SR. in press. Sexual dimorphism in diaphyseal cross-sectional shape in the Medieval Muslim population of Écija, Spain and Anglo-Saxon Great Chesterford, UK. *International Journal of Osteoarchaeology*

Rhodes, JA and Knüsel, CJ. 2005. Activity-related change in medieval humeri: cross-sectional and architectural alterations. *American Journal of Physical Anthropology* 128: 536-546.

Ricklan, DE. 1988. *A Functional and Morphological Study of the Hand Bones of Early and Recent South African Hominids*. PhD Dissertation. University of the Witwatersrand, Johannesburg.

Robb, JE. 1998. The interpretation of skeletal muscle sites: A statistical approach. *International Journal of Osteoarchaeology* 8: 363-377.

Román, L. n.d. El sector suroestse. In Romo, A (ed.) *Intervención Arqueológica en la Plaza de España, Ecija. Memoria Final. Volumen 1: Memoria 1*. 195-233. (Unpublished site report on excavations in the Plaza de España, Écija).

Roy, TA, Ruff, CB and Plato, CC. 1994. Hand dominance and bilateral asymmetry in the structure of the second metacarpal. *American Journal of Physical Anthropology* 94: 203–211.

Ruff, CB. 2000. Biomechanical analyses of archaeological human skeletons. In Katzenberg, MA and Saunders, SR (eds) *Biological Anthropology of the Human Skeleton*. New York: Wiley-Liss. 71-102.

Sarringhaus, LA, Stock, JT, Marchant, LF and McGrew, WC. 2005. Bilateral asymmetry in the limb bones of the chimpanzee (*Pan troglodytes*). *American Journal of Physical Anthropology* 128: 840-845.

Schwartz, JH. 1995. *Skeleton Keys: An Introduction to Human Skeletal Morphology, Development and Analysis*. Oxford: Oxford University Press.

Steele, J. 2000. Skeletal indicators of handedness. In Cox, M and Mays, S (eds.) *Human Osteology in Archaeology and Forensic Science*. London: Greenwich Medical Media Ltd., pp 307-323.

Steele, J. and Mays, S. 1995. Handedness and directional asymmetry in the long bones of the human upper limb. *International Journal of Osteoarchaeology* 5: 39-49.

Stirland, AJ. 1993. Asymmetry and activity-related change in the male humerus. *International Journal of Osteoarchaeology* 3: 105-113.

Stock, JT and Shaw, CN. 2007. Which measures of diaphyseal robusticity are robust? A comparison of external methods of quantifying the strength of long bone diaphyses to cross-sectional geometric properties. *American Journal of Physical Anthropology* 134: 412-423.

Susman, RL. 1988. Hand of *Paranthropus robustus*. *Science* 240: 781–784.

Trinkaus, E, Churchill, SE and Ruff, CB. 1994. Postcranial robusticity in *Homo*: Humeral bilateral asymmetry and bone plasticity. *American Journal of Physical Anthropology* 93: 1–34.

Returning Remains: A Curators View

Quinton Carroll

Historic Environment Team, Cambridgeshire County Council, Box ELH1108, Shire Hall, Cambridge, CB3 0AP
quinton.carroll@cambridgeshire.gov.uk

Abstract

Cambridgeshire's archaeology service operates an archaeological store that accessions all archives from fieldwork in the county, in support of the strong network of local museums. In recent years, questions have been asked about our storage and use of human remains, that have resulted in requests for reburial of some of our assemblages. In 2004, we undertook a survey to ascertain the range of public opinion on this issue.

The issues surrounding the treatment of human remains from overseas indigenous populations held in UK museums and other institutions have been around for many years. Recently however, developments at a national level have raised similar questions about remains archaeologically excavated in this country. This propelled a village in South Cambridgeshire to the forefront of the debate, and gave voice to individuals from the pagan community that is contrary to those expressed by archaeological and curatorial professionals.

In 2006, we referred a case to the newly created Human Remains Advisory Service (HRAS). After much deliberation the HRAS declined to offer an opinion, and we are still in discussion with the local community. This paper narrates our experiences at the sharp end of the debate, our views on the role of national bodies and guidance such as the HRAS, and the difficulties of trying to find a mutually acceptable path through a highly charged arena. Finally, it will ask what we can learn from our experiences in Cambridgeshire, and what lessons we feel the wider scientific and archaeological communities can take on-board.

Keywords: Cambridgeshire, curation, Melbourne, repatriation, reburial, skeletons

This paper provides an additional perspective on the debates relating to the repatriation of human remains within the UK. It is not written by a biological anthropologist, or an osteologist, or even a museum professional, but by a curatorial archaeologist.

I am the Historic Environment Team Manager for Cambridgeshire County Council. Curatorial archaeology has found itself at the forefront of many recent debates in this country. The role of the Curatorial Archaeologist is to operate on the front line of archaeology, liaising with developers, planners and contractors in the commercial sector, and to interact and present the historic environment to the wider public. The legislative framework that controls our work varies from the Ancient Monuments Act, to the ubiquitous Planning Policy Guidance note 16 (PPG16).

Archaeology in the noughties is driven by commercial development, and it is undoubtedly the case that there has been more excavation since the advent of PPG16 in 1990, than in the previous decades. The amount of work varies across the country, and naturally counties with higher rates of development have more archaeological work.

I would like to give some idea of the scale of work undertaken. Between 2003 and 2007, we have initiated over 800 archaeological interventions in Cambridgeshire, averaging around 170 per year. These range from small scale watching briefs, to open area excavations that can cover in excess of 50 hectares. Apart from adding to our knowledge of the historic environment, these also generate archives.

We are unusual in that Cambridgeshire has no county museum. We have the University of Cambridge and a strong network of local museums, often run entirely by volunteers. This has resulted in a lack of facilities for the storage of archaeological material. In the early 1990s, the decision was taken to open a storage facility for archaeological archives and other material in support of the wider museums' provision in the county. This suits all parties, as the small museums have access to recently excavated material without the logistical problems of storing them, and we, as curatorial archaeologists, can disseminate the results of excavations.

Since opening, we have accepted over 5000 boxes of material from over 500 fieldwork projects. The store is operated as part of the Cambridgeshire Historic Environment Record (CHER), and we see access to excavated objects as an integral part of public archaeology. We store the complete archive, including pottery, animal bone, metalwork, building material, small finds and human skeletal remains. We have supplied material to several museum exhibitions and displays, but the main use of our collections has been by researchers.

Our collections contain over 1500 human remains. These have come to us from excavations and stray finds, and cover the whole variety of types from prehistoric barrow burials, to post-mediaeval churchyards. The periods most represented in our collections are Roman and Anglo-Saxon, which account for over 75% of the collection. Several of our assemblages are of regional significance, and at least three are of national importance. We accept the Department of Culture, Media and Sport (DCMS) guidelines for the treatment of human remains, and are currently looking at the most suitable way to adopt our facilities and policies to incorporate them (DCMS 2005).

Our human remains assemblages are the most actively used part of the collection. We currently supply teaching assemblages to two Higher Education institutions. We have supported the English Heritage projects on advanced Accelerator Mass Spectrometry dating for the Saxon period, and also on radiocarbon dating anomalies from prehistoric features. We have supplied samples for a study on leprosy, and over the past two years have supplied material to several research students. We have also supported a student undertaking postgraduate study in forensic science, as their own institution was unable to do so due to their strict application of the Human Tissue Act (2004).

The key point is that our human remains assemblages are actively studied, and make contributions to research and knowledge in a wide variety of fields, from medicine to forensics, in addition to archaeology and anthropology. Anecdotal and hearsay evidence suggests that access to collections appears to becoming more difficult, especially for postgraduate students, and we are proud to be able to offer the support that we do. Although not a subject for this paper, it appears that that the issue of student access to collections needs assessment, for if a consequence (intended or otherwise) of recent legislation and guidance is to limit such access, then this has serious consequences for the future of our respective professions.

Like most curators of human remains collections, issues of repatriation and reburial have figured prominently in our thinking in recent years. Excavated assemblages have been reburied on two previous occasions in Cambridgeshire: one was undertaken on ecclesiastical land (CHER ref. MCB15021) and the other the reburial of a pagan Saxon assemblage in the mid-1990s (CHER ref. MCB12822), but these are exceptional. Our standard procedure for the preparation and deposition of archaeological material does not permit the unilateral disposal of any element of the archive, and we deal with any requests for such action on an individual basis.

In 1999/2000, two assemblages were excavated in Cambridgeshire that raised this issue. These were from Cherry Hinton (Cambridge), an assemblage of over 650 burials from a late Saxon cemetery (CHER ref. MCB14531), and Melbourn (South Cambridgeshire), comprising 60 skeletons from a previously known early Saxon cemetery (CHER ref. MCB15238). Both were excavated as part of the development process as defined by PPG16 by commercial contracting organisations, registered with the Institute of Field Archaeologists, and under a Home Office exhumation licence. In Cherry Hinton, stray finds of human remains are not uncommon and have were regarded as finds from nearby mediaeval plague pits. We now know that this is not the case. At Melbourn, excavations in the 1950s have uncovered other areas of the same cemetery (CHER ref. MCB15556).

Both excavations had high profiles within the local communities. At Cherry Hinton, the then incumbent of the parish church initially raised the issue of reburying the assemblage, but the assemblage had not been sufficiently studied to allow any such action, and the matter was dropped. Melbourn has an active local history society, and the parish council expressed an early interest in reburying the assemblage within a planned new village cemetery. The proposal was to bury the skeletons together under a mound with a plaque detailing their history. As the original cemetery had used the focus of a Bronze Age barrow, it could be seen as coming full circle.

Both assemblages have been assessed for their significance by appropriate experts, and are considered to be of national importance. Although smaller, the Melbourn remains have been professionally excavated under modern conditions, and are in an excellent state of preservation (Duncan et al. 2003). The Cherry Hinton remains are also in excellent condition and excavated under modern controlled conditions, and their value is further enhanced by the fact that there are no comparable assemblages of a late Saxon/early mediaeval rural population from the eastern region. It has been favourably compared to Wharram Percy for its research potential.

As local government officers, we are obviously accountable to the public, and we have to balance this obligation with the professional requirements of curating archives. When we received these approaches, we were aware of the activities of the DCMS sponsored Human Remains Working Group (HRWG) and the English Heritage/Church of England Advisory Panel (APACBE). We decided that the responsible approach would be to wait for the outcome of these consultations, in the hope that they would provide a framework against which to consider these requests. Melbourn Parish Council was advised accordingly; Cherry Hinton had, by this stage, gone quiet.

When the initial report and consultation paper from the Human Remains Working Group was released (DCMS 2003), we were concerned about the tone and direction of the report. We felt that the members had not grasped the issue of domestic reburial, focussing instead on issues relevant to overseas indigenous populations such as Native Americans, Maori and Aborigines. The initial report went so far as to say that the matter was non-contentious in this country, a claim that several organisations, including us, strongly refuted. We were also concerned that the HRWG seemed to feel that the English Heritage/Church of England report would address any issues that may arise, despite the latter focussing on remains from after AD 597, which clearly excluded pagan Saxon, Roman (Christian or pagan) and prehistoric remains. However, our main anxiety was that the HRWG appeared to be moving towards a 'one size fits all' approach based on assumptions that were erroneous.

At about the same time as this consultation, we were asked to attend a local village fair and bring remains excavated in the local area for display. This included skeletons from a small Anglo-Saxon cemetery excavated in the village (CHER ref. MCB11678). Although we did originally agree to this, we became uncomfortable with the nature and type of publicity this generated, so we took the decision that it was inappropriate to display human remains under these circumstances. Our conservator was also concerned about the state of preservation of the remains and their robustness for public display. On the day of the event, we took along objects and finds, but had to explain our decision.

The public reaction was varied. There was some disappointment, and a few people said they had come specifically to see the remains. Some were frustrated by what they saw as local government interference with 'their' remains. Conversely, others were grateful that we had not exposed the deceased to this type of public scrutiny, and that the dead were not to be treated as a source of entertainment. We had recently withdrawn human remains from other displays believing that there was a strong movement against them. The reaction experienced on this occasion showed that this issue was more complicated than we, and the HRWG, had realised.

As there had been little research on this issue, we decided to undertake a survey of public opinion. We devised a questionnaire that covered the basics of the issues, and over the summer of 2004 took this out to our public

events, circulated it through museums and via our website. We deliberately did not direct it at heritage professionals, or ask the opinion of organisations, but accepted responses from individuals associated with these bodies. It was stressed that human remains referred to archaeological material only.

The survey ran for four months and we received over 220 responses. The questions and percentage breakdowns of responses are presented in Table 1.

- Question 1 was asked to see how many people did not know human remains were stored.
- Question 2 is the main question. Although the 70% in favour of reburial may seem high, that 71% of those felt that reburial should only take place once archaeologists agreed it was appropriate is interesting.
- Question 3 had a different focus, with human remains being retained for scientific and not outreach purposes.
- Question 4 supported our experiences in Cambridgeshire, where we have found reburial requests were made not only on religious grounds, but because the skeletons 'belonged' to that community and so should be reburied there.
- Question 5 and 6 covered Outreach and distinguished between museums and archaeological events. There appears to be wide support for the use of human remains in exhibitions and other events.

Table 1. Results of the Cambridgeshire survey

	Question	Yes	No
1	Were you aware that skeletons excavated by archaeologists are frequently kept after the fieldwork?	85%	15%
2	Do you think that skeletons should be reburied?	70%	30%
	If YES, at what point in time:		
	Immediately after excavation	5%	
	If requested by the local community	25%	
	A set time after excavation (say two years)	27%	% of 'Yes' responses
	When the archaeologists decide there is no further scientific or research use for them.	71%	
	Other (please state)	2%	
3	Human skeletal remains can aid future scientific study. Do you think it is appropriate to keep skeletons for future scientific work?	88%	12%
4	Do you think that the buried person's religion should make a difference to how the skeleton is treated?	56%	44%
5	Do you expect to see human skeletons displayed in Museums?	79%	21%
5a	Do you think this is appropriate?	73%	27%
6	Do you expect to see human skeletons displayed at one-off public events hosted by archaeologists?	71%	29%
6a	Do you think this is appropriate?	69%	31%

Hence, 80% of respondents felt that human remains should not be reburied, or that reburial should only occur when archaeologists said there was no further scientific or research use for them. There were similar levels of support for displaying human remains in museums and at archaeological events. This is a vote of confidence in the professionals, with the public trusting us to do the right thing with human remains, such as research, study and appropriate presentation.

Of the options that took control away from archaeologists, support for immediate and total reburial was minimal, and although support for reburial at the request of the local community was marked, it is still a minority view. We were encouraged that what has been perceived as a popular view for the reburial of human remains may be incorrect, and that we, as archaeological professionals, may have had our view points skewed by a vocal, yet minority, opinion. Certainly, these results suggest there is not the groundswell of opinion that has been previously claimed, and we thought this was a vote of confidence in the professionals in the museums' and archaeological communities.

This survey is subjective for several reasons. It was not 'scientifically' prepared or carried out, and the questions were devised based on the issues as we saw them, and written accordingly. By using our events and contacts in museums as the means of dissemination we were playing to our active audience, and not the wider public. Finally, the results have not been statistically determined across the responses to questions. We accept these are valid criticisms, but we believe it was right to carry out this survey.

The results have been widely circulated, being published in British Archaeology (Carroll, 2005) and subsequently picked up by Professor Norman Hammond in a Times article (2005). We were encouraged that other organisations, most notably the Museum of London, have undertaken similar exercises with equally useful results, and call upon the national agencies to follow up these independent efforts with a wider, national survey.

After this survey and publicity, the DCMS released the Guidance for Treatment of Human Remains as the final product of the HRWG consultation process (DCMS 2005). Around the same time, the English Heritage/Church of England working party (APACBE 2005) released their own guidance. We were encouraged to see that some of our concerns raised earlier had been addressed, and overall we thought it a useful document in most areas. We are in the process of adopting some of its recommendations on storage and policies. Our stores are not a registered museum, but accept the principle in the guidance that good practice should be applied uniformly. However, we do have concerns about the section of the report that deals with repatriation.

Apart from the Guidance document, the other outcome was the Human Remains Advisory Service (HRAS). This body was set up to offer an opinion on repatriation cases, especially to smaller organisations that did not have access to appropriate advice themselves. Whilst it may seem strange to regard a County Council as a small organisation, it is the case that we do not have access to relevant advice. Hence, in 2006 we referred the Melbourn case to the HRAS for advice.

Ours was the first case sent to the HRAS. The HRAS initially declined to give an opinion, but after further representation they agreed to take the case. The HRAS appointed a panel of three people, two specialists in the field, and a non-specialist arbiter. We were advised that each specialist who submit a written opinion to the arbiter who would compile a single opinion and summary that would come to us. The process became fairly drawn out, and in April 2007, almost one year after our original request, the HRAS wrote advising that it could not offer an opinion, and that it considered the whole issue of UK excavated human remains to be problematic. This response has serious implications. In order to ascertain why, we should look at the criteria as set down in the Guidance document used to consider claims for repatriation, and how they relate to the Melbourn claim.

The Status of those making the request and continuity with remains
There are several ways in which a claimant can demonstrate this, being genealogical descent, cultural community of origin and country of origin. Evidently, there is a common country of origin, but demonstrating genealogical descent would require extensive scientific testing, and a cultural community of origin is very difficult given the lack of continuity of belief, customs and language between the Saxon and current populations.

The cultural, spiritual and religious significance of the remains
The remains are pagan Anglo-Saxon so this is very difficult to demonstrate. This clause has resulted in the involvement of the pagan movement, most notably Honouring the Ancient Dead (HAD), but the main strength of any claim, under this criterion, would appear to be the cultural significance of archaeological remains to a local community.

The Age of remains
The Guidance indicates that remains older than 500 years would be unlikely to be considered for repatriation.

How the remains were originally removed and acquired
This assemblage was excavated archaeologically under a Home Office Licence.

The status of the remains within the museum/legal status of institution
The remains are held in an archaeological store that is not a registered museum, but meets the requirements and guidelines for storage.

The scientific, educational and historical value of the remains to the museum and the public
English Heritage has submitted a paper demonstrating that the remains have a very high research potential.

How the remains have been used in the past
Postgraduate and other researchers have studied the remains.

The future of the remains if returned
This is under discussion, and together with Melbourn Council, we are investigating the feasibility of a bone store in the village, so the remains can be accessible for future study.

Records of the remains
There is a good report, but the assemblage would benefit from some further study.

Other options
The remains could be kept in the archaeological store.

Policy of the country of origin
This is not applicable

Precedent
Our concern here is that we are setting a precedent. There is a need for any decision to be reasonable and based on robust evidence, by a process that has been transparent and fair. This is the first test of the HRAS criteria for a UK repatriation claim, so to a certain extent we need to be more vigorous in our assessment.

It is evident from the above discussion that, based upon a strict interpretation of the HRAS criteria, there is no case for the repatriation of the remains to Melbourn. The only valid aspects are that the claimants occupy the same geographic area as the remains, and that they believe that they have a sense of ownership as a result. In every other area, including cultural and religious connection and, most crucially, age of the remains, it falls down. This then needs to be balanced by the stated expert opinion of English Heritage and other professionals that the assemblage is significant and should be retained for future study.

It would be too easy to take on board this view and dismiss the claim, but we feel that this process has thrown up a serious issue with the suitability of the criteria for claims of this nature. The criteria have been established to consider applications for the return of overseas populations, where the age of remains is likely to fall within the threshold for claims, and claimants can demonstrate a cultural connection. But, these same criteria make it very difficult for any archaeologically excavated remains to be successfully repatriated. Put simply, one size does not fit all, and we believe that by stating there is a need for further consultation the HRAS have also recognised this. This is important; as one fear was that the HRAS would seek to establish a precedent by applying inappropriate guidance, with the result that future claims would become more contentious. We

congratulate the HRAS for accepting that its own guidance is not suitable for this purpose.

This does not help us resolve the Melbourn claim, but it does raise a lot of issues applicable to the wider professions. We have communicated the outcome of the HRAS consultation to the parish, and began further discussions with them about the feasibility of a bone store. The parish council have also visited our own stores to see the remains. The outcome of the consultation has unfortunately left a vacuum that we are gradually filling, but it has provided an opportunity for third parties to enter the debate. Whilst some input has been constructive, some has resulted in several ill-informed and inappropriate interventions via various channels. The discussion is ongoing.

We consider the key lessons from our experiences are firstly, that the criteria set out in the DCMS Guidance document are not reasonable to consider claims originating in the UK, and it is incorrect to mix historical anthropological collections with archaeological archives and excavated materials. In addition, the presence of APACBE alongside the HRAS is confusing. In our dealings with the pagan movement, we had the Church of England guidance quoted back at us. We would consider this inappropriate, and would question whether having two bodies operating in a similar arena is useful. Linked to this is the need for a strong lead at a national level, with policies and guidance delivered by a single advisory panel. We consider that English Heritage should take this lead, and establish dialogue with interested parties and organisations accordingly.

Throughout, we have endeavoured to be the neutral party. We are the current custodians of these remains, and we have to consider their value to different people, and we are not operating to any agenda. This latter viewpoint has been extremely difficult to put across on occasion. We also feel that there should be an obligation on the scientific community to justify the claim of 'future research potential'. It is very difficult for those of us on the front line to defend this seemingly vague statement in the face of strong local feeling. After all, as local government officers, one of our core objectives is the greater involvement of the public in the historic environment, and debates such as the Melbourn one certainly achieve this. Conversely, there can be a feeling of pride when a community sees that what they regard as their remains are being used to add to knowledge. What communities do not like is a blanket response that remains are kept on shelves just because they may be useful, when in reality they are often forgotten and ignored. I can sympathise with this view.

We believe the scientific community should seek to develop a research framework for human remains, and establish priorities for the development and application of new techniques, and compile details of issues to be addressed. This could even go so far as establishing a national reference collection of human remains, beginning with a full catalogue of what is already held in stores and collections. Ideally, in future when new assemblages are excavated or repatriation claims made, an assessment can be made against developed and accepted priorities that reinforce the claim of future research potential. Again, we believe that English Heritage is the appropriate organisation to take the lead on this.

Ultimately, we need to establish a national dialogue that is constructive and reasonable. In the past, the question of UK claims for repatriation has been ignored or disregarded, with the inevitable outcome that the archaeologists and curators who are suddenly faced with it are not dealing from a position of sound practice or strength. Another consequence is that centre stage has been ceded to extreme views, and the potential for constructive debate can be overwhelmed by confrontation and accusation. Our experiences show aspects of all of this, but I am encouraged by conferences such as this where sensible debate can take place.

I would like to end with a personal observation. I do not think that the majority of the general public are concerned about this issue. But I do believe that a significant section those dealing with archaeology, heritage and culture are concerned. There is a rising debate about our actions and policies as a result of our own perceived faults, and through the rise of pressure groups exposing those faults. We are seeing a failure on two fronts: as professionals we have been afraid to tackle this issue and develop policy and strategy, and secondly, we have failed to communicate with wider audiences. With the possibility of further consultation by DCMS on the specific issue of UK remains, we have an opportunity to address all this. This is an opportunity we should eagerly take.

Acknowledgements
This paper is the product of our experiences over the past few years, and I would like to thank the archiving officers of CAM ARC, the Cambridge Archaeological Unit and Albion Archaeology for their input. Additionally, Joseph Elders (Church of England), Simon Mays and Sebastian Payne (English Heritage) have been extremely helpful with advice on this issue. I also acknowledge the patience of Melbourn Parish Council in waiting for this to be resolved.

Literature cited

CHER - Cambridgeshire Historic Environment Record. www.heritagegateway.org.uk

Carroll, Q. 2005. Bodies - Who wants to rebury old skeletons? *British Archaeology* 82: 11-12

Church of England, English Heritage 2005. *Guidance for best practice for treatment of human remains excavated from Christian burial grounds in England.* London: Church of England and English Heritage.

DCMS. 2003. *Report of the Working Group on Human Remains.* London: Department of Culture, Media and Sport

DCMS. 2005. *Guidance for the Care of Human Remains in Museums.* London: Department of Culture, Media & Sport

Duncan H, Duhig C, and Phillips M. 2003. A late migration/final phase cemetery at Water Lane, Melbourn. *Proceedings of the Cambridge Antiquarian Society* 92: 57-134

Hammond N. 2005. *Visitors Demand the Bare Bones.* The Times, 27 June 2005.

HMSO 1990. *PPG16: Archaeology and Planning.* London: HMSO

Authority and Decision-Making over British Human Remains:
Issues and Challenges

Piotr Bienkowski and Malcolm Chapman

Manchester Museum, University of Manchester, Oxford Road, Manchester M13 9PL
piotr.a.bienkowski@manchester.ac.uk

Abstract

Manchester Museum has long been active in the debate on human remains. Recently, through its new human remains policy and in other activities, and inspired by its experience of repatriations to Australia and New Zealand, it has engaged with diverse UK communities in the decision-making process around human remains from UK contexts. This stance has been criticised from outside the museum sector.

This paper explains Manchester Museum's principles and practice with regard to human remains, particularly those of UK origin. Eschewing a 'genealogical model' which requires evidence of lineal descent in order to make a 'claim', we offer a 'relational model' which regards human remains, found or stored in a particular area, as the collective responsibility of all that area's modern residents. No one group or individual – including archaeologists and museums – has any special claim to possession, and decisions about excavation, retention, analysis, display and reburial should be made through consultation. All interested groups should be involved in this process, including the growing migrant and refugee communities. This is a positive reaction by museums to the wider social inclusion agenda, enabling people to become more involved in local heritage and collections, and to develop a connection to the landscape and identity of their home.

In this way, different value systems and types of benefit of human remains become part of the decision-making process and are accorded equal value, whether they are of scientific importance, remains of ancestors, or parts of geographical communities.

Keywords: Human remains; genealogy; museums; consultation; communities; authority

The Manchester Museum has long been active in the debate on human remains. This paper explains the Museum's principles and practice with regard to policy development and to human remains.

Our practice is based on current museological thinking; part of our vision is to be a laboratory for museum practice and this is underpinned by the Museums Association's *Code of Ethics,* which states that museums should: "seek the views of communities, users and supporters and value the contribution they make...actively involve them in developing policy, and balance this with the role of museums in leading and promoting debate" (Museums Association 2001: 12). Within such thinking museums are not seeing themselves as isolated from a community or culture, they are not externalised, but are becoming more transparent, more explicit and more accountable. Essentially, the Museum has been constructing 'communities of practice' where "collective learning results in practices that ...are... the property of a kind of community created over time by the sustained pursuit of shared enterprises'" (Kelly and Gordon 2002: 153). While consultation has a strong tradition within anthropology and social history museums, it has not often been applied to the natural sciences and had not been applied to policy development at the Manchester Museum until a few years ago.

Back in 2004, as required for the Accreditation Standard administered by the Museums, Libraries and Archives Council, the Museum wrote a new *Acquisition and Disposal Policy* which involved widespread consultation with its communities and users. The resulting policy has consultation central to it; all proposed acquisitions and disposals require discussion with communities external to the Museum. These have varied from local special interest groups, academics at the University, to the Museum's own Community Advisory Panel.

To the Museum, the process of consultation over policy development is an essential element of its transparent practice. However, it is one which has brought a number of criticisms. Many of these are based on an outdated view of the role of museums and their collections, one in which the museum has multiple collections, each specific to a group of users: the display collection for the general visitor, the handling collection for the schoolchild, and the research or reserve collection for the *bona fide* researcher. In practice, the museum now has a single collection but multiple audiences and users, each engaging with and interpreting it in their own way and for their own purposes.

Museum stakeholders (their communities) are made up of visitors, staff, trustees, donors, benefactors, "the scholars and academics who use them for research, the producers, societies, and cultures whose creations are preserved there, and those persons, past and present, whom they represent" (Hein 2000:38). These are wide, diverse and often overlapping groups. The Museum's Community Advisory Panel is made up of individuals from diaspora communities, the socio-economically excluded, and academics based at the University.

Lavine (1992:145) has noted that "even when museums consult representatives of minority cultures…they still must consider how and on what basis their selection of such representatives has been made". However, the "desire to achieve equal representation can only *remain* a desire…for there will always be some group who will find itself unrepresented" (Witcomb 2003:80), through a number of means, not least choice, or being unaware there was an option to participate in the first place. Despite the efforts of a museum there will always be some who elect to remain excluded. Part of our dilemma is that, while attempting to resolve issues of exclusion, museums are seen as part of the problem (Young 2002). That is to say, as part of the authoritarian fabric of society. Thus, any community work they carry out can be seen in terms of 'state interference'. One question, therefore, is: who does the individual represent when they elect to represent a community? The short answer is that they only ever speak for themselves, and this applies equally to the scientific community. For example, one respondent on the consultation on Manchester Museum's Human Remains Policy was more concerned with a database mentioning the presence or absence of teeth than anything else.

Dialogue between museums and communities is not necessarily simple and straightforward. An individual community may have "many factions with differing views based upon…religion, political outlook, and status… [but can]…give people a feeling of ownership" (Simpson 2001: 48-49). What defines a community is the sense of belonging, that there is some form of relationship between the members. It follows, therefore, that the "notion of community is inherently 'othering'" (Hein 2000: 39), that there is a non-community, which in itself is a community of outsiders. Hein (2000) has noted that if museums attempt to expand their boundaries to include such outsiders, either self-selected or determined by socio-economic or cultural criteria, then this challenges the "parameters that made it a community of insiders in the first place" (Hein 2000: 39). That is, the museum ends up reflecting upon itself and its relationships with others.

Groups and communities are increasingly demanding their rights as citizens and to have "their contribution to society recognized, and their children's rights to see their cultures represented in a serious and respectful manner" (Hooper-Greenhill 1997:2). This has been seen as the liberation of culture itself and "not only about giving back or restoring a people's right to and control over their own management of their cultural heritage…the aim is to open the field to multiple voices, which represent a wide range of experiences and perspectives, and to give credence to bodies of knowledge…that have been historically overlooked and devalued" (Kreps 2003: 145).

Particularly contentious, at least amongst those from outside the museum sector, was the statement in the draft Human Remains Policy that the Museum would only acquire human remains in exceptional circumstances, a position that was called by one respondent 'extreme and uncompromising'. In practice, most archaeological excavations within the Manchester area are based around post-industrial sites undergoing redevelopment, and the acidic soils rarely preserve human remains well, so the discovery of human remains within this context would be exceptional. There is no suggestion within the policy that the Museum would reject scientifically important human remains excavated locally, or elsewhere. The discovery of another preserved body at Lindow Moss would of course be exceptional, and any proposed acquisition of this would follow the procedures laid out in the *Acquisition and Disposal Policy*; that is the Museum would consult interested communities, academics, researchers, and others and make a decision based upon the use of those remains in the Museum's and University's learning and research programmes.

It is evident that the criticisms from some communities were based upon a fear that the Museum would re-inter all archaeological human remains without proper consideration; that consultation with so-called 'non-specialists' would lead the Museum to make the wrong decision over the retention and care for the remains. In practice this is unfounded. As stated before, the Museum has multiple communities of interest, most of whom are actively involved in its programmes and practices. It is to misunderstand the Human Remains Policy to think that consultation means the Museum delegates its decision-making to others. On the contrary, decisions are made for sound curatorial and museological reasons, but are always based upon evidence and the views of those consulted. Consultation is undertaken for ethical reasons: the Museums Association *Code of Ethics* states that museums should "consult and involve groups from communities they serve and their representatives to promote a sense of shared ownership in the work of the museum" (Museums Association 2001:12). It should be noted that the final decision on ethically sensitive acquisitions and disposals lies with the Board of Governors of the University. Following the consultation process, the Policy has now been fully endorsed by the University's Senior Executive Team: indeed they commended the "evident care with which it had been developed" (Gordon 2007:1).

A major issue of concern, again from outside the museum sector, was that the draft Human Remains Policy contained proposals that went beyond those of the *Department of Culture, Media and Sport Guidance for the Care of Human Remains in Museums* (DCMS 2005). This is a conscious decision on the part of the Museum and acknowledges the difficulty of accommodating the multiplicity of opinions and beliefs. There is growing interest in the fate of human remains among many communities based in the UK, as well as outside, and growing interest and awareness of this amongst the UK's museums.

What are valued as human remains in many of these communities go beyond the strict scientific definition contained in the DCMS Guidance, and we believe that any definition and consultation should be extended to include those with alternative views. The extension of the definition of human remains to include ashes, blood and hair acknowledges the view of some communities that these have sacred importance, and as such there should be an increased duty of care on the part of any museum housing them. Hair, in particular, was left out of the DCMS Guidance as it would bring artefacts such as mourning jewellery within the definition, and thereby create unnecessary problems for some museums and galleries. But, would it be problematic in reality, or is it part of an assumption that the Guidance applies to ethnographic human remains of non-UK origin, whilst UK human remains are dealt with elsewhere? The Museum has holdings of human remains in its Zoological and Palaeontological collection areas as well as in Archaeology and Living Cultures; any policy needs to be applicable and transparent throughout the organisation, rather than being full of exceptions to the rule which can only lead to confusion.

It is a mistake to interpret the DCMS Guidance as anything other than guidelines. It is not a legal requirement nor is it compulsory for the management of human remains in a museum context, a context which by its very nature of engagement with audiences of many kinds is inherently different to that of a pure research institute. This is acknowledged in the introduction to the Guidance itself: that it represents best practice, but museums should "adapt it to their needs" (DCMS 2005: 7). What must be remembered is that the Manchester Museum's Human Remains Policy only applies to the Manchester Museum. It may be our self-defined role to participate in and promote debate, but it is not our role to determine the policies of other museums.

At the Manchester Museum we intend to involve, as far as is achievable, all interested groups in the consultation process, including the growing migrant and refugee communities, because we feel it is the right of everyone to feel a connection to the people who lived here before them. Human remains should be treated primarily as the antecedents of all the current residents of the area. The discussions the Museum has been having with local communities over the interpretation of Lindow Man in a forthcoming exhibition are a demonstration of this. The connection these communities feel to a body discovered in their locality is a strong one which the Museum should acknowledge, even though there is no direct cultural or genealogical link. The Museum is being pro-active in consulting with a wide range of views over the management of human remains in the collection. This should be seen as a positive approach to social inclusion, enabling people to become more involved in local heritage and collections, and through this to develop an interest in the landscape and identity of their home.

A more broadly based decision-making process now needs to be put in place for human remains without modern genealogical and cultural descendants. This sees human remains, found or stored in a particular area, as the collective responsibility of all that area's modern

residents. Some groups will inevitably have a greater interest in certain types of human remains, but no one group or individual has any special claim to guardianship of them. We now move on to discuss Manchester Museum's human remains policy, and the issues it raises, from a wider perspective.

The dead body has many meanings to different people: it is a cultural artefact shaped through social structures, treated and disposed of according to cultural rules and beliefs for dealing with the dead (see Peers in press). If we consider this as a spectrum of opinions and experiences (and perhaps we should not, since such a view tends to imply irreconcilable polarisation of perspectives which are often in practice a complex, even messy, mix), at one end human remains are 'things', the stuff of evidence, data to be analysed and recorded; at the other end, they are 'persons', someone's family and ancestors, who can be experienced (and perhaps themselves have experiences) as still part of a community (Bienkowski 2006; Tarlow 2006).

Yet the current criteria in the Guidance (DCMS 2005) are based on a genealogical model, which effectively restricts the meaning of human remains to communities. The genealogical model ties the notion of a legitimate claim for ownership to tightly defined definitions of lineal descent and kinship. The criteria were drafted to respond to claims by source communities from Australia, New Zealand and North America, but are also being applied to requests from UK communities (Bienkowski 2007a).

There are two serious deficiencies of using genealogy as the sole criterion. The first is that the demands of proof are offensive to some source communities. The Tasmanian Aboriginal Centre, for example, in its recent case with the Natural History Museum, stated that:

> It is deeply offensive to Aboriginal claimants to demonstrate to the satisfaction of museum officials the significance to our people of the remains of our ancestral dead (TAC 2006).

The second deficiency is that the genealogical model fundamentally misrepresents the ways in which peoples whom we class as indigenous actually constitute their identities. As Ingold (2000) observes, the genealogical model favours claims based purely on proof of prior presence, judged in terms of the principle of human descent and a linear concept of time and history. Yet indigenous peoples draw their being and identity from ongoing relationships with the land, not from fixed lineage. Furthermore, 'ancestors' are not just direct human kin, but can be human, non-human, spirits, mythic beings, animals or plants (Ingold 20001). The genealogical model implies that people do not draw their substance and knowledge from the land or from their ongoing relationships with it, but from their immediate (static) genealogical antecedents, and reduces the activity of dwelling to mere occupancy, not relationship (Ingold 2000).

Ingold (2000:151) criticizes the genealogical model as fundamentally a colonial model: indeed, the very notion of a genealogical 'legitimate claimant' comes from the biomedical consent model (as represented in the Human Tissue Act), which developed in the context of specifically western ideas of possession and relatedness. A particular tool of the genealogical model, the concept of blood quantum to determine tribal enrolment, is similarly highly contested by Native Americans as 'an imposition of the victor's essentialized reckoning of identity' (Strong and van Winkle 1996: 552) and an identity-creating apparatus with 'tremendous potential for exclusion, stigmatization, division, and fragmentation' (Strong and van Winkle 1996: 554). Introduced in the 1800s, explicitly to liquidate tribal lands and eliminate government responsibility to tribes, blood quantum is calculated on the basis of the immediacy of one's genetic relationship to ancestors whose bloodlines were supposedly unmixed (Garroutte 2001: 225). This official (government) discourse is fixed, rigid, essentialized and bureaucratized, individuals marked as belonging to a tribe only through demonstrating possession of at least one-quarter degree of tribal blood (Strong and van Winkle 1996: 558). It stands in stark contradiction to indigenous social and situational understandings of identity which are grounded more in shared history, social ties, and attachment to land than in objectified ancestry (Strong and van Winkle 1996: 555). Blood quantum offers legal rights and protections only to those who are able to make claims to Indianness that are formally judged as legitimate within federal definitions of identity (Garroutte 2001: 229). However, many individuals who are recognized by their tribes as tribal citizens are nevertheless considered non-Indian for some or all Government purposes, and the converse can also be true (Garroutte 2001: 227).

Blood quantum, together with the concept of genealogy as the (sole) criterion of determining membership, kinship and relationships within indigenous groups, closely reflects nineteenth and early twentieth-century theories of race introduced into indigenous American cultures by Euro-Americans (Myer 1999).

In place of the genealogical model, Ingold (2000) offers a relational model more consonant with the lived experience of inhabiting the land: for indigenous peoples themselves, it is in their relationships with the land that their history and identity unfold. In a relational model, ancestry can be human and non-human, in the present or in the distant past. The importance of connection to the land, to a particular place and environment, is key. The inhabitants draw their identity, personhood and energy from the land.

Replacing the current genealogical model with a relational one in terms of decision-making in the human remains discourse would entail a much more sophisticated comprehension and extensive dialogue with indigenous groups overseas, and require a deeper commitment to developing a reciprocal relationship of mutual understanding than the simplistic evidence-based

genealogical model allows for. Yet it also has implications for UK communities who wish to be involved in decision-making around human remains. The challenges to the current system in the UK are coming from communities who similarly have a deep commitment and connection to *place*, whether they are geographically based communities like parish councils, or religious communities like British Pagans. This experience of place can be based on inhabiting the same land, feeling a connection to and responsibility for those who lived there before them, feeling that living and dead are still part of the same community, or on religious sensitivities which experience the dead of a particular place as ancestors of that land (similarly, in a modern East European context, Verdery (1999) notes that kin, descendants, territory and burial sites are inseparable from each other). They are effectively excluded by the genealogical model, especially for human remains over 500 years old where it is difficult to trace direct biological ancestry. Yet, in a relational model, their sense of connection can be valued in the same way we value and accept the connection to land and ancestry of indigenous communities overseas.

Relationship to land for UK communities, as a criterion for feeling a connection to ancient human remains, has been dismissed as 'a naive and unworkable principle for assessing claims' (Smith 2007). Yet this dismissal ignores the wider social agenda within which museums increasingly work, and which archaeology needs to take account of.

The British government has identified as one of five priorities for all English museums their 'role in fostering, exploring, celebrating and questioning the identities of diverse communities' (DCMS 2006). In this sense, museums have an important role, both nationally and locally, in a wider social agenda: especially in terms of social inclusion, working with disadvantaged communities, migrants and refugees, using their collections to help establish a sense of identity, safety, belonging, multiculturalism and community, in which different groups can both express their own traditional values, and be exposed to different groups with different values (which are nevertheless accorded *equal*, or at least equitable, value). Museums are now less about the collections themselves, than about using their collections to develop reciprocal relationships with communities.

Human remains are part of this changing approach, and Manchester Museum's human remains policy (http://www.museum.manchester.ac.uk/aboutus/reportspolicies/). is the relational model in action as a positive approach to social inclusion It gives collective responsibility over ancient human remains to all of an area's modern residents, but without excluding the voices (and values) of scientists and archaeologists. But how can such different understandings of value be compared when making decisions about individual human remains?

Section 47 of the Human Tissue Act, which enables national museums to de-accession and repatriate human remains less than a thousand years old, has huge implications of principle. The precise wording is significant. The museums may transfer human remains 'if it appears to them to be appropriate to do so for any reason, whether or not relating to their other functions'; furthermore, closely associated material (e.g. artefacts buried with the human remains) that it is 'undesirable, or impracticable, to separate', may also be transferred. The reference to museums' 'other functions' refers to the traditional roles of research, education and display – roles firmly embedded in museums' scientific 'enlightenment' paradigm. Thus, the Human Tissue Act acknowledges the principle that human remains and closely associated artefacts, up to a thousand years old (and therefore, largely beyond the scope of a descent-based genealogical model). They have value to communities other than the scientific, archaeological and educational, and this value is afforded equal consideration alongside the demands of science.

Archaeological scientist argue that human remains have research potential, some of which may only be unlocked with new research questions and new techniques, hitherto undreamt of: it is therefore imperative that human remains be retained in perpetuity (Hubert 1989, 1992; Fforde 2004). There are three problems with this 'scientific potential' argument:

1. The stores of museums and archaeological units are overflowing with human remains (and other collections) that have been retained for their potential. This approach is inherently unsustainable, both in terms of long-term storage space and cost, and the cost of specialists, especially conservators, to monitor the conditions and undertake preventative conservation. Most museums are now considering disposal of certain unused collections as a necessary and prudent part of sustainable collections management. Unless there is existing use, or clear, measurable potential for use of collections, including human remains, then it is legitimate, and sensible, that they be considered for disposal.

2. Many collections of human remains in museums do not have useful associated, contextual information, which is necessary to ask meaningful research questions. Many human remains were excavated in the nineteenth and early twentieth centuries, and often even their provenance is unknown. The clear scientific benefits of retaining such remains have never been articulated.

3. To whom do the benefits of ancient human remains accrue? Museums and archaeologists claim that they are keeping, researching and displaying human remains on behalf of the 'whole community', but rarely do they involve representatives of any community in their decisions, and only then, by and large, on the basis of a scientific value system. When they do consult with diverse communities with alternative values – as Manchester Museum has done with its exhibition of Lindow Man

(www.museum.manchester.ac.uk/aboutus/ourpractice/lin dowman/) – the resulting narratives are much richer, bringing in different worldviews and perspectives, which enhance the archaeological perspective rather than detract from it. Published scientific research on human remains, on the other hand, from our experience of assessing countless sampling requests over the years, tends on the whole to focus on research questions that are of interest to other specialists, but rarely can it be said to be a clear 'benefit' to a wider community. We made this point in our paper presented at the 2007 BABAO conference: in the ensuing discussion, other delegates defended the wider benefits of research on human remains, but eventually conceded that archaeologists need to explain and justify their case for such benefits more transparently. Against that we must set the groups for whom the ancient dead are experienced as still part of their communities. Those communities have interests and needs now, in the present, not some uncertain future potential, and their involvement in decision-making around human remains, based on their relational values of respect, honour, responsibility, and connection to land would offer them a clear, measurable benefit (see Brooks and Rumsey 2007:266). Reburials in the UK, for example, as in other European contexts (Verdery 1999), are major community events, reaffirming connections between living and dead (Bienkowski 2007b; Restall Orr 2007).

Until relatively recently, the 'right' to retention and use of human remains as 'evidence' and as 'objects' of display by museums and archaeologists was uncontested. Now, however, there is a plethora of interests from different groups with different value systems. Museums and archaeology in the UK need to accommodate that change and alter their practice and decision-making processes. As Groarke and Warrick (2006) argue, archaeologists (and museums) are only one among several interest groups whose competing claims might better be decided more appropriately in a political arena, and on the basis of different values and benefits equally ranked. Archaeologists cannot at one and the same time be the prime beneficiaries and users of human remains, set the criteria for other groups, and be adjudicators in disputes.

A balanced view surely acknowledges the current social injustice: that authority over human remains is vested firmly, and unequally, in museums and archaeology, who generally claim to represent wider interests but do not involve other communities in their decisions. The implications of the 2004 Human Tissue Act are that equal consideration should be afforded to a complex range of meanings that people attach to human remains, and we now need to put in place a practical mechanism to ensure that decision-making around human remains is also equal. A relational model – like the one we use at Manchester Museum, is also better archaeology, bringing in wider perspectives on human remains, often phenomenological, which cannot be addressed scientifically (Thomas 2004).

Literature cited

Bienkowski, P 2006. Persons, things and archaeology: contrasting world-views of minds, bodies and death. *Paper presented at the conference 'Respect for Ancient British Human Remains: Philosophy and Practice', Manchester Museum*, 17 November 2006. Electronic document: http://www.museum.manchester.ac.uk/aboutus/ourpractice/respect/, accessed 18 July 2007.

Bienkowski P 2007a. Authority over human remains: genealogy, relationship, attachment. *Archaeological Review from Cambridge* 22 (2): 113-30.

Bienkowski P 2007b. Care assistance. *Museums Journal*, June 2007: 18.

Brooks MM. and Rumsey C 2007. The body in the museum. In: Cassman, V, Odegaard, N and Powell, J (eds.) *Human Remains: Guide for Museums and Academic Institutions*. Lanham: Altamira Press, pp 261-89.

DCMS 2005. *Guidance for the Care of Human Remains in Museums*. London: Department of Culture, Media and Sport.

DCMS 2006. *Understanding the Future: Priorities for England's Museums*. London: Department of Culture, Media and Sport.

Fforde, C 2004. *Collecting the Dead: Archaeology and the Reburial Issue*. London: Duckworth.

Garroutte, EM 2001. The racial formation of American Indians: negotiating legitimate identities within tribal and federal law. *American Indian Quarterly* 25 (2): 224-39.

Gordon, D 2007. Communication from University of Manchester Senior Executive Team to Dr Nick Merriman, Director of The Manchester Museum. 24 July 2007.

Groarke, L and Warrick, G 2006. Stewardship gone astray? Ethics and the SAA. In: Scarre, C and Scarre, G (eds.) *The Ethics of Archaeology: Philosophical Perspectives on Archaeological Practice*. Cambridge: Cambridge University Press, pp 163-77.

Hein, H 2000. Museums and communities. In: Hein, H *The Museum in Transition*. Washington: Smithsonian Institution Press, pp 37-50.

Hooper-Greenhill, E 1997. Towards Plural Perspectives. In: Hooper-Greenhill, E (ed.) *Cultural Diversity: Developing Museum Audiences in Britain*. London: Leicester University Press, pp 1-14

Hubert, J 1989. A proper place for the dead: a critical review of the 'reburial' issue. In: Layton, R (ed.) *Conflict in the Archaeology of Living Traditions*. Abingdon: Routledge, pp 131-66.

Hubert, J 1992. Dry bones or living ancestors? Conflicting perceptions of life, death and the universe. *International Journal of Cultural Property* 1:105-27.

Ingold, T 2000. Ancestry, generation, substance, memory, land. In: Ingold, T *The Perception of the Environment: Essays on Livelihood, Dwelling and Skill*. London/New York: Routledge, pp 132-51.

Kelly, L and Gordon, P 2002. Developing a Community of Practice: Museums and Reconciliation in Australia. In: Sandell, R (ed.) *Museums, Society, Inequality*. London/New York: Routledge, pp 153-174.

Kreps, C 2003. *Liberating Culture: Cross-Cultural Perspectives on Museums, Curation and Heritage Preservation*. London: Routledge.

Lavine, S 1992. Audience, ownership, and authority: designing relations between Museums and communities. In: Karp, I, Lavine, S and Kraemer, C (eds.) *Museums and Communities: The Politics of Public Culture*. Washington: Smithsonian Institution Press, pp137-57.

Museums Association 2001. *Code of Ethics for Museums*. London: Museums Association.

Myer, ML 1999. American Indian blood quantum requirements: blood is thicker than family. In: Matsumoto, VJ and Allmendiger, B (eds.) *Over the Edge: Remapping the American West*. Berkeley, CA: University of California Press, pp 231-49.

Peers, L in press. On the treatment of dead enemies: indigenous human remains in Britain in the early 21st century. In: Macdonald, M and Lambert, H (eds.) *Social Bodies*. Oxford: Berg.

Restall Orr, E 2007. Reburial at Highworth. Electronic document: http://www.honour.org.uk/projects/highworth/index.php, accessed 18 July 2007.

Simpson, MG 2001. *Making Representations: Museums in the Post-Colonial Era*. London: Routledge.

Smith, M 2007. Letter in *Museums Journal*, July 2007, 14, in response to Bienkowski P 2007. Care assistance. *Museums Journal*, June 2007: 18.

Strong, PT and van Winkle, B 1996. 'Indian Blood': reflections on the reckoning and refiguring of Native North American identity. *Cultural Anthropology* 11 (4): 547-76.

TAC 2006. *Tasmanian Aboriginal Centre submission to the Natural History Museum (NHM)*, published by the NHM in its press pack which accompanied its announcement in November 2006 that it would repatriate its collection of Tasmanian human remains. October 2006.

Tarlow, S 2006. Archaeological ethics and the people of the past. In: Scarre, C and Scarre, G (eds.) *The Ethics of Archaeology: Philosophical Perspectives on Archaeological Practice.* Cambridge: Cambridge University Press, pp 199-216.

Thomas, J. 2004. *Archaeology and Modernity.* London: Routledge.

Verdery, K. 1999. *The Political Lives of Dead Bodies: Reburial and Postsocialist Change.* New York: Columbia University Press.

Witcomb, A 2003. *Re-Imagining the Museum: Beyond the Mausoleum.* London: Routledge.

Young, L 2002. Rethinking heritage: cultural policy and inclusion. In: Sandell, R *Museums, Society, Inequality.* London/New York: Routledge, pp 203-12.

Ethical dimensions of reburial, retention and repatriation of archaeological human remains: a British perspective

Simon Mays,[1] and Martin Smith[2]

[1]English Heritage, Portsmouth PO4 9LD, UK
[2]School of Conservation Sciences, Bournemouth University, Talbot Campus Poole, Dorset, BH12 5BB, UK.
simon.mays@english-heritage.org.uk

Abstract

As the physical traces of once living people, human remains are distinct from other kinds of archaeological evidence, invoking ethical considerations over and above those afforded to other types of material. The management of collections of human remains is consequently a complex area where decisions may sometimes be required which balance the needs of science and the wider public interest against the wishes of claimants or other concerned parties. After discussing the role and development of current guidelines for the treatment of archaeological human remains in Britain we consider the nature of current debates and the wider ethical background within which such guidelines are required to operate. Following this, we discuss further recent developments in Britain in relation to calls for changes in the way claims relating to human remains are assessed. In particular, we address recent claims by some modern practitioners of Pagan beliefs for the reburial of some British remains, in addition to calls from some parts of the museums sector for an alternative model for assessing such claims. The respective arguments are explored at both a practical and a philosophical level and are argued to be misplaced and incoherent on both counts.

Keywords: Reburial, repatriation, ethics, guidelines, Pagan, museums

Introduction

The special status of human remains as the remains of people rather than objects, means that their treatment invokes ethical considerations over and above those pertaining to other classes of archaeological materials. These considerations mean that treatment of human remains is one of the most complex and emotive areas of archaeological practice. In some parts of the world (e.g. Australasia, North America) archaeological human remains have been the subject of often, quite polarised, debate for more than 30 years (see reviews in Ubelaker and Grant, 1989; Jones and Harries, 1998; Walker, 2000). The ethical debate concerning remains in Britain is, by comparison, less developed. Collections of human remains in museums and other institutions in Britain comprise those of British origin (the great majority), plus some from overseas.

In Britain, pressures on land for development are intense, particularly in urban centres. Britain has been heavily populated for many centuries, and most urban centres were founded more than 1000 years ago. Therefore, ancient burials, usually in long-forgotten burial grounds which have since been built over, are frequently threatened by modern redevelopment. In such instances, the response is normally to excavate the burials archaeologically in advance of destruction of the burial ground. The great majority of British archaeological human remains held in museums and other institutions were acquired in this manner. Debates in Britain on ethics and human remains have tended to focus, not on whether burials should be disturbed, but whether after excavation, they should be retained in museums or other institutions for future study. The debate has largely been confined to academic and professional circles. It is not, at present, a high-profile public issue.

Remains from overseas housed in British museums were acquired in various ways, including transfer from overseas museums and direct acquisition by British museum employees or researchers, often during the colonial period. Requests for repatriation of human remains held in UK museums, mainly from indigenous groups from North America and Australasia, have in the past, been few (33 were made up to 2003 – Palmer, 2003), but recently have been growing. For example, in the last two years, claims have been made for Australian remains to the Natural History Museum and the British Museum in London, and to various provincial museums including Exeter, Oxford, Newcastle, Edinburgh and Aberdeen. These matters have begun to receive some coverage in the national press and other media in Britain (e.g. Kohn, 2006; various articles listed on www.babao.org.uk), so that the ethical issues have a rather higher public profile than those surrounding archaeological burials from Britain. In this article, we focus on retention/reburial of human remains of British origin, and also on aspects of the debate regarding overseas remains held in British museums and other institutions.

Guidelines on ethical matters and human remains

Archaeologists have long been conscious that the treatment of human remains is an important issue, but ethical considerations with regard to British remains have only been debated in print in the last decade (e.g. Morris, 1994; Parker-Pearson 1995; Cox 1996). In England, feedback from professionals involved in archaeological fieldwork, to professional organisations and heritage bodies, indicated that guidelines were needed for best practice in this area. As a result, a collaborative document (Mays, 2005) was prepared by English Heritage (the statutory organisation responsible for heritage in England) and the Church of England. It provides guidance on the treatment of human remains from Christian burial grounds in England. It attempts to cover legal and archaeological best practice as well as addressing ethical issues, chiefly from the point of view of Christian theology. This guidance document was aimed specifically at Christian remains because they comprise the majority (about 75%) of those excavated in England, and they provide a coherent body of material for which a consistent theological framework can be applied to inform ethical treatment.

Another stimulus to the provision of guidelines in Britain has been the debate surrounding the reburial and repatriation of indigenous remains in North America and Australasia. This lead to Historic Scotland (the Scottish counterpart of English Heritage), to wish to clarify its own stance regarding human remains excavated from Scottish archaeological sites, and to set out the legal position regarding human remains in Scotland (Historic Scotland, 1997).

In 2000, the British and Australian Prime Ministers made a joint declaration to increase efforts to repatriate human remains held in UK museums to Australian Aboriginal groups when appropriate. One outcome of this was that, in 2004, legal changes gave nine national museums (including the London Natural History Museum) powers, which they had previously lacked, to de-accession human remains under 1000 years old. A second was that the British Government set up a working party to produce a code of practice providing guidance for the care of human remains in museums and, particularly, for assessing claims presented to museums for repatriation/ reburial of remains. The guidance (Swain, 2005), published by the Governmental Department of Culture, Media and Sport (DCMS), emphasises that it is the responsibility of museums, as current guardians of the material, to make decisions over their future, albeit in consultation with the scientific community, claimants and other interested parties. The guidance on procedures for assessing claims was specifically aimed at helping museums balance the need to respect the culture and wishes of claimants with the needs of science. The framework it promulgates applies not only to remains of overseas origin in British museums but also archaeological remains of British origin (Swain, 2005).

The DCMS guidelines were assembled by a panel with a wide range of expertise, and were only finalised after broad consultation. They have support at Governmental level, and are also endorsed by major professional organisations in the UK including the Museums, Libraries & Archives Council and the Museums Association. They have now begun to be used to assess claims. For example, the guidelines were used by the London Natural History Museum in 2006 as a framework to assess a claim by a Tasmanian Aboriginal group (the remains were repatriated - see http://www.nhm.ac.uk/about-us/news/2007/may/news_ 11682.html for further details), and were also the basis of advice given by English Heritage to a county council in England regarding a request by a (secular) parish council for reburial of remains from a pre-Christian English archaeological site. The DCMS document is a pivotal contribution to the handling of claims for reburial/repatriation in Britain. However, before discussing its utility in more detail, it is pertinent to recapitulate some of the arguments that have been put forward, both for retention of remains for research and for reburial of remains.

Retention versus reburial

The value of research on human remains for archaeology, medical history, forensic science and other disciplines has been summarised elsewhere (e.g. Mays, 2005: 35-36). The importance of such work is widely recognised, even in policy statements that otherwise seek to emphasise the rights of indigenous communities to human remains (e.g. World Archaeology Congress, 1989). What we set out below is the necessity for curated collections to be retained long-term in museums or other institutions if the needs of scientific research are to be met.

When human remains are excavated from an archaeological site in Britain, they are normally examined soon after excavation by an osteologist who prepares a scientific report on them. It is a common misconception that this osteological report represents the definitive scientific work on a collection, and it is sometimes even suggested that it is appropriate to rebury skeletal material once the report has been completed. However, this misunderstands both the purpose of an osteological report and the nature of scientific enquiry. The main purpose of an osteological report is to address research questions pertinent to the site from where the remains were excavated, and the specific population of which they are a mortality sample (Mays et al., 2002). A secondary purpose is to make osteological data available to the scientific community. It is, of course, impossible for an osteologist to predict what future researchers, working on projects as yet unformulated, might require in the way of data. Therefore, an osteological report, no matter how carefully prepared, cannot substitute for the long-term retention of the skeletal material itself. This is illustrated on the broader scale by the wide-ranging osteological recording initiated on remains from North America in the 1990s in response to the threat of repatriation and reburial of skeletal material under The Native American Graves Protection and Repatriation Act (NAGPRA) and other legislation. Data from this recording exercise has been available to scholars since the mid 1990s, but scanning the scientific journals suggests its impact on osteological research has been minimal. Research in osteology is reliant on the collection from curated skeletal material of data specifically relevant to the research problems being investigated.

It is fundamental to the scientific method that observations of earlier workers can be checked so that errors or deficiencies may be remedied. Re-analysis of collections plays a central part in this process (Buikstra and Gordon, 1981; Palkovich, 2001). The retention of skeletal collections also permits the application of new methods of analysis which may have been unavailable at the time of excavation. Such innovations in techniques enable completely new data to be obtained from old collections. Recent developments that are yielding new information include DNA analyses to investigate genetic relationships and infectious disease, and stable isotope analyses to investigate diet and mobility amongst past populations. In addition, research is an iterative process in which as well as addressing *a priori* aims, new questions are raised which entail re-analysis of skeletal material. For example, a recent study (Mays et al., 2008) showed that there was a difference in growth patterns between a 19th century British urban group and their rural counterparts. One possible explanation was differences in breastfeeding practices; however, this possibility could not be evaluated by stable isotope analysis as the urban collection had been reburied. In the longer term, changes in theoretical orientation of academic disciplines mean that we continue to ask new questions of old material. For example, many Neolithic tombs in Britain were excavated 100 years ago or more when the main focus of examination of skeletal material was to reconstruct population affinities using cranial measurements. Whilst this remains a valid approach, more recent re-examination of these Neolithic skeletal collections has yielded new insights, focussing on areas such as mortuary rites, subsistence, mobility and conflict amongst early agricultural communities (e.g. Schulting and Wysocki, 2005; Smith, 2006; Richards and Schulting, 2006; Smith and Brickley, forthcoming).

Turning to the issue of claims for reburial/repatriation of remains, claimants who make such requests present diverse cases and each needs to be treated on its merits. Nevertheless, perusal of the literature (e.g. Besterman, 2003; Smith, 2004; Pickering, 2006; Heywood, 2006; Kohn, 2006; Mansell, 2006) indicates a number of common themes. The aim from the claimant's point of view is to bring back remains, which they perceive as theirs, to the region from which they originated so that they can be reburied or otherwise 'laid to rest' according to the cultural traditions of the claimant group. Repatriation is often seen as a step toward restitution for injustices suffered by ancestors of the claimant group during the period of colonial domination. There is also usually a spiritual dimension. For example, it may be asserted that continued retention of remains in a museum perpetuates grief in the claimant community, which can only be healed by the repatriation of the remains. There may be a political dimension whereby return of remains helps claimants to assert their cultural identity, and may be part of other political processes aimed at bolstering the rights of indigenous groups in former colonies of European powers. It may also be a step toward recognising past wrongs and aiding reconciliation.

Claims for human remains: an ethical overview

Retention of collections is ethically desirable in that it permits future generations to learn from them, whereas reburial, or other actions which place the remains beyond the reach of science, denies future generations this option. Such destruction of knowledge is ethically undesirable. Set against this are the wishes of particular groups or individuals who have links with remains which may confer them rights over their disposal, and who may desire reburial. There are also a number of subsidiary considerations which bear on these central issues, such as the perceived scientific value of the remains, the age of the remains, the way in which the remains were initially acquired, as well as their future if returned (Swain, 2005: 27-29).

One of the most difficult aspects for a museum or other institution considering a claim is assessing the status of the claimant group in terms of their links with the remains they are claiming. Unless museums are content simply to give away remains to whoever asks for them, formal criteria for evaluating claimants are needed. To ensure equitable treatment of cases, avoid charges of discrimination, and to ensure transparency of decision-making, evaluation criteria need to be explicit and broadly applicable. One of the core purposes of the DCMS document (Swain, 2005) was to set out such criteria. This document defines two types of linkage, genetic descent and cultural connections.

Giving close relations authority to make decisions regarding the recent dead appears to be a cultural universal (Walker, 2000). By analogy, if a claimant group can demonstrate a close genealogical link to human remains, their wishes would normally be accorded strong weight. For remains of any antiquity, descendants are likely to be many, and the holding institution would need to assess the potential range of claimants and gauge how their interests might best be balanced (Swain, 2005: 26). For most archaeological remains, personal identities are unknown, and evaluation of cultural links is therefore critical, as this may be the only level at which it is possible to make reliable statements regarding their identity. A clear demonstration of continuity of culture between a claimant and the remains is of key importance in making a claim. Of course, cultures change over time, but in such instances there is usually archaeological or historical evidence for culture change. For a valid claim, it would normally be expected that the claimants demonstrate continuity of beliefs, customs or language, or else demonstrate why this was no longer the case (e.g. due to disruption of indigenous culture in the colonial period) (Swain, 2005: 26-27).

The DCMS criteria emphasise the need for decisions to be made on a case by case basis, and to seek compromise solutions where appropriate. This latter is echoed in the policy outlined by English Heritage and the Church of England for Christian remains from England (Mays, 2005). For human remains recovered from Christian burial grounds, the view of the Church is that they should

Figure 1. The public space housing the exhibition of human remains at the redundant church at Barton-upon-Humber, England.

be returned to consecrated ground. Upon burial, in a churchyard or other ecclesiastical burial area, responsibility for the remains was effectively handed over to the church. The Christian Church in England was founded in the 7th century AD, and the current Church of England is the legal successor to the pre-Reformation mediaeval church. The continuity of belief and continuity of care of remains gives the church a strong moral locus for Christian remains dating from the 7th century AD onwards. As a compromise between the wish on the part of the Church for reburial, and the preservation ethic for remains of scientific value, a policy of deposition in redundant or partially redundant churches (which, theologically speaking, remain consecrated) has been reached, so that the remains would continue to be accessible to researchers (Mays, 2005: 5). One such depository is in the church at Barton-on-Humber, Lincolnshire, England. The church has been declared redundant (i.e. it is no longer used for worship). It is under the care of English Heritage and is open to the public. During the 1980s, more than 2000 skeletons, dating from 10th-19th century AD, were recovered by archaeological excavations in the church and churchyard. This collection is of considerable scientific value (Waldron, 2007). Originally the plan was that these skeletons should be reburied, but in the light of the English Heritage / Church of England policy document's recommendations, they are now stored in a specially constructed area within the church, separate from the public space (Mays, 2007). They are available for study by *bona fide* researchers. A committee which includes

English Heritage collections managers, clergy and archaeological scientists, regulates access to the collection. A permanent exhibition on the history of the church and the burials, which includes displays of human remains, has been mounted in the public area of the church (Fig. 1) to educate and inform the public about the excavations and particularly the human remains.

Modern paganism and claims for reburial of prehistoric British remains

Four years ago, in an article on the ethical dimensions of claims for repatriation of overseas remains, Don Brothwell made the following comment:

> *"Perhaps it is only a matter of time before the Druids of Stonehenge or those who...soak up the primeval energy of the Avebury stones, will begin to make claims for reburial of their local prehistoric Ancestors. This may seem absurd and unlikely, but it is certainly not beyond the realms of possibility"* (Brothwell, 2004: 416).

Recently, this possibility appears to have become a reality, as some modern British practitioners of Pagan beliefs have indeed begun to press for reburial of prehistoric British human remains, apparently having been influenced by recent developments regarding the repatriation of overseas material:

"At present many museums in this land display the remains of our ancient cultural ancestors under spotlight in glass cases or in a dusty box in archaeological archives. The Council of British Druid Orders believes that it is time for these remains to be returned to their rightful place of rest within the earth." Paul Davies, Council of British Druid Orders[1] (www.cobdowest.org/reburial.html).

Modern Pagans are a somewhat disparate group, although they share spiritual beliefs which are broadly 'nature orientated'; specific examples include Wicca and Druidism. Whilst many take their cues from what they perceive to have characterised 'pre-Christian' beliefs, the modern Pagan movement essentially dates from the 1950s and 60s (for example, Wicca was invented in the 1950s by a retired British Civil Servant), but its ethos can arguably be traced to the Romantic movement of the late 18th and 19th century (McIntosh, 2004). Numbers of adherents are hard to estimate, but there may be 1-4 million worldwide (McIntosh, 2004) although, given the wide range of belief systems, followers of any one are very much fewer than this.

As might be expected, given the diversity of Pagan belief systems, there is also a diversity of views among Pagans concerning what constitutes respectful treatment of remains, and whether reburial is desirable:

"Not all Pagans feel strongly that ancient human remains should be reburied. Yet those who do not feel that way do not lack respect for their ancestors, they just show that respect differently" (Aburrow, 2007).

"I was appalled to read that some museums are considering performing neo-Pagan rites on human remains upon reburial..." "...I do not think it is acceptable for rituals to be performed in connection with people whose original beliefs are unknown." (Diedriech, 2007)

"They are just bones - honestly I would have no cares or concerns if people dug me up...cause I am going to be long gone and on to other things...If someone can learn something from my dead leftovers - have at it" (Tenebrae, accessed Dec. 2007).

It is difficult to assess the extent to which reburial of prehistoric remains is supported by Pagans in Britain, but what is clear is that those who are pressing for reburial are becoming more vocal and more organised in pressing their claims.

When the DCMS guidelines (Swain, 2005) were drafted, the section on claims for repatriation was written taking a

view that such claims would be few in number and relatively simple to administer. There is no doubt that some human remains of overseas origin in current British museum collections were acquired in highly dubious circumstances during the colonial period. Where the provenance of such material is clear, and a claimant group exists with strong and verifiable links to the material, it is often right that such remains should be repatriated. This is not to suggest that such remains have little or no scientific potential. On the contrary, many of the human remains recently repatriated by museums in Britain hold considerable potential for learning about humanity's recent past in a variety of circumstances and world regions. However, in such cases, the wider social and cultural issues surrounding these remains are felt to outweigh the contributions to knowledge that could be derived through their retention. This part of the DCMS guidelines was intended to help resolve a fairly small number of relatively clear-cut cases in an efficient and amicable manner, and where the guidelines have been applied correctly, they have so far worked well.

In relation to the date of human remains (regardless of provenance) the guidelines state:

"...it is very difficult to demonstrate clear genealogical, cultural or ethnic continuity far into the past, although there are exceptions to this. For these reasons it is considered that claims are unlikely to be successful for any remains over 300 years old, and are unlikely to be considered for remains over 500 years old" (Swain, 2005: 27).

Like the DCMS guideline as a whole, this statement clearly applies, not only to overseas human remains, but also those found in Britain, which is entirely appropriate. The fact that it is hard to make successful claims for older human remains of British origin is deliberate. The small number of human remains which survive from prehistoric periods in Britain are the ancestors of everyone and hold great potential for current and, more importantly, future generations to learn about our collective past. No case for reburial was felt to exist which outweighs the scientific case for retention of such remains.

Despite the care with which the DCMS document was drawn up, some British Pagans now appear to believe that its approach is inadequate (e.g. Restall-Orr, 2006), and they are receiving support in this from some museums (e.g. Manchester Museum), which appear sympathetic to their cause. Cynics might suggest that calls from such quarters to "move beyond" the confines of the DCMS document are simply prompted by the realization that their claims for remains are likely to fail under these criteria. Modern Pagans are obviously unable to demonstrate continuity of beliefs with those of prehistoric people, and have no stronger genealogical links to such remains than the rest of the population of Britain. However, some are attempting to make the intellectual case.

---

[1] Although there are in fact two organisations calling themselves the Council of the British Druid Orders.

Genealogical versus relational models
The fact that claims for older remains are unlikely to succeed under the current guidelines may partly explain recent calls for an alternative model to replace the current 'genealogical model' for guiding such decisions:

> *"Eschewing a 'genealogical model' which requires evidence of lineal descent in order to make a 'claim', [Manchester Museum's human remains policy] offers a 'relational model' which regards human remains found or stored in a particular area as the collective responsibility of all that area's modern residents".* (Bienkowski, 2007).

The notion of using a "relational" model as a conceptual tool for discussing the cultural identities of indigenous peoples has been discussed most explicitly by Ingold (2000a). Ingold notes various problems with relying solely on genealogy to assess the ethnic distinctiveness of people claiming 'indigenous' status. For example, there is the question of what proportion of more recent colonists (such as Australians of European origin) one can number among one's ancestors whilst still qualifying as 'indigenous'. He argues that such a system will ultimately result in "ever finer lines of discrimination and exclusion" (Ingold, 2000a: 137). The present authors would not wish to dispute this observation. There are indeed problems that may arise with the practical application of such a model. However, an obvious question this prompts is what alternative could replace it?

Ingold (2000a, b) discusses various efforts by modern national governments to relocate 'genealogically' indigenous peoples away from their perceived homelands. He argues that such a view of the transmission of indigenous culture fails to understand that such peoples' relationships with their environment are as important as their relationships with each other. He goes on to argue that culture is not something static that exists independently. Rather, it is acquired through engagement with the community and environment in which individuals live. As 'indigenous' culture is therefore acquired, at least partly, through the experience of inhabiting a particular landscape, defining such peoples purely on genealogical grounds is consequently deemed inadequate (Ingold, 2000a). This argument clearly has validity and does make sense on its own terms. However, recent attempts to take this train of thought and transpose it directly onto current debates regarding the fate of archaeological remains are considerably less coherent. In this latter context, such arguments may be neither appropriate nor useful.

Taking the stance that they hold their archives on behalf of their local communities, some museums are arguing that these 'communities' (presumably including representation from local Pagans) should be involved in discussions and decisions regarding human remains.

> *"...it is the right of everyone to feel a connection to the people who lived here before them"*

(Manchester Museum Human Remains Policy, 2007: 3).

Whilst attempting to foster dialogue and find compromises between groups whose opinions differ is undoubtedly a worthy goal, at its most basic level a system for assessing claims regarding human remains is not a means for dealing with groups and individuals who agree with each other. Whether a framework based on genealogical/cultural continuity or some other model is chosen, the essential function remains the same - a system for making decisions regarding the relative correctness of potentially opposing claims according to an agreed set of principles. The key point is, what weight to attach to the views of groups who may demand reburial of remains or some other say in their future? Firstly, in order for a system of arbitration between competing claims for human remains to function effectively, it needs to be based upon clearly defined terms. Terms such as "community", "local", "area" and even "here" are vague and highly subjective. This raises the obvious question of where to draw the boundaries when attempting to apply such terms. In addition, the place where the remains were found, and the museum that houses them, may be in quite different locations. For example, the preserved prehistoric body Lindow Man, found in a peat bog in Cheshire, is currently housed 200 miles away at the British Museum in London. Secondly, according greater weight to 'local' views (however these may be defined), ignores the wider truth that important collections of human remains have significance beyond their 'local' area. Study of the past using archaeological remains enriches us all, not just those who happen to live near the museum where the remains are kept, or the archaeological site where they were found. Thirdly, if claims are to be handled equitably then they need to be evaluated on criteria that are generally applicable. In this light, the principal of local participation in decision making is found wanting. For example, should a UK museum, faced with a claim for repatriation of Australian Aboriginal remains consult specifically with people who live within a short distance of the museum to assess their views, and with Australians of European or other non-Aboriginal descent who happen now to live near the site where the bones were originally found? In our view, these are hardly key aspects in evaluating such a claim. Lastly, whilst we would not contend that a model stressing genealogical relationships and cultural continuity in evaluation of claims is beyond criticism, a system which proposes to settle claims simply on the basis of current geographical proximity to the place where remains were found (or are curated), is simplistic and unsatisfactory. It would be very much more subjective, illogical and potentially discriminatory, whilst offering no guiding principle to turn to when individuals or groups (who may each consider themselves local to the remains) disagree.

Relativist and Social Constructivist perspectives

Taking a broader view of the current debate, some recent criticisms of current practice regarding the retention and curation of archaeological human remains from Britain appear to draw heavily on two philosophical strands; relativism and social contructivism. These two schools of thought have been used in tandem in order to argue that:

1. All views have equal validity (relativism)
2. All world views are contingent upon the social conditions in which they were created. Therefore, they are all 'correct' on their own terms (social constructivism).

Dealing with these in reverse order, constructivist views can be defined by the general idea that: "facts are socially constructed in a way that reflects contingent needs and interests" (Boghossian, 2006, 20). Ultimately, such views are characterised by some degree of refusal to accept (or at least engage with) the idea that reality is objective, and that the world exists as it is, independently of human opinion. During recent years such views have become prominent in a variety of guises in academic debates and particularly the humanities (Boghossian, 2006; Levitt, 2006; Benson and Stangroom, 2006[2]). Sokal (2006) groups such thinking under the general term 'postmodernism' and notes that whilst this covers a wide range of ideas and approaches they are united by a general tendency to:

> *"reject the idea that assertions about the natural or social world can be objectively (and hence transculturally) true or false; rather they insist that "truth" is relative to some social or cultural group"* (Sokal, 2006: 289).

Boghossian (2006) produces a similar summary of such views in that they claim that:

> *"there are many radically different yet equally valid ways of knowing the world with science being just one of them"* (Boghossian, 2006: 23).

Some recent arguments regarding archaeological human remains appear to be based upon such a standpoint:

> *"They [museums and archaeologists] need to accept that pagans experience the world differently...otherwise museums are no more than arrogant mouthpieces of one particular way of engaging with the world"* (Restall-Orr and Bienkowski, 2006)

> *"Any story that is reconstructed from [archaeological] data will be an imagined past, which usually turns out to be a blueprint of the present imposed upon the past"* (Paul Davies, Reburial Officer, Council of British Druid Orders, quoted by Randerson, 2007).

[in discussing pagan claims for reburial]: *"It is a different world view which, actually, like the scientific world view can be neither proved nor disproved. It is actually our responsibility to take those views into account."*(Bienkowski, quoted by Randerson, 2007).

Following several years of the promotion of such views in a range of academic discourse, a number of writers have more recently come out in defence of the opposing position, 'fact objectivism'. Such writers have pointed out that there are undoubtedly aspects of reality which are independent of human opinion. To give a very simple example, the fact that the earth revolves around the sun is not dependent on us but is, rather just a natural fact that obtains without any help from us.

Having said this, there is no doubt that a great many notions which are widely accepted, are at the same time no more than social constructions. Examples include concepts as diverse as 'biological' races, gender roles, monetary economies and star constellations. It is also true that the type of questions asked, and the style in which observations are expressed within a scientific discipline, may be influenced by various social and institutional factors (Benson and Stangroom, 2006). However, this does not mean that all facts are in themselves socially constructed, or at least we have no reason to think so. We have no reason to think that there is not an independent reality. Nor is there any convincing evidence to suggest that we are not able to make at least some accurate observations about that reality, and to reject radical alternatives which are inconsistent with observed evidence. In fact as Boghossian (2006: 25) observes:

> *"properly understood, fact constructivism is such a bizarre view that it is hard to believe that anyone actually endorses it."*

In fact, everyone experiences the world in exactly the same way. What differs is the opinions people form on the basis of such experiences. When reworded in these terms this becomes a rather bland and obvious statement. There can be no doubt that there can be many different but equally true descriptions of the world (or aspects of it) at any one time. An example of this can be seen in Ingold's (2000b) juxtaposition of scientists' definitions of "climate" with indigenous people's experience of "the weather". In this case, these two definitions are, in fact, referring to different aspects of the same, or at least closely related, phenomena, (which again is ultimately rather obvious). However, this is not the same as saying that *all* descriptions are equally true or equally valid. It does not follow from such a statement that no description of the world (or aspects of it) "could be any closer to the way things are in and of themselves than any other" (Boghossian, 2006: 31). Some statements are simply incompatible with the evidence and must, therefore, be rejected.

Turning to relativism, there are undoubtedly some aspects of philosophical debate where relativism is entirely

---

[2] See Benson and Stangroom (2006) in particular for a detailed discussion of this trend.

appropriate, such as in some areas of morality or etiquette. However, the above statements (about different ways of experiencing the world) invoke 'epistemic relativism' which is a very different proposition. Epistemology deals with the area of what can be classed as knowledge, and the sort of justification required in order for a statement or belief to be accepted as true. Epistemic relativism rejects the idea that it is possible to take a truly objective view of anything, as no 'external' standpoint exists from which to take such a view. All opinions are formed within the culture and method of reasoning to which the person making the observation is accustomed.

Perhaps the most commonly cited counter-argument to epistemic relativism hinges on the point that it is ultimately self-refuting. To put this briefly, an argument which essentially states that 'no view is any more valid than any other' must include itself. Consequently, such arguments have been claimed not to warrant a response as they have already contradicted themselves:

> *"we need not offer any reason* [for disagreeing with a relativist] *since he has offered us no reason to accept"* (Nagel, 1997).[3]

We should like to state firmly that it is not Pagan beliefs themselves (or any other beliefs), that we would wish to take issue with. People are free to believe anything they like. The point we wish to make here, rather concerns the use of postmodernist arguments to promote specific, often religiously motivated agendas by attempting to confer a veneer of academic credibility which they would otherwise lack. Sokal (2006: 286) notes that:

> *"advocates of pseudoscience* [within which definition he includes religion] *sometimes fall back on postmodernist arguments when the reliability or credibility of their evidence is challenged (this stratagem is admittedly second best from their point of view but at least it manages to avert outright refutation)"* (Sokal, 2006: 286).

Rather than 'moving the debate on', the claim that 'Pagan spirituality' has an equal intellectual footing with science is surely just such an argument of last resort, made in order to avoid having to defend this position through rational debate. Perhaps most telling is the attempt to assert that differing models regarding the nature of mind and consciousness are equal in the sense that they cannot be disproved. Bienkowski (2007) cites four such models, Dualism, Materialism, Idealism and Panpsychism (or Animism). The last of these four is of greatest relevance for some recent Pagan arguments concerning human remains, on the basis that this view holds mind, body and soul to be inseparable. Consequently, the excavation of

human remains is argued to "deny the sanctity of nature" and to block the course of a "journey of dying" (Restall-Orr, 2006).

The implication that that these four views are all on an equal footing, in so far as none is disprovable (Bienkowski, 2007), is a rather weak argument at best. The fact that a statement cannot be disproved ultimately has no bearing on its likelihood of being true. The existence of any number of improbable occurrences and supernatural entities (e.g. alien abductions or fairies) cannot be disproved, but this does not make their existence any more likely. As famously pointed out by Bertrand Russell (1952), the burden of proof falls upon the believers to make their case positively, rather than upon non-believers to disprove it. The acceptance of the intellectual validity of relativist arguments has widespread and, in our view, undesirable ramifications. For example, should museums with important fossil collections change their displays to take account of Biblical Creationism as an 'equally valid' world view? By the same token, should Creationism, or its pseudoscientific incarnation, Intelligent Design, be taught in British school science courses as an equally valid alternative to evolution, as is already the case in some States of the USA? The absurdity of this latter has been famously exposed in a light-hearted, but highly effective, manner by scientists in Kansas. In response to the 2005 decision of the Kansas State School Board that the 'theory' of Intelligent Design should be taught in schools as an alternative to evolutionary theory, a group of physicists requested that classroom time also be devoted to teaching a further alternative theory, i.e. that the world was created by a "flying spaghetti monster" (Church of the Flying Spaghetti Monster, 2005) (Fig. 2). This request was supported using the same argument for equal validity by which Intelligent Design was purportedly being justified, pointedly demonstrating the fatuity of such a stance.

The UK has not yet faced the widespread threat from creationism to the teaching of science that has been seen in the USA.

However, there are disturbing suggestions that creationism inspired by Christian- or other religious-fundamentalism may soon become an issue in UK and some other countries (Cornish-Bowden and Cárdenas, 2007).

Conclusions

Reburial of human remains denies future generations the opportunity to study and learn from them. However, reburial may in some cases be desirable in order to respect the wishes of groups with strong links to the remains. It is therefore, mistaken to characterise, as some have (e.g. Baxter, 2007), matters of reburial of archaeological human remains as a dilemma between an "ethical desire" to rebury and the research value of collections of human remains. Ethical considerations

---

[3] However, there are also a number of other more complex and specific arguments as to why epistemic relativism is untenable. For a more detailed exploration of these see Boghossian (2006).

Figure 2. Creation of Adam by the now famous "Flying Spagetti Monster" (Reproduced by kid permission of www.Venganza.org)

often point, not toward reburial, but to retention of collections. Whether retention or reburial of remains is the more ethically desirable course of action will vary in different situations, and the correct response needs to be carefully evaluated in each case. In the decision-making process, all views have an equal right to be expressed, although this does not mean that all opinions should be accorded equal weight. The amount of weight attached to the views of different groups, who may demand reburial of remains or some other say in their future, should depend on the strength of a group's links with the remains. A model based on genealogical and cultural links has recently been agreed for remains in UK museums (Swain, 2005), and this resembles broadly that used in other parts of the world, such as the USA (Walker, 2000). Of course, the ethical treatment of human remains is a developing area in which policies need to be continually reviewed, but we know of no better models that have been proposed. To our knowledge, all policy documents regarding the treatment of human remains acknowledge the value of scientific research on them, so it is right that any claimant who may potentially wish to rebury, or otherwise remove remains from the reach of research, be required to demonstrate strong links with them.

The ethical treatment of archaeological human remains is complex and involves balancing a variety of concerns and objectives, some of which may be in conflict. Decisions may at times, need to be made which balance the needs of science and the wider public interest against the wishes of claimants or other interested parties. Where these conflict, finding a compromise may be difficult. Curators and other professionals need also to be aware of public opinion at a broad level, as this may differ from that expressed by smaller groups of potential claimants. In making decisions about collections, we must also recall that archaeological collections are unique and irreplaceable. As temporary custodians of the small quantity of remains which have survived from our past, we have an obligation towards future generations which is just as great as any obligation to those who lived before us.

Literature cited

Aburrow, Y. 2007. "What does "respect" mean? A discussion of responses to the reburial question". paper presented at the Association of Polytheist Traditions Conference: *Gods and Sacred Places*.

Baxter, K. 2007. "Reburial of ancient British human remains". *Museum Archaeologists News* 42: 3-4.

Benson, O. and Stangroom, J. 2006 *Why Truth Matters*. London: Continuum.

Besterman, T. 2003. "Returning the Ancestors". http://www.museum.manchester.ac.uk/ourcollections/humanremains/fileuploadmax10mb,120894,en.pdf

Bienkowski, P. 2007. "Authority and decision-making over British human remains: issues and challenges" paper presented at *Diversity & The Past: progress, challenges and the future*, Manchester University (abstract).

Boghossian, P. 2006. *Fear of Knowledge: Against Relativism and Constructivism*. Oxford: Clarendon Press.

Brothwell, D. 2004. "Bring out your dead: people, pots and politics". *Antiquity* 78: 414-418.

Buikstra, JE and Gordon, CC. 1981. The study and restudy of human skeletal series: the importance of long-term curation. *Annals of the New York Academy of Sciences* 376: 449-465.

Church of the Flying Spaghetti Monster. 2005. http://www.venganza.org/ (accessed December 2007).

Cornish-Bowden, A, Cárdenas, ML. 2007. The threat from creationism to the rational teaching of biology *Biological Research* 40: 113-122.

Cox, M. 1996. Crypt archaeology after Spitalfields: dealing with our recent dead *Antiquity* 70: 8-10.

Diedriech M. 2007. No-one can speak for ancient Britons. *Museums Journal*

Heyward, F. 2007. Homeward bound *Museums Journal*, November 2006: 34-37.

Historic Scotland. 1997. *The Treatment of Human Remains in Archaeology* Historic Scotland Operational Policy Paper No. 5. http://www.historic-scotland.gov.uk/humanremains.pdf

Ingold, T. 2000a. *The Perception of the Environment: Essays on Livelihood, Dwelling and Skill* London: Routledge.

Ingold, T. 2000b. Perceiving the environment in Finnish-Lapland *Body & Society* 6: 183-196.

Jones, DG, Harris, RJ. 1998. Archaeological human remains: scientific, cultural and ethical considerations. *Current Anthropology* 39: 253-264.

Kohn, M. 2006. Grateful dead. *New Statesman*, 6th November.

Levitt, N. 2006. The colonization of the past and the pedagogy of the future" In: Fagan, G.G. (ed.) *Archaeological Fantasies: How Pseudoarchaeology Misrepresents the Past and Misleads the Public.* London: Routledge, pp 259-285.

Manchester Museum. 2007. *Policy document for the strategic development of the Manchester Museum: Policy on Human Remains.* http://www.museum.manchester.ac.uk/aboutus/reportspolicies/fileuploadmax10mb,120796,en.pdf

Mansell, M. 2006. *Submission by the Tasmanian Aboriginal Centre to the Trustees of the Natural History Museum for the repatriation of Tasmanian Aboriginal Human Remains.* http://www.nhm.ac.uk/about-us/corporate-information/assets/nhm-hrap-tasmanian-submission.pdf

Mays, S. (ed) 2005. *Guidance for Best Practice for Treatment of Human Remains Excavated From Christian Burial Grounds in England.* English Heritage / Church of England. http://www.english-heritage.org.uk/upload/pdf/16602_HumanRemains1.pdf

Mays, S. 2007. United in Church. *British Archaeology* 96: 40-41.

Mays, S, Brickley, M and Dodwell, N. 2002. *Human Bones from Archaeological Sites. Guidelines for Producing Assessment Documents and Analytical Reports.* Swindon: English Heritage.

Mays, S, Brickley, M and Ives, R. 2008. Growth in an English population from the Industrial Revolution. *American Journal of Physical Anthropology* 136, 85-92.

McIntosh, C. 2004. The Pagan revival and its prospects. *Futures* 36: 1025-1048.

Morris, R. 1994. Examine the dead gently. *British Archaeological News* 17: 9.

Nagel, T. 1997. *The Last Word* Oxford: Oxford University.

Palkovich, AM. 2001. Taking another look: the reanalysis of existing collections. In: Williams, E. (ed) *Human Remains: Conservation, Retrieval and Analysis. Proceedings of a Conference held in Williamsburg Va., November 7-11th 1999.* British Archaeological Reports International Series 934. Oxford: BAR Publishing, pp 143-149.

Palmer, N. (ed). 2003. *Report of the Working Group on Human Temains.* London: Department of Culture, Media and Sport.

Parker Pearson, M. 1995. Ethics and the dead in British archaeology. *Field Archaeologist* 23: 17-18.

Pickering, M. 2006. Repatriation at the National Museum of Australia. Paper delivered at the Australian High Commission, London.

Randerson, J. 2007. Give us back our bones pagans tell museums". *The Guardian* (5th February).

Restall-Orr, E. 2006. Human remains: the acknowledgement of sanctity. Paper delivered at the conference '*Respect for Ancient British Human Remains: Philosophy and Practice*' Manchester Museum, 17 November 2006

Restall-Orr, E. and Bienkowski, P. 2006. Respect for All *Museums Journal* (May 2006, 18)

Richards, MP and Schulting RJ 2006. Against the grain? A response to Milner et al. (2004). *Antiquity* 80: 444-458.

Russell, B. 1952. Is There a God? In: Slater, JG and Köllner, P. (eds.) *The Collected Papers of Bertrand Russell, Volume 11: Last Philosophical Testament, 1943-68.* London: Routledge., pp 543-48.

Schulting, R. and Wysocki, M. 2005. 'In this chambered tumulus were found cleft skulls…' an assessment of the evidence for cranial trauma in the earlier Neolithic *Proceedings of the Prehistoric Society* 71: 107-138.

Smith, .L 2004. The repatriation of human remains-problem or opportunity. *Antiquity* 78: 404-413.

Smith, M. 2006. Bones chewed by canids as evidence for human excarnation: a British case study *Antiquity* 80: 671-685.

Smith, MJ. and Brickley, MB. 2009. *People of the Long Barrows: life, death and burial in earlier Neolithic Britain.* Stroud: The History Press.

Sokal, AD. 2006. Pseudoscience and postmodernism: antagonists or fellow travellers? In: Fagan, GG (ed.) *Archaeological Fantasies: How Pseudoarchaeology Misrepresents the Past and Misleads the Public* London: Routledge, pp287-345.

Swain, H. (ed) 2005. *Guidance for the Care of Human Remains in Museums.* DCMS. http://www.culture.gov.uk/NR/rdonlyres/0017476B-3B86-46F3-BAB3-11E5A5F7F0A1/0/GuidanceHumanRemains11Oct.pdf

Tenebrae, E. What is all the fuss about? On the issue of respect for the ancient dead. http://pagantheologies.pbwiki.com/What+is+all+the+fuss+about? (accessed December 2007).

Ubelaker, DH, Grant, LG. 1989. Human skeletal remains: preservation or reburial. *Yearbook of Physical Anthropology* 32: 249-287.

Waldron, T. 2007. *St Peter's Barton-upon-Humber. A Parish Church and its Community. Volume 2: The Human Remains.* Oxford: Oxbow.

Walker, P. 2000. Bioarchaeological ethics: a historical perspective on the value of human remains. In: Katzenberg M, Saunders S, (eds.) *Biological Anthropology of the Human Skeleton.* New York: Wiley-Liss., pp 3-39.

World Archaeology Congress, 1989. *The Vermillion Accord – human remains motion approved at the first inter-congress on the disposal of the dead*, Vermillion SD. http://www.worldarchaeologicalcongress.org/site/about_ethi.php#code2

The Problem of Provenance: inaccuracies, changes and misconceptions

Margaret Clegg

Human Remains Unit, Department of Palaeontology, Natural History Museum, Cromwell Road, London SW7 5BD
e-mail:m.clegg@nhm.ac.uk

Abstract

When human remains are being considered for repatriation it is important that only remains affiliated to the claimant group are included in this process. The documentary evidence in collection registers, index cards and databases tend to be sparse, and may be either incomplete or inaccurate. It is therefore important that a wider archival search is conducted before the number of human remains included is finalised. This paper presents one case where the basic information was both incomplete and inaccurate. In the course of an earlier re-cataloguing exercise, one individual had changed not only ethnic group, but sex, age and lost their name as well. This would have resulted in the return of a named individual to the wrong part of the world. This would be unethical to both the claimant group, and to the possible descendants of the individual. This case highlights the possible pitfalls associated with too heavy a reliance on the basic information in collection records.

Keywords: Repatriation, human remains, provenance, museum records.

There is an implicit assumption, particularly by those outside museums, that the basic records kept within museums will accurately reflect the information about human remains they hold. This is not always so. Inaccuracies, transcription errors and other mistakes can creep into the basic records. These errors are compounded when the human remains in question have passed through several institutions, as the complete record may not accompany the collection or partial collection when they are transferred between institutions. Also, record keeping in the past within museums and other institutions was not to the standard we would expect today, index cards were small and so the minimum of information was copied to them. It is therefore important, that when human remains are considered for repatriation, a wider archival search is conducted to ensure that the provenance of the remains is correctly established. This is important because only remains affiliated to the claimant group should be included in this process. The

documentary evidence in collection registers, index cards and databases tend to be sparse, and may be either incomplete or inaccurate. It is essential to ensure that the records are as complete and accurate as possible before the number of human remains included in any repatriation claim is finalised.

Undertaking such archival research is often a long process, but allows for the origin of the remains and their history, (particularly how they come to the museum), to be determined with greater confidence. This would also assist in determining if the affiliation of the human remains in the museum collection is with the group making the repatriation claim. Unless we can be confident that the information available can adequately do this, then we can not ensure that only remains affiliated to a particular group are considered for repatriation. This is an ethical issue, it is essential that only remains affiliated to a claimant group are returned to

them. Repatriation is forever; if remains are returned to the 'wrong' group, and should this group bury or cremated the remains, then it would not be possible for the 'true' descendents to ask for the remains to be returned.

There are also issues of provenance that impact on research questions. It is important that when research is conducted on remains, that the researchers can be sure that the remains do belong to the group to which they have been assigned, or some research questions may not be answered correctly by the data.

There are a variety of potential errors that can occur within the basic information held on any set of human remains. They can be as simple as a transcription error, very likely to occur when handwritten documents are transferred to computer records in databases. Some handwritten records can be very difficult to decipher, particularly when unfamiliar names or terms are used. Sometimes, the basic record for the remains does not contain all the information given at the time of donation. This is usually the simplest error to correct by looking again at the original documentation. Human remains are also often transferred between institutions. Provenance problems can occur if the documentary evidence from the original institution is not transferred with the remains. There are also occasions when deliberate changes are made to records either by accident or design.

The repatriation process is often the main reason that the provenance of human remains is investigated within museums and other institutions. It is essential that additional checks are made during this process. Ideally, such checks should be made during cataloguing exercises to ensure that complete and accurate information is collected and held by the museum. This does slow down the rate at which specimens are entered into the new database, but is an important part of the cataloguing process. The need to input accurate information, rather

A.

PA PHR 336
Tribe: Australian Aboriginal.
Sex: Male.
Maturity: Adult.
Tasmania, Australia, Australia.
Associated: Oxford Colln.
Nature of Acquisition to NHM: Presd.
Acquired from: Oxford Collection.
See also: Williamson Collection.
Original Collection: Oxford AUS 80/5
Cranium
Dentition

B.

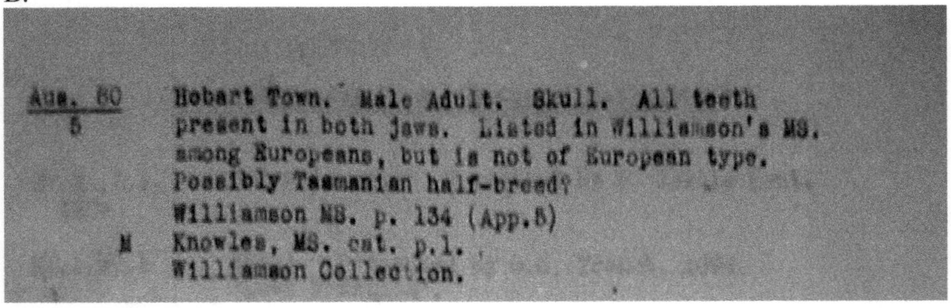

Aus. 80
5

Hobart Town. Male Adult. Skull. All teeth present in both jaws. Listed in Williamson's MS. among Europeans, but is not of European type. Possibly Tasmanian half-breed?
Williamson MS. p. 134 (App.5)
M Knowles, MS. cat. p.1.
Williamson Collection.

Figure 1. A. Database entry for the skull. B. Index card for the same individual.

than unchecked original records, can sometimes be overlooked in the drive to get as much information entered into a new database as possible.

There are a large number of other sources of information that can be used to collect additional information on human remains. These include the institution's own archives, which would allow information in the basic record to be checked against the original source; for example, donation letters, trustees' minutes and purchase ledgers. The archives and catalogues of previous holding institutions should also be visited to ensure that all information about any particular human remains have been transferred with them. In the past, it was not unusual for human remains to be transferred without the full documentation. This was especially true when only part of a collection was being transferred between institutions. This often means that the donating institution provides only edited highlights, usually hand written, from the original papers. Such extracts may have essential information missing for the sake of brevity. If possible, the donor's papers and journals should also be examined to ascertain if they passed on all relevant information at the time of donation. The information in such accounts often more accurately reflects what actually happened at the time, as the events are clear and fresh in the writer's mind.

It is also a good idea to make a literature search for journal articles that have been written about the remains from any particular group. Early research on the remains may also have valuable additional information. The author may, for example, have been able to speak directly to the donor, and ask the questions we would like answered. These papers can be difficult to obtain, however, JSTOR and other archival sites are a good starting point in tracking down such papers. You may also need to visit large national libraries such as the British Library for the older volumes of journals. Other sources relevant to the remains should also be checked; for example, accounts of voyages, archives of the donor's employer, such as, missionary societies, government departments, universities and the armed forces.

The potential consequences of not taking care when a repatriation claim is made can be illustrated through an intriguing case we uncovered recently at the Natural History Museum in London. The archival research conducted as part of the provenancing of the Tasmanian repatriation claim showed that the same individual had two possible identities attributed to them. The index cards and database entry described this individual as a male Tasmanian, 'possibly half-breed' (Fig 1).

This information had been provided by Oxford University on transfer of the remains to the Natural History Museum. However, the remains were previously part of a transfer of the large Williamson Collection from the Royal Army medical Corp to Oxford University. The original catalogue shows clearly that these remains were not of a Tasmanian man, but a British woman (Fig 2)! This discrepancy had previously been documented by Plomley (1962) who had given both versions in his paper on Tasmanian human remains in Museum collections, and by Fforde (1992), in her paper on the current holdings at the Natural History Museum.

E2/5 Louisa Ferris British Twice attempted to commit murder Hobart Town 6th November 1855
Donor: Dr. Atkinson DSG

Figure 2: Extract from Williamson Manuscript Catalogue

Family Name	Given Names	See Surname	See Given Names	Date of Arrival	Ship Name	Date of Departure	Port of Departure	Remarks	Database Number
Ferris	Louisa			02 Jan 1848	Cadet (2)	09 Sep 1847	London		23102

Figure 3. Details of convict voyage Index to Tasmanian Convicts Tasmanian State Archives

Some basic research at the National Archives at Kew, and the online search facility of the Tasmanian State Archives, confirmed the information in the Williamson catalogue. Further research in the archives of the Times newspaper gave much more information about this woman, the crime and her victim. Louisa Ferris had been a lodging housekeeper and had killed one of her lodgers, a policeman, in a fit of jealousy on 2nd November 1846. She then went straight to the police station and confessed her crime. She was the step-daughter of a policeman and appears to have lived a blameless, or at least non-criminal, life up to that point. The press reports (The Times, 1846) are as lurid as they would be today, but give a huge amount of background information, about her family and other circumstances, which can be readily verifiable from census returns, police archives and parish records. The trial was at Gloucester Assizes (Oxford Circuit) on 5th April 1847 and the court records give details of the trial, the verdict of manslaughter, and of the sentence of 'transportation for life' (National Archive Kew, 1847). Louisa sailed from London on the convict ship Cadet, in September 1847 (Fig 3) aged 29, (National Archive Kew 1808-1849), and arrived at the female factory in Tasmania in January 1848, after a voyage lasting four months (Tasmanian State Archives, 1848).

After her arrival in Tasmania Louisa disappears, (although more information may exist in the records at the Tasmanian State archive), until her death in 1854 at the hospital in Hobart. Her skull was donated to Royal Army Medical Corp by Dr Atkinson, the Deputy Surgeon General (DSG) in charge of the hospitals in Tasmania (Johnston, 1968). During the 19th century in Tasmania, all convicts who died with an unexpired sentence, or who re-offended after expiry of sentence, were liable to dissection if they died in hospital, or in custody (MacDonald, 2006) .It is likely that this is what happened to Louisa, and as was so often the case, only the head was retained for further study. The hospitals in Tasmania, particularly those for the convicts, came under the jurisdiction of the Army. The DSG was an army medical officer and had the disposition of the remains under his care (MacDonald, 2005). During the 19th century it was quite common for such officers to send the heads of those who died back to the Royal Army Medical Corp. In this

way, their collection covered many continents and many different nationalities.

Further examination of the Williamson catalogue and the later records from Oxford, showed that during an earlier cataloguing exercise after the remains had been transferred to Oxford, the designation of this and other skulls was changed (Ellis, 1953). The curator or researcher who made the alterations did so because, in his words, the skull was "not typical of the European" The skull is quite large and robust, and so on these grounds alone, was changed to male, this despite the evidence from the donor of the nam, age and sex of the individual, together with her known and alleged crimes.

This case highlights the problems of over-reliance on the basic information in record cards, and databases taken from those cards. If no additional research had been conducted prior to repatriation this individual would have been erroneously returned with the correctly assigned Tasmanian remains. It is important to all concerned that this process is undertaken.

To ensure that the correct affiliation is made for any human remains claimed for repatriation, it is essential that the person dealing with the claim goes further than the basic records to establish provenance. This can be a time-consuming exercise, research for the Tasmanian remains took approximately two months, but it is important to examine other sources of evidence. The researcher should never assume anything in relation to the completeness or accuracy of the records. Repatriation is forever, you can not bring the remains back should you get it wrong, so it is essential to get it right!

Literature cited

Ellis F. 1953. Tasmanian Skulls NHM Archive file DF 141/26

Fforde C. 1992. Some Current Holdings at the Natural History Museum London. *World Archaeology Bulletin* 6 37-52

Johnston, W 1968. *Commissioned officers in the medical services of the British Army.* Vol. 1 London: The Wellcome Historical Medical Library

MacDonald, H 2005 *Human Remains: Episodes in Human Dissections,* Melbourne: Melbourne University Press

MacDonald H 2006 *Human Remains: Dissection and Its Histories* Yale: Yale University Press.

National Archives Kew (1808-1860) Tasmanian list of convicts.

National Archives Kew (1847) Court Register for Gloucester Assizes ASSI 2/34

Plomley NJB (1962) A list of Tasmanian Aboriginal material in collections in Europe *Records of the Queen Victoria Museum*, Launceston 15 1-18

Tasmanian State Archives online http://www.archives.tas.gov.au/ Index to Tasmanian Convicts

The Times Digital Archive http://www.jisc-collections.ac.uk/timesdigital

Native American Human Remains in UK Collections:
Implications of NAGPRA to consultation, repatriation, and policy development

Myra J. Giesen

International Centre for Cultural and Heritage Studies, Newcastle University, Newcastle upon Tyne, NE1 7RU
myra.giesen@ncl.ac.uk

Abstract

The past 30 years has witnessed a dramatic shift in attitudes towards excavating (pre)historic cemeteries, the study of human remains, and the retention of remains in formal collections, as well as their placement on public display. However, legislation and policy on their treatment varies dramatically, especially across international boundaries. For example in 2004, the British parliament passed the Human Tissue Act, which enabled nine national museums the discretionary power to deaccession human remains under 1000 years old. The *Guidance for the Care of Human Remains in Museums* was then published the following year as a 'best practice' document to aid institutions in England, Wales, and Northern Ireland by providing a legal and ethical framework for the treatment of human remains. Most repatriation claims in England are not domestic, but are actually related to human remains from overseas. In this case, the *Guidance* advises that institutions become aware of relevant foreign legislation, especially as it relates to local policy and claimants' expectations. Greater awareness is particularly critical with Native American human remains in the United States, which are broadly governed by the Native American Graves Protection and Repatriation Act (NAGPRA, Public Law 101-601), a law that is both complicated and quite different from other countries. The goal of this paper is to inform UK institutions on NAGPRA terms and concepts, expectations among Native Americans, and available support resources. The paper will then provide recommendations on how to work within NAGPRA, so that consultations on Native American human remains will be most fruitful.

Keywords: human remains, NAGPRA, Native American, repatriation, United Kingdom

Introduction

Laws and policies regulating the treatment of human remains held in institutions (i.e., museums, academic institutions, research laboratories, antiquarian societies, government agency, or any organized entity holding human remains) are highly variable and seldom apply beyond domestic borders. Additionally, the protocol for communicating between interested parties varies between cultures and administrators, which create further differences and possible disparities. As repatriation requests for indigenous human remains continue to increase, institutions and claimants must better understand formal legal processes and learn to communicate effectively to avoid legal and other conflict.

Australian Aborigines long campaigned for the repatriation of human remains held in British institutions (Fforde and Ormond-Parker 2001). In 2000, these efforts finally gained political clout when the Australian and British governments agreed to increase efforts to repatriate human remains to Australian indigenous communities (DCMS 2005), with the Australian government assuming a formal role in facilitating international repatriations (Australian Government 2005). The increasing number of repatriations back to Australia from the UK bares witness to the success of this formal agreement (DCMS 2005: 23). However, the responses of British institutions to claims from other native peoples are less clear, especially Native North Americans. The United States (US) and British governments have no formal agreement related to Native American human remains, nor has the US government assumed a leadership role in coordinating such repatriations to Native Americans. Despite this lack of infrastructure, large numbers of indigenous human remains originating from the Americas reside in UK institutions (Weeks and Bott 2003).

The 2003 *Scoping Survey of Historic Human Remains in English Museums and Other Organisations* (Weeks and Bott 2003) is the only published study that attempts to document the number and place of origin of human remains in collections in the UK. It only included information from 146 English museums; however, it found that 41.7% of the institutions that responded had human remains of indigenous peoples from North and South America who died between 1500 and 1947 (Weeks and Bott 2003: 13), which roughly equated to 1,800 individuals. Weeks and Bott also gathered information about individuals who died prior to 1500, with 46.2% of the responding institutions indicating they held 'ancient' human remains (>4,000 individuals) from overseas. Locations of origin were not available and it is not possible to say how many of those individuals were from the US or North America, or broadly from the Americas.

Although the exact number of Native American human remains in UK institutions is unknown, it is just a matter of time before inquires and/or claims start arriving at UK institutions regarding them, and no national approach exists within the UK for addressing such actions. UK institutions (except those in Scotland, where independent guidance is under development) seeking guidance on such international repatriations most likely will turn to the *Guidance for the Care of Human Remains in Museums* (2005). This Guidance provides a legal and ethical framework for the treatment of human remains. Additionally, it has a section entitled "Policy of the country of origin" (Section 3.2K), which states that "[s]ome nation states have developed domestic legislation or policy to govern claims for the return of remains…[and should] be aware of any policies of the national government from which a claim originated" (DCMS 2005: 28). Furthermore, the Guidance recommends that museums be aware of how claims are resolved in the native country, as well as expectations of claimants based on the practice in their country of origin.

A need for greater awareness is especially true for human remains originating from the US, where legislation and policy for the repatriation of Native American human remains is well established (Table 1) under the Native American Graves Protection and Repatriation Act (NAGPRA, Public Law 101-601) and its implementing regulations (43 CFR Part 10). NAGPRA affects almost all Native American repatriations and is legally complicated, requiring considerable expertise for successful consultation. Given this background, the goal of this paper is to inform British institutions of key terms, concepts, and expectations within NAGPRA as a guide for consultations, but also to present for discussion NAGPRA as a model for future repatriation claims.

US repatriation legislation

The desire to repatriate human remains resulted from the strong conviction of many Native Americans and others that the long-term curation, display of, and research on human remains is not an appropriate treatment of the dead.

Political pressure and heightened awareness among the public increased the power of indigenous groups over the disposition and treatment of cultural items, and led to the enactment of progressively broader and more complicated laws associated with the issue of repatriation. Historically, individual US states were the first to respond to increasing concerns about long-term curation, display, and research on Native American human remains. Local actions most often were through legislation aimed to protect unmarked burial sites, and later through actual repatriation law. This resulted in very different laws from state to state, although the core of most state law mandates special treatment of burial sites and similar cultural resources, and provides significant penalties for failure to comply.

Due to growing national pressures, federal legislation was finally put forward and passed in 1989. The first law was the National Museum of the American Indian Act (NMAI Act). This law mandated Smithsonian museums to identify, and consider for return, if requested by a Native community or individual, American Indian, Alaska Native, and Native Hawaiian human remains and associated funerary objects. Furthermore, federal funds

Table 1. Key US repatriation laws, regulations, and policies

- 1989 **National Museum of the American Indian Act** (NMAI Act) www.nmnh.si.edu/anthro/repatriation/pdf/ nmai_act.pdf

- 1990 **Native American Graves Protection and Repatriation Act** (NAGPRA), plus regulations www.nps.gov/history/nagpra/MANDATES/ INDEX.HTM

- 1997 **State Statues** – "Update of Compilation of State Repatriation, Reburial And Grave Protection Laws" www.nrcs.usda.gov/technical/ECS/culture /rebury.pdf

- 2007 – **Policy Statement Regarding Treatment of Burial Sites, Human Remains, and Funerary Objects** www.achp.gov/docs/hrpolicy0207.pdf

being provided to cover the cost of the actions under this law.

Congress later broadened the scope of law through the passage of NAGPRA in 1990, which established a similar mandate to all US federal agencies and US museums that receiving federal funding. NAGPRA also targets human remains and associated funerary objects, but also added unassociated funerary objects, sacred objects, and items of cultural patrimony to the list of potential repatriable items. Although operational ramifications were daunting, only limited funds were appropriated to cover the cost of NAGPRA actions, which has become very significant in efforts to implement the law.

The NMAI Act Amendment of 1996 further added provisions for the inventory and repatriation of unassociated funerary objects, sacred objects, and objects of cultural patrimony. The NMAI Act and its amendment are most often applied to the Smithsonian museums, which have large American Indian collections, specifically located in the National Museum of American Indian and the National Museum of Natural History. Both museums have repatriation offices that follow similar NMAI Act guidelines, yet each museum manages a separate and distinct repatriation program.

Broadly speaking, NAGPRA and the NMAI Act affirms the rights of lineal descendants, Indian tribes, and Native Hawaiian organizations to custody of Native American human remains, funerary objects, sacred objects, and objects of cultural patrimony (collectively referred to as Cultural Items). In enacting this legislation, the federal government acknowledged that over the course of the nation's history, Native American human remains and funerary objects have suffered from differential treatment compared with related materials from other groups. They also acknowledged the failure of US law to recognize traditional concepts of communal property used by many Indian tribes. In a nutshell, NAGPRA and the NMAI Act aim to help affected parties resolve issues surrounding the custody of Cultural Items in an equitable manner. Specifically, NAGPRA requires federal agencies and museums to consult directly with lineal descendants, Indian tribes, or Native Hawaiian organizations and, in many cases, transfer custody of Cultural Items to them.

For simplicity, one can break NAGPRA into four basic parts. The first deals with identifying and defining terms. The second part deals with new and existing collections of Cultural Items. The third part deals with the protection of Native American graves, and describes procedures that federal agencies must follow when they intentionally excavate or remove Cultural Items, or when they inadvertently discover Cultural Items on federal or tribal land. The fourth part describes criminal penalties for illegally trafficking in Cultural Items. The first and second parts (i.e. Definitions and Collections) are of greatest interest here, although tribes may have different expectations depending on experiences with the third part (Discoveries/Excavations), which will be specifically discussed under expectations below.

Key NAGPRA Terms and Concepts

In order to understand NAGPRA and its regulations, one must first become familiar with the terms they use. Although some definitions will be provided, it is highly recommended one returns directly to the law and its regulations to understand fully their context, meaning, and relationship with each other. Below are some general questions that may set the stage for informed communication with Native Americans.

1. What must US museums do if they have human remains in their collections?

This answer is "it depends." If the museum receives federal funds (after November 16, 1990) and the human remains are Native American, then NAGPRA applies. However, if the museum does not receive federal funds or the human remains are not Native American, the museum policy or applicable state laws apply. Although these options appear clear, terms within NAGPRA have specific legal meanings, which must be understood to answer the above question correctly in a given case.

For example, *Native American* is defined as "of, or relating to, a tribe, people, or culture that is indigenous to the United States" (25 USC 3001 (9)) and "of, or relating to, a tribe, people, or culture indigenous to the United States, including Alaska and Hawaii" (43 CFR 10.2 (d)). A disagreement over the meaning of *Native American* was central to the Kennewick Man controversy (Holden

2004, Watkins 2004, Zimmerman 2005, Edgar et al. 2007). Furthermore, *human remains* mean "the physical remains of the body of a person of Native American ancestry." The term does not include remains or portions of remains that have been freely given or naturally shed by the individual from whose body they were obtained (e.g., hair made into ropes). Furthermore, "for the purposes of determining cultural affiliation, human remains incorporated into a funerary object, sacred object, or object of cultural patrimony must be considered as part of that item" (43 CFR 10.2 (d)(1)). *Control* means to have "a legal interest in human remains . . . [that is] sufficient to lawfully permit the museum . . . to treat [them] . . . as part of its collection for purposes of these regulations whether or not the human remains . . . are in the physical custody of the museum" (43 CFR 10.2 (a)(3)(ii)). Finally, *Indian tribe* means "any tribe, band, nation, or other organized group or community of Indians, including any Alaska Native village (as defined in, or established pursuant to, the Alaska Native Claims Settlement Act), which is recognized as eligible for the special programs and services provided by the United States to Indians because of their status as Indians" (25 U.S.C. 3001 (7)). The current list of eligible tribe is available at www.narf.org/nill/resources/fr2007.pdf, although this list changes periodically as the Bureau of Indian Affairs approves tribal petitions for recognition, or as recognition is conferred through legislation.

In summary, the terms *Native American, human remains, control,* and *Indian tribe* have explicit legal meanings, which in total, narrows the scope of NAGPRA. Consequently, care and experience is needed to fully appreciate the many intricacies of NAGPRA. In fact, these terms are all potentially contentious because one is often dealing with limited information and interpretations that are subject to the bias of observers. Many of the litigations and disputes within the US have resulted from a lack of understanding or challenges of these terms (Ackerman 1997, Goldman 1999, Owsley and Jantz 2001, Watkins 2004). As such, UK institutions would benefit from knowing the legal meaning of these terms, especially given that they are familiar to most Native Americans likely to make claims to Native American remains.

2. How do you know which Native American group(s) to consult?

The answer to this question also is not straightforward. Using NAGPRA as a model, the range of Native American groups to be consulted differs depending whether the human remains are being dealt with as a Collection or a Discovery/Excavation. Table 2 provides a summary of these differences. Note that much disagreement exists regarding the scope of consulting parties identified in NAGPRA, with many advocating that non-federally-recognized tribes should be included in the process. Native American views on recognition are split, but for differing reasons.

Table 2. NAGPRA consulting parties

43 CFR 10.9(b) Collections	43 CFR 10.5(a) Inadvertent discoveries and planned excavations
• **Lineal descendants**; • Indian tribe officials and traditional religious leaders from whose **tribal lands** the human remains originated; • Indian tribe officials and traditional religious leaders that are, or are likely to be, **culturally affiliated** with human remains; and • Indian tribe officials and traditional religious leaders from whose **aboriginal lands** the human remains originated.	• **Lineal descendants**; • Indian tribes on whose **aboriginal lands** the planned activity will occur or where the inadvertent discovery has been made; • Indian tribes and Native Hawaiian organizations that are, or are likely to be, **culturally affiliated** with the human remains; and • Indian tribes and Native Hawaiian organizations that have a demonstrated **cultural relationship** with the human remains.

According to Watkins (2004: 69), "many tribes feel that non-federally-recognized tribes are no less Indian than their federally-recognized counterparts, while others are afraid that to allow standing under NAGPRA would allow such groups to bypass the normally tedious process of federal recognition."

3. Where can one obtain more information about NAGPRA, especially related to identifying consulting parties?

The National NAGPRA Program hosts a website, which provides all sorts of information about NAGPRA and useful databases for NAGPRA implementation. The *Native American Consultation Database* is particularly relevant to consultation, which identifies current official contacts for Indian tribes, Alaska Native villages and corporations, and Native Hawaiian organizations; and includes names and addresses of tribal leaders according to the current information kept by the Bureau of Indian Affairs.

Also useful is the *Notices of Inventory Completion Database*, which is a searchable library of published Federal Register notices pertinent to Native American human remains. Within the notices are consultation lists that are relevant to human remains that have been assigned cultural affiliation. Equally helpful is the *Culturally Unidentifiable Native American Inventories Database*, which provides information about Native American human remains, determined to be culturally

unidentifiable. See Table 3 for a detailed list of web addresses for these and other online resources.

Noteworthy too is that Native American human remains found as inadvertent discoveries or planned excavations on non-federal or non-tribal lands do not fall under NAGPRA. In those cases, state laws often provide a different set of consulting parties, including tribes that fall outside federal recognition. Details of state-recognized tribes can be obtained at www.ncai.org/State_Recognized_Indian_Tribes.285.0.html.

Table 3. Online resources

- National NAGPRA www.cr.nps.gov/nagpra
- Native American Consultation Database http://home.nps.gov/nacd/
- Tribal Leaders Directory http://library.doi.gov/internet/tribaleaders9.pdf
- Indian Land Cessions 1784-1894 www.nps.gov/history/nagpra/onlinedb/land_cessions/index.htm
- Federal Lands and Indian Reservations Map http://nationalatlas.gov/printable/images/pdf/fedlands/fedlands3.pdf
- Indian Reservations in the Continental US Map www.nps.gov/history/nagpra/DOCUMENTS/RESERV. PDF
- Judicially Established Indian Lands Map http://rockyweb.cr.usgs.gov/outreach/mapcatalog/images/culture/indian_land_judicial_areas_11x15.pdf
- NAGPRA Notice of Inventory Completion Database www.nps.gov/history/nagpra/fed_notices/nagpradir/ index.htm
- NAGPRA Culturally Unidentifiable Native American Inventory Database http://64.241.25.6/CUI/index.cfm
- NMNH Cultural Affiliation Reports www.nmnh.si.edu/anthro/repatriation/reports/summaries.htm
- NMAI Repatriation Office www.nmai.si.edu/subpage.cfm?subpage=collaboration&second=repatriation

4. How do you make a cultural affiliation determination?

Cultural affiliation is defined as "a relationship of shared group identity which can be reasonably traced historically or prehistorically between a present day Indian tribe or Native Hawaiian organization and an identifiable earlier group" (25 U.S.C. 3001 (2)). Under NAGPRA, cultural affiliation is "established when the preponderance of the evidence…based on geographical, kinship, biological, archeological, linguistic, folklore, oral tradition, historical evidence, or other information or expert opinion…reasonably leads to such a conclusion" (43 CFR 10.2 (e)). The National NAGPRA Program databases, particularly the *Notices of Inventory Completion Database*, are useful in assessing what others have done with respect to making cultural affiliation determination. Equally helpful are the repatriation reports of the Repatriation Office of the National Museum of Natural History. Web links to these resources are found in Table 3. It should be noted that determining cultural affiliation is among the most difficult components of NAGPRA because the evidence ones uses can be contradictory or often open for interpretation. Weighing out the lines of evidence is in an unbiased manner is exceedingly challenging.

5. Does a priority system exist regarding repatriation or disposition claims?

Yes, but like consultation, priority depends upon whether the human remains are identified as a Collection or as a Discovery/Excavation (see Table 4 for a comparison of priorities). At this moment, repatriating Native American human remains in Collections is fairly straightforward with priority going to lineal descendants and then to culturally affiliated Indian tribes. However, human remains that are culturally unidentifiable (the term used in NAGPRA) will be less clear until the reserved section of the NAGPRA Regulations (43 CFR 10.11) is finalized.

Table 4. Custody priorities

43 CFR 10.10(b) Collections	43 CFR 10.6(a) Inadvertent Discoveries & Planned Excavations
1. Lineal Descendant 2. Culturally Affiliated Indian Tribe 3. Retain culturally unidentifiable until 43 CFR 10.11 is finalized, or recommendation to do otherwise is obtained from the Native American Grave Protection and Repatriation Review Committee.	1. Lineal Descendant 2. Indian Tribe on whose tribal land cultural items were found 3. Culturally Affiliated Indian Tribe 4. Indian Tribe with stronger cultural relationship, unless another tribe has a stronger one 5. Indian Tribe aboriginally occupying the land, as determined by the Indian Claims Commission of US Court of Claims 6. If custody cannot be determined or no claim is received, then the agency retains unclaimed remains and objects.

Currently, culturally unidentifiable human remains can only undergo disposition after the Native American Graves Protection and Repatriation Review Committee provides recommendations to support such an action. A proposed rule for this section of the NAGPRA Regulations was published in the Federal Register in October 2007 with comments due in January 2008.

6. Who can make a claim under NAGPRA?

NAGPRA only recognizes claims by lineal descendants, Indian tribes, and Native Hawaiian organizations. *Lineal descendant* means "an individual tracing his or her ancestry directly and without interruption by means of the traditional kinship system of the appropriate Indian tribe or Native Hawaiian organization or by the common law system of descendance to a known Native American individual" (43 CFR 10.2 (b)(1)). Whereas, *Native Hawaiian organization* means "any organization that (a) Serves and represents the interests of Native Hawaiians; (b) has as a primary and stated purpose the provision of services to Native Hawaiians; and (c) has expertise in Native Hawaiian affairs" (43 CFR 10.2(b)(3)). *Indian tribe* was defined in Question 1 above. Who can claim under NAGPRA can be contentious; therefore, the above definitions need to be clearly understood by institutions involved in consultation and repatriation.

7. What are some tips for achieving successful consultations?

Know what is meant by federally-recognized tribe - It is centrally useful to know which tribes are considered sovereign Nations with whom the US government has unique legal relationships. Federal agencies are obligated to work with these tribal governments on a government-to-government basis, and strongly support and respect tribal sovereignty and self-determination. Museums do not have the same legal relationship with Indian tribes; instead, they tend to engage in consultation more on a business level. Also, refer back to the response provided to Question 2.

Seek out established support documents - Two helpful documents written on tribal consultation include *Tribal Consultation: Best Practices in Historic Preservation* at www.nathpo.org/PDF/Tribal_Consultation.pdf, and *Guidelines and Procedures for Repatriation* at www.nmnh.si.edu/anthro/repatriation/pdf/guidelines_and _procedures.pdf.

Document collection and management procedures *a priori* – Know your collection and document it clearly through inventories. Additionally, it is always good practice to have formal written procedures and collection management policies in place prior to consultation, which sets the stage for open and transparent discussions. Additionally, it is very helpful to have organizational charts that clearly identify who has authority to make decisions about the treatment of human remains within any museum or institution. It also is prudent to maintain formal administrative records of correspondence, meetings, and decision processes that occur.

Make sure whom you are consulting with is who you think they are - Tribes (like museums) have numerous individuals on staff and not all of them have the authority to make decisions. Be sure the persons with whom you are sharing information have the authority to represent the tribe you are consulting. Note also that many tribes have traditional leaders, elected officials, and NAGPRA coordinators who will have some say about human remains; the latter two positions usually are appointed and change with tribal elections. Finally, confirm you are consulting with the current administration.

Expectations of Claimants

Under NAGPRA, lineal descendants, Indian tribes, and Native Hawaiian organizations have some clear expectations of which UK institution must be aware. For example, they expect to be provided item-by-item inventories of Native American human remains, which are likely culturally affiliated with them or originated from their tribal or aboriginal lands, regardless of age of the remains (historic and ancient). Additionally, they imagine such inventories will include details about associated funerary objects. Similarly, Indian tribes and Native Hawaiian organizations assume they will be consulted on Native American human remains *and* associated funerary objects regardless of the age of the collections. They expect the opportunity to contribute information relevant for the museum to make a cultural affiliation determination and that tribal government officials, Native Hawaiian organization officials, Alaska Native groups, and traditional religious leaders will be invited to take active roles in the consultation process. Finally, expectations exist relating to public notices about inventory completion and cultural affiliated determinations. Museums and federal agencies in the US must publish such notices in the Federal Register – the official daily publication for rules, proposed rules, and notices of federal agencies and organizations; see http://www.gpoaccess.gov/fr/index.html. These notices allow open and equal access to information, plus allow tribes to make claims to collections. Finally, tribes expect to have an advisory committee available to voice concerns and facilitate dispute resolutions.

Once cultural affiliations are determined, the affiliated Indian tribes or Native Hawaiian organizations expect timely repatriation of the human remains and associated funerary objects to occur following submission of their written claims. Additionally, Indian tribes and Native Hawaiian organizations anticipate the return of culturally unidentifiable Native American human remains, and, in many cases, the associated funerary objects (Office of the Secretary, Interior 2007). However, such expectations are not consistent with UK Guidance (DCMS 2005: 27), which states, "that claims are unlikely to be successful for any remains over 300 years old, and are unlikely to be considered for remains over 500 years old, except where

a very close and continuous geographical, religious, spiritual and cultural link can be demonstrated." This incongruity demonstrates why UK institutions need to establish their own policies regarding US repatriations because Native American expectations can differ from the Guidance recommendations and even the legal obligations of NAGPRA.

Conclusion and recommendation

UK institutions should expect increasing claims for Native Americans human remains and associated funerary objects from their collections, whether these items are historic or ancient because Native Americans are becoming more active and successful at making claims in the US under both state and federal laws. This reality impacts UK institutions with Native American remains and greater knowledge of NAGPRA is demanded. However, the relative success of NAGPRA also might provide a framework for UK institutions to model their own practices. Clearly, the UK and US legal systems differ, but evidence from other quarters suggest the systems are becoming more similar (e.g., medical litigation); therefore, lessons from NAGPRA may be very important for future UK repatriation activities. Furthermore, better understanding NAPGRA is critical and requires increased awareness and education.

Pertinent to this, one can find many overviews of NAGPRA as policy (Trope and Echo Hawk 1992, Carter 1999, Lovis et al. 2004, Ousley et al. 2005) and other issues related to practice (Echo Hawk 2002). However, the best way to understand NAGPRA is to read the statue and its implementing regulations. Although this is generally useful, the regulations are still incomplete; therefore, also expect change. In fact, the pending Proposed Rule for Disposition of Culturally Unidentifiable, 43 CFR 10.11 promises some interesting and possibly controversial changes, as can be seen by the number of disparate responses to it publication (see comments at

http://www.regulations.gov/fdmspublic/component/main? main=DocketDetail&d=DOI-2007-0032).

Regardless, proactively sharing information about Native American collections will play a significant role in setting the appropriate tone and likely reduce expense of consultation activities in the future. As such, compiling and publishing inventories of institution holdings of human remains is a desirable starting point as is stated in the Guidance. Establishing a web-based clearinghouse to post inventories and notices would be highly beneficial. It is clear both federally-recognized and non-federally-recognized Indian tribes have an interest in and seek the repatriation of Native American remains. In the US, NAGPRA focuses on who should be consulted, but also limits the potential claimants of Native American human remains. No similar restrictions exist in UK law; consequently, each UK institution has complete discretion on such matters. Consequently, when it comes to Native American human remains in their collections, it would be useful for institutions to 1) decide whether it will consult with all interested parties, or only NAGPRA-defined legal claimants; and 2) fully understand the consequences of such a decision.

Ultimately, managing human remains in our increasingly litigious world comes down to establishing internal policies and procedures. The Guidance does provide practical advice. Nevertheless, it is up to each institution to formalize its practices in written policy and procedures, thereby lessening the potential for disputes or possibly litigation by being consistent and transparent. At a minimum, UK institutions controlling Native American human remains should become knowledgeable of US policy and procedures and then develop their own that specifically address 1) how to and who will make cultural affiliation determinations (including the types of evidence needed); 2) who are acceptable consulting parties; 3) who can or cannot make claims; 4) how will associated funerary objects be dealt with; 5) how are dispute resolved; and 6) what type of notifications are needed in the process.

Managing and researching human remains is a unique opportunity, which comes with complex and often contradictory viewpoints. It is important that decisions in response to claims for repatriation be made equitably and transparently. Such decisions are not simple. Better understanding NAGPRA a key step in simplifying such decisions, both related to contemporary repatriations with Native Americans, but also as a guide for UK institutions in setting up an effective infrastructure for addressing repatriation claims in the future. NAGPRA has been relatively successful in the US for the last seventeen years, and deserves consideration as a model for equivalent policy in other domains.

Literature cited

Ackerman, D 1997. The meaning of 'Cultural Affiliation' and 'Major Scientific Benefit' in the Native American Graves Protection and Repatriation Act. *Tulsa Law Journal* 33: 359–83.

Australian Government 2005. *Strategy and Procedures on the Management of Overseas Repatriation of Indigenous Human Remains*. Electronic document, http://www.oipc.gov.au/programs/documents/Strategy_April06.pdf accessed 07 February 2008.

Carter, NC 1999. Native American graves protection and repatriation act: law, analysis, and context. *International Journal of Cultural Property* 8: 285-306.

DCMS 2005. *Guidance for the Care of Human Remains in Museums*. London: Department of Culture, Media and Sport DCMS. Electronic document, www.culture.gov.uk/NR/rdonlyres/0017476B-3B86-46F3-BAB3-

11E5A5F7F0A1/0/GuidanceHumanRemains11Oct.pdf, accessed 07 February 2008.

Edgar, HJH, Jolie, EA, Powell, JF, and Watkins, JE 2007. Contextual issues in Paleoindian repatriation: Spirit Cave Man as a case study. *Journal of Social Archaeology* 7: 101-122.

Echo-Hawk, R 2002. *Keepers of cCulture: Repatriating Cultural Items under the Native American Graves Protection and Repatriation Act*. Denver: Denver Art Museum. Electronic document, http://www.denverartmuseum.org/files/File/nagpra.pdf, accessed 07 February 2008.

Fforde, C and Ormond-Parker, L 2001. Repatriation Developments in the UK. *Indigenous Law Bulletin* 5(6). Electronic document, http://www.austlii.edu.au/au/journals/ILB/2001/10.html, accessed 07 February 2008.

Goldman DE 1999. The Native American Graves Protection and Repatriation Act: A benefit and a burden, refining NAGPRA's cultural patrimony definition. *International Journal of Cultural Property* 8: 229-244

Holden, C 2004. Kennewick Man: court battle ends, bones still off-limits. *Science* 305 (5684): 591.

NAGPRA. 2007. Native American Graves Protection and Repatriation Act Regulations - Disposition of culturally unidentifiable human remains. Office of the Secretary, Interior. *Federal Register* 72(199): 58582- 58590. http://www.nps.gov/history/nagpra/MANDATES/FR%20Notice%20Proposed%20Reg%20%20CFR%2010.11%20 0-16-2007.pdf, accessed 07 February 2008.

Ousley, SD, Billeck, WT, and Hollinger RE 2005. Federal repatriation legislation and the role of physical anthropology in repatriation. *American Journal of Physical Anthropology* 128(41): 2-32.

Owsley, D and Jantz R 2001. Archaeological politics and public interest in paleoamerican studies: lessons from Gordon Creek Woman and Kennewick Man. *American Antiquity* 66(4): 565–675.

Lovis, WA, Kintigh, KW, Steponaitis, VP, and Goldstein, LG 2004. Archaeological perspectives on the Native American Graves Protection and Repatriation Act: underlying principles. In: Richman, JR and Forsyth MP (eds.) *Legal Perspectives on Cultural Resources*. Walnut Creek: Altamira Press, pp 165-184.

Trope, JF and Echo Hawk, WR 1992. The Native American Graves Protection and Repatriation Act: background and legislative history. *Arizona State Law Journal* 24(1): 35-77.

Watkins, JE 2004. Becoming American or becoming Indian? NAGPRA, Kennewick and Cultural Affiliation. *Journal of Social Archaeology* 4(1): 60–80.

Weeks, J and Bott, V 2003. *Scoping Survey of Historic Human Remains in English Museums undertaken on behalf of the Ministerial Working Group on Human Remains*. Electronic document, www.culture.gov.uk/NR/rdonlyres/4503143F-8A56-4DA6-A96D-7DF46A700083/0/ScopingSurveyWGHR.pdf, accessed 07 February 2008.

Zimmerman, L 2005. Public heritage, a desire for a "White" history for America, and some impacts of the Kennewick Man/Ancient one decision. *International Journal of Cultural Property* 12: 265–274.

Repatriation - A View from a Receiving End: New Zealand

Nancy Tayles

Department of Anatomy and Structural Biology, Otago School of Medical Sciences, University of Otago, Dunedin, New Zealand
nancy.tayles@otago.ac.nz

Abstract

This paper is essentially a personal experience of repatriation of Maori remains to and within New Zealand, from the viewpoint of a *pakeha* (New Zealander of European descent) biological anthropologist. The history of the creation of collections of *koiwi tangata* (skeletal remains of Maori) both nationally and internationally is briefly reviewed, along with the recent development of repatriation programmes in New Zealand. The role of Maori within these programmes and their success is considered. The paper includes a brief review of my experiences on both sides of the repatriation process, and considers the future for the place of the study of human remains in New Zealand.

Keywords: Repatriation, Maori, New Zealand, *Koiwi Tangata*

Introduction

This paper is a personal story, relating my experiences and perceptions as a biological anthropologist and *pakeha* (New Zealander of European descent) with and about repatriation of Maori human skeletal remains, both within and to Aotearoa-New Zealand. My aim is to present a first hand account of my view from the receiving end, and to suggest some actions that can be taken which may be of benefit to both Maori and the wider scientific community in reconsidering the finality implied by the word 'repatriation'.

Firstly, a very brief background to the New Zealand situation. For a more comprehensive review of both prehistory and history, there are numerous publications available, including Belich (2001) and King (2003). New Zealand Maori are Polynesians who settled the country, probably less than 1000 years ago, from a homeland known as Hawaiki, an unidentified location accepted as being in Polynesia. Maori are the *tangata whenua*, the people of the land. Settlement of New Zealand by Europeans dates from approximately 200 years ago, and from the very first contact, the origin of Maori in particular, and Polynesians in general, was a source of much interest and conjecture by western scientists and anthropologists. This was primarily because of their very different physical appearance, and social and cultural customs from those of the nearest neighbours in Melanesia and Australia (Forster 1996). This interest stimulated the collection of skeletal remains (*koiwi tangata*) of Maori, and their cousins in the Chatham Islands, the Moriori.

History of collection and repatriation in New Zealand

During the 19th century, Pakeha soon became numerically, economically and politically dominant in New Zealand. By the second half of the century the institutions of western education, scholarship and science, including the University of New Zealand, the Royal Society and National (initially 'Dominion') and regional museums, were established and followed their overseas counterparts in desiring collections of skulls of the 'dying race' (King 2003). The methods used to research Maori origins and to place these people in the human taxonomy from their skeletal remains were those used universally to categorise human populations, principally craniometrics (Buck, 1938). Naturally, skulls were particularly valued and every museum worth its salt in Europe and North America strove to include examples in their collections during the 19th and early 20th century (Tapsell 2005). In the context of 19th century science, the craniometric data would have been desired, not only for this purpose, but also simply to add to the range of examples of different populations so that the races of the world could be categorised, and no doubt placed in the appropriate stage of evolution towards the ideal represented by white Europeans (Gould 1997).

The methods of acquisition of the skeletal remains have been documented thoroughly and appropriately elsewhere (Tapsell 2005, Hole 2007), but in summary, it included what was perceived to be justified collecting, often from caves which were favoured by Maori as either primary or secondary burial sites, or were sold by *Pakeha* or disaffected Maori. Initially, tattooed heads (*Moko Mokai*) were the focus of international interest, but over time the supply ceased and the attention moved to skeletons, especially skulls. These were at first sent to Museums in Europe and the USA in exchange for natural history specimens and items of material culture, as New Zealand institutions sought to build up comprehensive international collections (Tapsell 2005). *Koiwi* were also deliberately stolen from burial sites, as in the example documented by King (1981) of the activities of Andreas Reischek, an Austrian taxidermist and 'collector' in the 1880s. There was no doubt that Reischek was aware of the feelings of Maori but deliberately ignored these in his quest to acquire the remains. This action, and those of others in the 19th century, was a reflection of the European attitude towards indigenous peoples at the time.

Later, in the 19th and early 20th century *koiwi* were
donated or sold to institutions in New Zealand, usually by
Pakeha, in the name of science. This included the
Medical School at the University of Otago, where the
morphology and origin of Maori was among the first
research topics. Sir Peter Buck (also known as Te Rangi
Hiroa), the first Maori to graduate in Medicine at the
University in 1904 records:

> "I remember well when a fellow Maori student
> and I first entered the taboo precincts of the
> Medical School and saw at the top of the stairs
> a notice offering various prices for Maori
> skulls, pelves, and complete skeletons. We read
> it with horror and almost abandoned our quest
> for western medical knowledge" Buck
> (1938:14)

For most Maori, the expectation of science that cranial
morphology could act as a surrogate for genetic
affiliation has no merit. Maori culture has a very strong
oral tradition that not only documents the origins of their
ancestors in the South Pacific, but also documents the
genealogy, the *whakapapa*, of every Maori. This is an
important aspect of being Maori, as *whakapapa* defines
an individual, detailing their relationship to family
(*whanau*), subtribe (*hapu*), tribe (*iwi*) and ultimately
through ancestors (*tupuna*) to the land (*whenua*). The
skeletal remains of *tupuna* are the physical embodiment
of *whakapapa* (Ngai Tahu 1993) and are sacred. Strong
emotional ties to *tupuna* mean that the idea of handling
koiwi tangata and storing them on museum shelves is
abhorrent to Maori. Their sequestration in museums is
seen as part of the process of colonisation (Smith 1999).

The founding document of New Zealand, the Treaty of
Waitangi, was drafted by representatives of the British
Crown in 1840 on the grounds that there were benefits for
both sides in the British establishing sovereignty over the
country (Orange 2004). It was hastily translated into
Maori and signed in 1840 by Lieutenant William Busby
and over 500 Maori chiefs. The English and Maori
versions have some contentious differences, but the point
relevant here is that:

> "Her Majesty the Queen of England confirms
> and guarantees to the Chiefs and Tribes of New
> Zealand the full exclusive and undisturbed
> possession of their Lands and Estates Forests,
> Fisheries and other properties"

This can be taken to include ancestral remains. Not only
is there a moral and ethical duty not to disturb these
remains, the Treaty provides a written contract between
Maori and the Crown. The Treaty was clearly disregarded
in many respects since 1840, not only in relation to *koiwi*.
Although the establishment of the Waitangi Tribunal in
1985, with the ability to hear claims dating from 1840,
and settlement since then of some longstanding claims by
iwi, has provided tangible evidence of the will to redress
the suffering meted out to Maori, at least as far as is

possible at this temporal remove, and with the constraints
of contemporary land ownership.

An important event for Maori (and *pakeha*) relationships
with museums and for attitudes towards the collection,
display and interpretation of Maori *taonga* (treasures)
was the international tour of the exhibition Te Maori
between 1984-1986. The reception this exhibition
received and the *mana* (in this context, prestige) it
carried, resulted in a general raising of consciousness in
New Zealand of Maori culture and Maori rights, and the
role of Maori culture in New Zealand museums (Butts
2002). This had profound and far-reaching consequences
in many aspects of New Zealand life, but for *koiwi
tangata* specifically, a conference held in 1990, '*Taonga
Maori*' established research programmes and discussed
repatriation with the Field Museum in Chicago, and the
Stuttgart Museum in Germany.

The first formal actions taken to acknowledge what had
happened to *koiwi tangata* were by Dr Maui Pomare, a
member, and ultimately chair, of the National Museum
Council 1978-1992. During his time in office, he pushed
for the creation of a repository, known as a *Wahi Tapu*
(place sacred to Maori), in the National Museum (now
known as Te Papa Tongarewa) in Wellington, for the
appropriate temporary storage of *koiwi tangata*. These
would be held in the Museum collection until such time
as provenance could be established and repatriation to
appropriate iwi could be completed. This facility became
the keeping place for *koiwi* currently deposited at the
Museum, and the transitional facility for repatriated
remains.

In 1999, a *Wananga* (workshop) involving Iwi, Te Papa
and NZ government agencies supported Te Papa's
involvement in repatriation, and in 2003, a Government
Order in Council established a repatriation programme,
with the Karanga Aotearoa Repatriation Research
Committee, based at Te Papa, the Government Agent.
The role of the Committee is to locate *koiwi* in
international institutions and to negotiate their return to
New Zealand. Where possible, they establish provenance
and return Tupuna to the appropriate *iwi*. The *iwi* then
has the authority to determine the disposition of the
remains, whether that be in a secure keeping place, as
discussed below, or for reburial (Te Papa n.d.). This work
is to be undertaken in a quiet, dignified manner with
appropriate adherence to *tikanga* (Maori customs and
protocol). Their success is evident in recent significant
returns from Oxford and other institutions in Britain
(Waatea News 2007, New Zealand Press Association
2008).

Other authorities have been acting independently of Te
Papa, such as the Auckland War Memorial Museum of
Auckland. The museum has under its own Act of
Parliament (Auckland War Memorial Museum Act
1996), representation from the local *iwi*, Ngati Whatua O
Orakei on its Trust Board (Tapsell 2005:166). The
Governance Policy issued by the Trust Board in 2002:
C1.7. states that (Para 3.11):

"The Museum will seek the cooperation of identified international museums and institutions to assist in the return of Auckland Museum-associated Ancestral Human Remains back to source."

Detailed record keeping of these exchanges by the Museum Director has provided a basis for identifying the international institutions holding the remains and their provenance, allowing appropriate repatriations to *iwi* and *hapu*. Tapsell (2005) is critical of the Te Papa repatriation programme on the grounds that it does not directly involve the local *iwi*. This criticism shows how delicate the situation is, and how easily protocol may be breached.

In 1993, the largest *iwi* in the South Island, Ngai ('Kai' in the local dialect) Tahu, developed a policy on Koiwi Tangata (Ngai Tahu 1993). They were the first *iwi* in New Zealand to do so. This policy iterates the rights of the iwi to manage the *koiwi* from their *rohe* (tribal area) under the Treaty of Waitangi, including the return of any *koiwi* that have been removed from their *rohe*. This policy has been accepted by regional museums within the rohe, which extends over most of the South Island of New Zealand, to the extent that *Wahi Tapu* have been established within the Otago Museum (Dunedin) and the Southland Museum and Art Gallery (Invercargill) since 1994 (Gillies and O'Regan 1994). Where the geographic origin within the rohe of *koiwi* from museum collections is known, the ultimate arbiters of the long-term disposition,, whether retention in Museum *Wahi Tapu* or reburial, will be the local *runanga* (council, assembly). The policy recognises the role of scientific investigation of *koiwi,* and reserves the right to control research access and to edit for reasons of cultural sensitivity any material proposed for publication, including illustrations.

My experience

My personal experience with koiwi Maori dates from the 1970s and 80s, when as an archaeologist, I participated in archaeological excavations where human skeletal remains were immediately reburied by representatives of local *iwi* after having been discovered accidentally.

In the early 1990s I was appointed lecturer in Biological Anthropology in the Department of Anatomy and Structural Biology at the University of Otago, and since 1996 I have been Curator of anthropological human remains in the department. This Collection dates from 1876 when the Medical School was established, and included many Maori and Moriori remains that were added to the collection, through purchase or donation, up until the mid twentieth century (Buck 1938). Subsequent additions were almost exclusively from archaeological excavations.

This collection has formed the basis for over 60 publications and research theses, starting from the earliest description of cranial morphology by Scott (1893). Interestingly, despite his earlier distress, Sir Peter Buck

published a paper on the diet of prehistoric Maori that drew on evidence from the collection published by Scott (1893: 20). The most prolific researcher, Professor Philip Houghton (1980) was the first to provide a thorough description of the singular character of the Maori cranial and postcranial morphology, which now forms the basis for identification of Maori and Polynesian remains in forensic cases. He provided a theoretical basis for the cranial morphology in the 1980s (Kean and Houghton 1982, Houghton and Kean 1987, Kean and Houghton 1987). Most of the publications based on the collection have contributed to understanding of the quality of life of prehistoric Maori through description of their health and demography, rather than purely the documentation of their craniometry, which is the only aspect of physical (which I prefer to call biological) anthropology acknowledged or discussed in most publications about repatriation. Unfortunately, there have been no Maori contributors to the research, with the exception of Buck himself.

In 1996, following the transfer of the collection at the Otago Museum to the control of Ngai Tahu, and in recognition of the Maori feeling about their *tupuna,* our Department initiated contact with Ngai Tahu about our collection. Negotiation began, not only about the disposition of the remains from their *rohe* (tribal area), but also unprovenanced remains, on the grounds that they were being held within their *rohe*. In 2003 agreement was reached that the relevant koiwi in the collection would be transferred to the *Wahi Tapu* at the Otago Museum. In 2003 this transfer took place. At the time, Ngai Tahu gave an opportunity for a discussion paper on the research potential of the *koiwi* and the value to Maori of the research. This was to be circulated among individual *runanga* who would determine the disposition of the *koiwi* from their *rohe*. We await word on their determinations. Tapsell (2005) records that, despite the vocal support for reburial of koiwi, there is a range of opinions among Maori and that there are certainly those who will argue for their retention in appropriately dedicated keeping places with access for research under the control of the local *iwi*. Why have no further 'repatriations' taken place from the University of Otago? Our initiation of contact with Ngai Tahu has shown our willingness to return remains to the appropriate *iwi* authority, and we anticipate contact from other *iwi* in due course.

In 2002, I was contacted by the Karanga Aotearoa repatriation Committee at Te Papa and asked to provide training for the Repatriation Committee in the analysis of human skeletal remains. In 2004 I attended Te Papa Wananga at Wanganui, North Island, and presented a talk on research on koiwi, with the theme 'Let the *tupuna* speak'. I suggested that as these *koiwi* had sat anonymously on museum shelves for many decades before being repatriated to New Zealand, it seemed to me to be appropriate to allow at least basic estimation of age at death and sex, and examination for evidence of health and disease. This was well received, although as yet has had no sequel. In 2007, I was formally appointed as consultant to the committee and have visited Te Papa to provide assistance with the collection currently held in the *Wahi Tapu* at Te Papa. This was carried out in the *Wahi Tapu*, with strict adherence to appropriate protocol, and involved assisting with the identification of remains as human or animal, establishing whether crania and mandibles match and sorting of commingled remains. This also provided an opportunity to build an understanding of the research potential of the remains. This was the first of what is expected to be a series of visits as more koiwi are repatriated to New Zealand.

Conclusion

So what is the future for *koiwi* repatriation in New Zealand? Small collections of remains that have been returned to *iwi* so far have been reburied but others, such as the collection at the Southland and Otago Museums, continue to be held under control of local *iwi* in *Wahi Tapu*. The future of research on these *koiwi* will depend on communication between anthropologists and Maori, with the building of mutual understanding and trust that can arise from such contacts. The collection at the Southland Museum has been accessed for at least one research project since the establishment of the *Wahi Tapu*.

An important issue is the ending of 'demonisation' of science and scientists. It has been clear, in many of the discussions and writing about *koiwi* in New Zealand, that the bodies seen as having an interest in the process, apart from Maori, are the museums. These discussions often refer to scientists or researchers as the perpetrators of 'unacceptable activities', but with no opportunity for the few biological anthropologists in New Zealand to be represented. More activities, such as the invitations to provide a review of the possibilities with research on human remains, and to present at the *Wananga*, provide an important route for establishing mutual understanding and trust between biological anthropology and Maori, so that we are recognised as possessing the ability to 'read' *koiwi* in a way that could be of interest to Maori.

Hole (2007) as a non-*Pakeha* European has provided an interesting, if somewhat rosy, review of repatriation of Maori remains in New Zealand. He suggests that the situation in New Zealand is very different from that in other post-colonial Commonwealth countries, because the populace has a much more open and accepting attitude towards the claims of Maori. Hole bases this largely on an *ad hoc* survey taken in the Auckland Domain, the site of the Auckland War Memorial Museum in the centre of Auckland. I would suggest that the people in the Domain are far from a cross-section of New Zealand society, and that he might well have got a very different opinion from a survey in suburban Auckland or elsewhere in the country. Hole's review of the current situation is influenced towards the Auckland situation and reflects the opinions of those in the Museum at Auckland. He cites issues with physical anthropology in New Zealand being separate from archaeology (which indeed it was,

historically, at the University of Otago), and takes issue with the archaeological community and their lack of interaction with *iwi*. This is despite there being no evidence that he discussed these issues with archaeologists, and certainly did not make contact with those of us working in biological/physical anthropology at Otago, the institution with the longest history of research in the field. These omissions notwithstanding, he appears to be in a position to make a disinterested assessment of the situation, and sees the degree of participation of Maori in museum governance and the repatriation process, as crucial to the positive and dignified atmosphere in which repatriation proceeds in this country.

As an adjunct issue, the University of Otago has also recently repatriated archaeological collections of human skeletons to Thailand and Fiji, and we are in active discussions with the National Museum of the Solomon Islands over a collection that has been in the Department for 20 years. Some of these collections were held in the Department on loan, but others were not. The return of the latter was in response to requests from the country of origin and was an act of good faith, as there is now evidence that the collections will be stored and available for future research. What goes around, comes around. There are institutions in other countries that are refusing, or at least delaying, returning skeletal collections to the country of origin, which taints the field for all of us.

I do not have any argument, nor would I have the right, to deny that Maori are the only people who should determine the future for their ancestors. Given that repatriation of *koiwi tangata* from overseas institutions is gaining momentum day-by-day, this process does not have to be a prelude to reburial. Maori could benefit from culturally appropriate retention of *koiwi tangata* in keeping places in New Zealand, and the opportunity for research being retained, as it does not need to carry with it the taint of 19th century craniometry, as the publications from the University of Otago have shown. It can contribute significantly to understanding how the *tupuna* lived and what their lives were like. The ideal would be for such research to be conducted by Maori and my colleagues, and I look forward to Maori being involved in this work.

Acknowledgements

Thank you to Sian Halcrow and Hallie Buckley for comments on this manuscript.

Literature cited

Belich, J 2001. *Making Peoples: a History of the New Zealanders : from Polynesian Settlement to the end of the Nineteenth Century*. Auckland: Penguin.

Buck, P (Te Rangi Hiroa) 1938. *Vikings of the Sunrise*. Philadelphia: Lippincott..

Buck, PH 1925. The pre-European diet of the Maori. *New Zealand Dental Journal* 20: 203-217.

Butts, D 2002. Maori and Museums: the politics of indigenous recognition. In: Sandell R (ed.) *Museums, Society, Inequality*. London: Routledge, pp 225-243.

Forster, JR 1996. *Observations Made During a Voyage Round the World*. Honolulu: University of Hawai`i Press.

Gillies, K and O'Regan, G 1994. Murihiku resolution of Koiwi Tangata management. *New Zealand Museums Journal* 24: 30-31.

Gould, SJ 1997. *The Mismeasure of Man*. London: Penguin

Hole, B 2007. Playthings for the foe: the repatriation of human remains in New Zealand. *Public Archaeology* 6: 5-27.

Houghton, P 1980. *The First New Zealanders*. Auckland: Hodder and Stoughton

Houghton, P and Kean, MR 1987. The Polynesian head: a biological model for *Homo sapiens*. *Journal of the Polynesian Society* 96: 223-247.

Kean, MR and Houghton, P 1982. The Polynesian head: growth and form. *Journal of Anatomy* 135: 423-435.

Kean, MR and Houghton, P 1987. The role of function in the development of human craniofacial form. *The Anatomical Record* 218: 107-110.

King, M 1981. *The Collector Andreas Reischek – a Biography*. Auckland: Hodder and Stoughton.

King, M 2003. *The Penguin history of New Zealand*. Auckland: Penguin.

Museum of New Zealand Te Papa Tongarewa 2001. *Museum of New Zealand Te Papa Tongarewa Annual Report 1 July 2000 – 30 June 2001*. Department of Internal Affairs: Wellington. 16.

New Zealand Press Association. 2008. Oxford to return Maori, Moriori remains. 2nd February.

Ngai Tahu. 1993. *Koiwi Tangata*. Unpublished Manuscript.

Orange, C 2004. *An Illustrated History of the Treaty of Waitangi*. Bridget Williams: Wellington

Scott, JH 1893. Contribution to the osteology of the Aborigines of New Zealand and of the Chatham Islands. *Transactions of the New Zealand Institute* 26: 1-64.

Smith, LT 1999. *Decolonizing Methodologies*. University of Otago Press: Dunedin.

Te Papa n.d. *Karanga Aotearoa Repatriation Programme. Resource kit*. Te Papa Tongarewa National Museum of New Zealand: Wellington.

Tapsell, P 2005. Out of sight, out of mind: human remains at the Auckland Museum – *Te Papa Whakahiku*. In: Janes, RR, and Conaty, GT (eds) *Looking Reality in the Eye: Museums and Social Responsibility*. Calgary: University of Calgary Press, pp. 153-173.

Waatea News Update. 2007. *Koiwi* home from Britain. 21st November.

www.ingramcontent.com/pod-product-compliance
Lightning Source LLC
Chambersburg PA
CBHW061000030426
42334CB00033B/3300